H O M E
Heaven On Mother Earth

by Patricia Diane Cota-Robles

New Age Study of Humanity's Purpose, Inc.
PO Box 41883
Tucson, AZ 85717

Website: www.1spirit.com/eraofpeace
Fax: (520) 749-6643
Phone: (520) 885-7909
E-mail: eraofpeace@aol.com

New Age Study of Humanity's Purpose, Inc.
PO Box 41883
Tucson, AZ 85717

Website: www.1spirit.com/eraofpeace
Fax: (520) 749-6643
Phone: (520) 885-7909
E-mail: eraofpeace@aol.com

Cover by Sharon Maia Wilson
Printed in the United States of America

Library of Congress Cataloging in Publication Data
ISBN: 0-9615287-7-x

First Edition: January 11, 2003

Dedication

This book is lovingly dedicated to the Sons and Daughters of God who are awakening and accepting responsibility for cocreating Heaven On Mother Earth.

Additional Books
by Patricia Diane Cota-Robles

Take Charge of Your Life

The Next Step...
Reunification with the Presence of God in our Hearts

Your Time Is At Hand

The Awakening...
Eternal Youth, Vibrant Health, Radiant Beauty

Stargate of the Heart

What On Earth Is Going On?

It Is Time For YOU To Be
Financially Free

New Age Study of Humanity's Purpose, Inc.
PO Box 41883
Tucson, AZ 85717

Website: www.1spirit.com/eraofpeace
Fax: (520) 749-6643
Phone: (520) 885-7909
E-mail: eraofpeace@aol.com

Acknowledgments

With deep love and appreciation I acknowledge...

Dickie, my precious husband of 38 years who is the love of my life and my best friend.

My son Joao and my daughter Victoria, who have filled my life with love and laughter.

My grandsons Dylan and Hayden, who prove to me that all is well in the world and that we are indeed going to make it.

Kay Meyer, my friend and the cofounder of the New Age Study of Humanity's Purpose, who works tirelessly to fulfill the administrative duties for our organization.

Margy Vaughan, my friend, who helps with the logistical arrangements for our Free Seminars and other facets of our Lightwork.

And I would like to give a very special "thank you" to the selfless volunteers who dedicate their time and energy to help us distribute the information pouring forth from the Realms of Illumined Truth, Mona Hoover, Sue Larson, Jim McAndrew, Terry Teal, Kim Kleving, Anna Schoen, Brenda Howard, Jacquie Brooks, Karen Bowman, Kay Eacker, Bonnie Schroeder, Pat Williams, Linda Cox and Susan Hughes.

Finally, I would like to thank all of the rest of my Earthly Family and my Heavenly Family who encourage and support me in myriad ways beyond their knowing.

GOD BLESS YOU ALL!

I LOVE YOU.

TABLE OF CONTENTS

⸻❦⸻

INTRODUCTION

It seems that everyday we are being flooded with fear-based information that reflects the dire possibility of economic collapse, terrorist attacks, war, environmental disasters, governmental and corporate corruption, crime, violence and myriad other potential dangers. It is very easy to become so overwhelmed with concern that we just wring our hands and muddle through our days in a state of anxiety and desperation.

The majority of people feel helpless when it comes to changing their lives or making a significant difference in the world. Everyone wants things to get better, but most people don't truly believe they can effectively assist in the process. Well, fortunately, nothing could be further from the Truth. We are ALL cocreators. We are on Earth during this unprecedented time for the explicit purpose of uniting with our Father-Mother God and the Company of Heaven to cocreate the wonders of Heaven on Earth.

Whether we consciously remember it or not, each and every one of us has been preparing for a very long time to assist in this mission. We all have unique skills and abilities that no one else on the planet possesses in exactly the same way we do. We have volunteered to assist in helping to change the old, obsolete behavior patterns that are responsible for the pain and suffering Humanity is enduring. This is being brought to our attention by our God Selves because the time for us to begin fulfilling our Divine Missions is NOW!

Traumatic experiences cause us to regroup and to reevaluate how we are living our lives. It seems we have fallen into the pattern of using pain as our motivator. As long as we are not in pain, we will just plod along, day after day, without much thought. We halfheartedly go through the motions of doing what we need to do to survive. We go to our jobs to make money to put food on the table and a roof over our heads. We take care of our families' physical needs, and with the little bit of time that is left, we try to take care of our selves.

When a tragedy happens, however, we are forced to put our lives into perspective. We stop for a moment and focus on what really matters to us. If we use the tragic event to change our mode of operation and to put more meaning in our lives, then something good will come out of even the most horrific experience.

The tragic events of September 11, 2001, transformed our lives forever. We have a choice as to whether we allow catastrophes of that nature to catapult us into lives of fear and dread or whether we use those experiences to motivate us into creating lives of fulfillment and joy. We have the ability to do both of those things; the path we choose is up to us.

The only reason we haven't been cocreating lives of joy, happiness, prosperity, loving relationships, financially and creatively rewarding jobs, vibrant health, fulfillment, enlightenment and every other positive experience is because we have forgotten that we can.

Not only *can* we create the lives we dream of, *this is our purpose and reason for being.* We are Children of God, and we have been invested with the gift of free will. Our thoughts and feelings are creative. Whatever we focus our thoughts, words, actions and feelings on, we bring into physical form. It is time for us to remember this Divine Truth and for us to consciously choose to create the lives we want instead of inadvertently manifesting, through our fears, the experiences we don't want.

It is time for us to reclaim our Divine Birthrights and to fulfill our Divine Potentials. As we take charge of our lives, we will be effective examples for our loved ones and friends. We will be positive catalysts, and the results of our efforts will be exponential. We are all One, and the Universal Law is *"As I Am lifted up, ALL Life is lifted up with me."* We can each make a difference. As we change our lives, we will change the direction for Humanity and for all life evolving on this planet.

Part 1

Chapter 1

Chapter 1

WHERE YOUR ATTENTION IS...
THERE YOU ARE!

The Light of God is increasing daily and hourly on Earth, and people everywhere are beginning to awaken to the Truth of who they are and why they are here. Contrary to what we have come to believe, we are not just fragmented, limited, dysfunctional facets of our fear-based human egos. We are Beloved Sons and Daughters of God, and all that our Father-Mother God has is ours. By remembering this fact and acting out of this inner knowing, we can turn around what is happening in our lives and on Earth. Together, we can change the course of history.

As Children of God, we have the responsibility of cocreating our physical reality. Through lifetimes of misunderstandings, we have developed the erroneous belief that we are just powerless victims of circumstance when, in fact, we are powerful cocreators of circumstance.

When we accept that we are on Earth during this unique moment to cocreate the wonders of Heaven on Earth, we become empowered instruments of God. Our acknowledgment of this Truth opens our hearts and allows our God Selves to increase the amount of Light flowing through our Earthly bodies.

As the Light of God flows through us into the physical plane, it enters the core of purity in every electron of precious life energy. The Light then pushes to the surface anything that conflicts with its frequencies of harmony, love and balance. As the discordant frequencies of energy surface to be healed and transmuted back into Light, they often create the illusion that things are getting worse. We can easily see the surfacing negativity, but what we don't see is the incredible Light that is pushing the negativity to the surface. That phenomenon has the effect of keeping our attention focused on the problems instead of the solutions.

When we are focused on the negativity instead of the Light, we empower and sustain the negative things that are surfacing. Instead of eliminating the problems, we actually intensify them. This has the tendency to make us feel desperate, overwhelmed and hopeless.

When we observe things through the eyes of our dysfunctional human egos, we mistakenly think that the physical plane is our only reality. Our human egos have forgotten that we are multidimensional and multifaceted Beings of Light who are functioning simultaneously in many diverse realities.

Our God Presence is the all-encompassing part of us that is created in God's Image. This aspect of our Being is a radiant Sun which resonates with the full perfection of our Father-Mother God. When it is time for us to embody on Earth, our God Presence projects one minuscule ray of Light into this physical plane to sustain our Earthly bodies. Our human egos have manipulated us into believing that all we are is that single ray of Light.

When we buy into that illusion, it is easy for us to feel limited and inadequate. We then readily accept the erroneous belief that we are just helpless victims who are being buffeted about by life's circumstances without any options or choices.

The physical plane is merely a reflection of our consciousness and, in fact, it is the *least* real of all of the realities we abide in. No matter how real our life challenges seem or how entrapped we are in the human miscreations of poverty, disease, low self-esteem, loveless relationships, hatred, corruption, ignorance, war, etcetera, those distorted expressions of life can manifest in our lives *only* if we sustain them through our thoughts, words, actions, feelings and beliefs. If we choose to empower the Light and all of the patterns of perfection contained in that Light instead of choosing to empower the things that cause our pain and suffering, our Earthly experiences will be transformed in *"the twinkling of an eye."*

This is not just religious rhetoric or wishful thinking. It is the tangible effect of the Universal Laws that apply to our Earthly experiences. This is true whether we believe in the Universal Laws or not. For instance, we are all subject to the law of gravity while we are abiding on this planet, but our belief in the law of gravity is immaterial. If we jump off a roof, we are going to fall to the ground regardless of what we believe. It is just that simple. The same applies to all of the other Universal Laws we are subject to in the physical plane as well.

The Law of the Circle

Through the Universal Law of the Circle, our thoughts and feelings create our life experiences. Our lifeforce continually flows through us with every heartbeat and every breath we take. We use that lifeforce to form thoughts, words, actions and feelings which go out from us on electromagnetic currents of energy very much like radio or television waves. As our thoughts and feelings pass through the atmosphere, they accumulate other thoughts and feelings which are vibrating at the same frequency. *Like attracts like*. Once our thoughts and feelings reach their point of destination, they return to us greatly magnified over what we originally sent out due to the accumulation of like vibrations.

World religions and science have tried to teach us about the Law of the Circle, which is the Universal Law that confirms we are cocreating this physical reality. Unfortunately, we haven't fully understood. For example, the religions of the East teach about the Law of Cause and Effect or the Law of Karma. Judaism teaches an eye for an eye, a tooth for a tooth or, in other words, what goes around comes around. Christianity teaches that we reap what we sow and that when we cast our bread upon the water, it returns to us. The Law of the Circle is also demonstrated in the science of physics which reflects the principles of like attracts like, action and reaction, radiation and magnetization.

The literal interpretation of the Law of the Circle simply means that every thought, word, action and feeling we express goes out into the world and returns to us in the form of our everyday life experiences. That is true whether we are focusing on lack, limitation, fear, grief, war, pain and suffering or prosperity, love, happiness, unity, compassion, oneness, peace, courage and strength. At any given moment, our lives are reflecting a sum total of everything we have ever thought, felt, said or done since we were first breathed forth from the Heart of our Father-Mother God. Just imagine!

If we are expressing positive thoughts and feelings, then those frequencies manifest in our lives as positive experiences, people and situations. If we are expressing negative thoughts and feelings, then those frequencies manifest as negative experiences, people and situations in our lives.

The events taking place at this time on Earth are unprecedented and profound. Even though many of us are awakening to the Truth of who we are and why we are here, when we turn on the news or read a newspaper, we are bombarded by the horrific things that are taking place all over the world. In spite of the fact that we know we are cocreating this reality and that we have the ability to change things, the information is shocking and causes us to sometimes sink into the emotional grip of anxiety, fear and dread. What we must keep in mind is that the information being reported in the news involves a very small portion of the six-billion souls evolving on this planet. Even though the governmental leaders claim that they are speaking for the millions of people they represent, that is not true.

There are literally hundreds of millions of souls who are attempting to live their lives the best way they can according to their wisdom and understanding. It is just that many of them have given their power away to their human egos who are manipulating them into believing they are helpless victims.

Reaching Critical Mass

In addition to the negative thoughtforms we are receiving from the media, there is another phenomenon that is causing Humanity to feel frustrated and powerless. When we awaken and begin to understand the power of our creative faculties, we attempt to control our behavior patterns. We put forth the effort to think positively, and we strive to focus our attention on what we want to manifest in our lives. Daily we envision the lives we aspire to, and we work to empower our visions of Heaven on Earth with positive thoughts and affirmations.

But often, after what seems like a valiant effort, we continue to experience many of our old problems. This causes us to become discouraged and to lose trust in our ability to change our lives. At this point, we feel like our efforts are futile, and we usually give up on trying to improve our situations. We let go of our visions and regress back into our old, negative thinking patterns. We dwell on our fears, problems and challenges instead of empowering our goals, hopes and dreams. As a result of that relapse, things get worse, and our situations appear even more hopeless. If we understand the Universal Law governing that particular phenomenon, it will give us the courage to persevere even in the face of apparent failure.

Everything is comprised of energy, vibration and consciousness. When we explore a portion of the vast science of quantum physics, we learn that when something reaches critical mass, there is an *unstoppable shift* that takes place. For instance, when an electron is increasing in vibration, the moment it reaches critical mass, the entire electron is pulled up into the higher frequency and nothing can stop it.

Critical mass is 51 percent. When 51 percent of an electron is vibrating at a higher frequency, the remaining 49 percent is instantly absorbed into the new vibration. So, how does this facet of quantum physics affect our ability to take charge of our own lives?

As we strive to improve our lives, the same laws of quantum physics apply. When empowering a vision or thoughtform, the moment 51 percent of our energy, vibration and consciousness is in alignment with our vision, it reaches critical mass, and nothing can stop it from manifesting. The problem is that we never know just when we are going to reach that magical moment of critical mass. There are often no outer-world signs, and it may even look as if we are very far away from that instant of transformation. This is when we usually feel our efforts are failing, and we give up. Sometimes we may be just a breath away from reaching critical mass, but we don't realize that, so we get discouraged and stop trying to change our lives. Then we end up never reaching our goal.

In very practical terms, critical mass means that when we are striving to create prosperity in our lives, the moment our thoughts, words, actions and feelings are vibrating with 51 percent prosperity consciousness instead of poverty consciousness, our life circumstances will shift, and we will begin to experience prosperity. The moment 51 percent of our energy is aligned with self-esteem and love, we will magnetize positive relationships into our lives. The moment 51 percent of our energy is aligned with peace, harmony and balance, we will manifest those Divine Qualities tangibly in our life experiences.

The key to our success is that we must *keep on keeping on* even in the face of adversity. It is vital for us to understand that the Light of God is infinitely more powerful than any fragmented human miscreation we may have inadvertently created. Poverty has no power over the limitless Abundance of God. Our Divine Potential is infinitely more powerful than disease, failure, dysfunctional relationships, hatred, greed, corruption, war or any of the other humanly-created maladies appearing on the screen of life.

As long as we choose the Light and consecrate our energy to empower only the positive experiences we want to create in our lives and not the negative experiences we don't want, we will manifest our visions and dreams faster than we can possibly imagine.

This information is being given to us by the Beings of Light in the Realms of Illumined Truth during this critical moment on Earth to help us remember that if we don't like what is happening in our lives, we have the option to do something about it. This is true for each of us individually, and it is true for all of us collectively as a global family.

It is important that we put things back into perspective and accept responsibility for turning our lives around. When we deliberately focus on cocreating our highest Divine Potential, our efforts are empowered by the unfathomable Light of our God Selves, and our success is assured.

We don't have to believe in the various Universal Laws in order to exist on Earth, but since we are ALL subject to them, it is just common sense for us to try and accept them. We don't have to believe that every single thought, word, action and feeling we have will go out and affect the world and then return to us to affect our personal lives, but this is happening scientifically, to the letter, in spite of our disbelief.

It doesn't matter whether we believe in reincarnation or whether we understand that we have an accumulation of experiences from other time frames and dimensions that are influencing our present lives; it is happening anyway. If we stop resisting this Truth and just accept it as a possibility, it will certainly be to our advantage. Even if we just say to ourselves, *"Maybe it is true. Maybe I can turn things around in my life by accepting the Law of the Circle and working with that principle instead of fighting against it,"* we will experience a positive shift in our lives. When we are willing to take this first step and genuinely put forth the effort to correct our behavior, the floodgates of Heaven will open to assist us in accomplishing our goals.

The Process of Conscious Cocreation

So how do we begin? Well, first of all, we must constantly remind ourselves that whatever we are thinking, feeling, saying or doing we are cocreating, empowering and magnetizing into our lives.

Let's contemplate this statement for a moment:

WHATEVER WE ARE THINKING, FEELING, SAYING OR DOING WE ARE COCREATING, EMPOWERING AND MAGNETIZING INTO OUR LIVES!

Are we empowering prosperity, abundance, vibrant health, loving relationships, fulfilling jobs, happiness, spiritual growth, world peace, global harmony, tolerance, planetary healing, reverence for all life and the vision of Heaven on Earth, or are we empowering hatred, war, dysfunctional relationships, poverty, disease, natural disasters, cataclysmic earth changes, governmental conspiracies, corporate corruption, economic collapse violence, crime, inhuman behavior toward each other and every other negative situation manifesting on Earth?

To begin *consciously* creating what we want, we must first evaluate our lives and decide what we like about them and what needs to be changed. Then, using our creative faculties of thought and feeling, we need to write a detailed vision describing exactly what we want to create and the type of lives we want to live.

Our visions must always reflect the highest good for ourselves and everyone involved. We must never be willing to attain our goals at the expense of another person or another living thing. We can easily fulfill that requirement by always striving for the most positive visions possible and then stating, *"I ask my God Self to be sure that my visions manifest in alignment with the highest good of all concerned."* Our God Selves will then have permission to intervene and safeguard our visions to fulfill our request.

Writing down our visions begins the process of creating new matrixes and archetypes. The very first step of changing any human experience or condition is to create a blueprint, a matrix and archetype that will shatter and replace the matrix and archetype of the old, dysfunctional situation or behavior pattern. As we focus the power of our attention on our visions and magnetize the Light of God into them daily and hourly with positive affirmations, the unformed primal Light from the core of Creation will flow into the new matrixes and archetypes, greatly empowering them. The moment our visions reach critical mass, they will manifest tangibly in our lives.

We can prevent our old patterns of limitation from sabotaging our visions by transmuting them with the Violet Flame from the Heart of God. This is accomplished by simply invoking the Violet Flame and asking our God Self to transmute all of our thoughts, words, actions and feelings from all time frames and dimensions, both known and unknown, that will, in any way, prevent or interfere with the manifestation of our visions.

The Violet Flame is the perfect balance of the masculine polarity of God, which resonates with a *sapphire blue* radiance and encompasses the God Qualities of Divine Will, Authority, Power and Protection and the feminine polarity of God, which resonates with a *crystalline pink* radiance and encompasses the God Qualities of Divine Love, Adoration and Reverence for ALL Life.

Together the pink and blue polarities of our Father-Mother God form the Violet Flame which manifests not only the masculine and feminine qualities of our God Parents, but the Divine Qualities of Limitless Physical Perfection, Transmutation, Forgiveness, Mercy, Compassion, Freedom, Liberty, Justice, Victory, Opportunity, Rhythm, Invocation and Divine Ceremony as well. This Sacred Fire is the most effective tool we can use to transmute the negative energy we have expressed throughout our lives.

Here is an example of a vision we can use to begin the process of transforming our lives, but this is just an example. It is important for each of us to create a vision to fit our own life path and heart's desire.

I Am Cocreating My Life!

*I remember who I Am, and I love and
respect myself as a Beloved Child of God.*

*I Am perpetually enveloped in the invincible protection of
God's glorious Light as I sojourn through my
Earthly experiences.*

*I Am limitless physical perfection. I Am vibrantly healthy,
eternally youthful and radiantly beautiful.*

I Am manifesting wonderful, loving relationships in my life.

*I Am prosperous, and I Am open and receptive to the limitless
flow of God's Abundance, which is now pouring into my life.*

I Am financially and creatively rewarded in my job.

*I Am an exponent and example of Divine Family Life,
including my place in the family of Humanity.*

*I Am reaching my highest Divine Potential as a Human
Being, son/daughter, wife/husband,
grandmother/grandfather, woman/man, friend, relative,
coworker, Earth steward, teacher, wayshower, Lightworker
and cocreator of Heaven on Earth.*

*I Am an Open Door for Divine Truth, Wisdom,
Enlightenment and Illumination.*

*I Am a living example of love, trust, integrity, honesty,
tolerance, acceptance and reverence for ALL life.*

*I Am able to listen, understand and communicate openly and
honestly with whomever I come in contact.*

*I Am effortlessly Ascending into the Divine Heart and Mind
of God with every Holy Breath I take.*

*I Am tapping into the Divine Guidance that will assist me in
fulfilling my Divine Plan and my purpose
and reason for being.*

I Am an instrument of God.

I Am the physical manifestation of Transfiguring Divine Love, Healing Through the Power of Limitless Transmutation, Mercy, Compassion, Forgiveness, Liberty, Victory, Justice, Understanding, Clarity, Purity, Hope, Divine Will, Authority, Power and Order, Harmony, Balance, Enthusiasm, Purpose, Joy, Transformation, Eternal Peace, Ministering Grace and every other Divine Attribute of God.

From moment to moment, I Am open to the Divine Guidance of my God Self and the Legions of Light in the Realms of Illumined Truth. I easily communicate with these Beings of Light through open heart and open mind telepathic communication.

I Am One with ALL Life, and I communicate openly with the Angelic and Elemental Kingdoms as well.

I Am daily and hourly fulfilling the Immaculate Concept of my Divine Plan and the Divine Plan for Beloved Mother Earth.

I Am expanding the borders of the Kingdom of Heaven on Earth with every thought, word, action and feeling.

I Am that I Am.

Sealing Affirmation

I now invoke the full-gathered momentum of the Violet Flame to transmute every thought, word, action or feeling I have ever expressed in any time frame or dimension, both known and unknown, that would in any way, shape or form interfere with or prevent my vision from manifesting tangibly in the world of form.

I Am the Immaculate Concept of my vision NOW made manifest and sustained by Holy Grace.

I Am the Immaculate Concept of my vision NOW made manifest and sustained by Holy Grace.

I Am the Immaculate Concept of my vision
NOW made manifest and sustained by Holy Grace.

I accept that this vision and invocation are
victoriously accomplished.

In God's most Holy Name, I Am.

Keep on keeping on!
Don't give up until your vision is manifest.

Coping with Negativity

Focusing on the positive things we want does not mean putting our heads in the sand and pretending that the negativity does not exist. There are a lot of things that need to be dealt with, but it is how we deal with them that determines whether we are part of the solution or part of the problem.

All life is interrelated, interconnected and interdependent. This means that every person, place, condition and thing affects every other person, place, condition and thing. Stop and think about this for just a moment. This is a critical point in our clarity and understanding.

We cannot have a single negative thought or feeling without it adversely affecting ourselves as well as the person or situation we are thinking about. Our negativity also adds to the accumulation of negative energy surrounding the Earth, which causes pain and suffering for everybody. Fortunately, the same principle applies to our positive energy as well. Our positive thoughts and feelings bless us and the person or situation we are thinking about, and they add to positive energy surrounding the Earth, which lifts everybody up.

WE ARE ALL ONE! There is NO *"us and them."* As soon as we deteriorate into thinking there is *"us and them,"* we become part of the problem.

The words "We are ALL One" have reverberated through the hearts and minds of Humanity in one form or another since the beginning of time. They do not express a sweet cliche, even though our lower human egos have often perceived them as such. They profess a profound Truth.

Daily and hourly we witness myriad atrocities happening in the world. It seems as though people everywhere are inflicting pain, suffering, injustice and even death on their fellow Human Beings. The *only* way that behavior could possibly make sense or be justified in anyone's mind is through their ignorance of the fact that *we are all One*. To inflict harm on another Human Being is totally and completely ludicrous in the face of that Truth. It is self-destructive and suicidal. It is unconscionable and uncivilized.

During this unprecedented moment of accelerated Light on Earth, these problems seem as though they are being exacerbated. This is occurring for a very specific reason.

What we call *God* is the omnipotent, omniscient, omnipresent Divinity that envelopes ALL life everywhere—All That Is. Every minute electron, atom and subatomic particle of life throughout infinity is a *cell* in the body of *God*.

All lifeforms pulsate as ONE unified energy in the Body of God. Therefore, what affects one part of life affects the rest of life. What affects one cell has an affect on all of the cells.

So why do things seem to be getting worse? *BECAUSE THE LIGHT OF GOD IS INCREASING ON EARTH!*

The Light of God is flowing into the physical plane at an accelerated pace through the hearts and minds of awakening Humanity. As it does, it activates the original Divine Potential in every electron of energy. No matter how distorted or mutated a lifeform is, it still has the original Spark of Divinity which contains the Immaculate Concept of its Divine Potential, or it couldn't survive. This is true of even the most degenerate souls or the most negative situations.

Within every electron of poverty still pulsates the potential of God's Limitless Abundance; within every electron of disease still pulsates the potential for vibrant health; within every electron of war still pulsates the potential of peace; within every electron of hate still pulsates the potential of Divine Love. When the Light of God flows into the Earth and pushes to the surface the things that conflict with our Divine Potential, we respond to the negativity in various and sundry ways.

For example, the frequencies that conflict with Divine Love are hatred, fear, jealousy, resentment, low self-esteem, envy, intolerance, prejudice, greed, selfishness, indifference, lack of compassion, disrespect and myriad other emotions that reflect a lack of reverence for life. If we contemplate the negativity being pushed to the surface as God's Love increases on Earth, we can see how many of the world's problems are associated with this phenomenon.

People often latch on to the surfacing negative patterns instead of transmuting them back into Light. Consequently, we are seeing a tremendous increase in hate crimes, ethnic cleansing, war, prejudice, intolerance, corruption, discrimination, road rage, physical abuse, dysfunctional families, violence, shootings, drug abuse, neglect and all manner of disharmony and imbalance. From outer appearances, it looks as if the world has gone amuck. That is why this time is referred to in the Bible as *"the time of screaming and the gnashing of teeth."*

It is certainly not the Divine Plan for God's Light to take us down the tubes. In fact, if there was even the slightest potential of that happening, the Light of God would not be increasing on Earth at this unprecedented pace.

We have been preparing for aeons of time to invoke the Violet Transmuting Flame and project it into the negativity that is coming up to be healed. We have also been trained to educate the masses and remind them of the *Oneness of ALL life*.

We must teach people that when we hate ANYONE, it is the same as hating ourselves. When we are prejudiced or discriminate against people because of the color of their skin or their religion, nationality, culture, gender, lifestyle, economic or social status, it is the same as hating ourselves. We are ALL cells in the One Body of God, and we each have unique gifts and purposes that serve various functions, all for the good of the whole.

To say that we hate people because they are different from us is like saying, *"I like lung cells, but I hate stomach cells and heart cells."* The lungs cannot survive without the stomach and the heart. All cells need to function in harmony with each other in order for the whole body to be vibrant and healthy. All cells are necessary and their diversity is vital.

We are born into various situations because of the lessons we came to Earth to learn and the experiences we volunteered to go through. Our physical body is merely the "car" we drive to navigate around in the physical plane. We have all probably been *every* race, religion, nationality and gender. To say we hate someone because of the color of their skin is like saying,

"I like people who drive blue cars, but I hate everyone who drives a green car." That sounds pretty silly, doesn't it?

We as Human Beings need each other to survive on this planet. We must recognize that we are all in this together. Instead of functioning out of fear and hatred, we need to learn about each other and revel in the wonder and beauty of our unique diversities.

So how do we address negativity without latching on and empowering it? First of all, we move out of the *"holier than thou"* consciousness of separation and acknowledge that the person or people involved, who are just other facets of ourselves, are out of sync.

Even if you or I would never think of picking up a gun and shooting someone or of being violent, committing a crime, hating another ethnic group, lying, being dishonest or corrupt, instigating a war, polluting the environment, abusing another person, betraying a loved one, hoarding our wealth while others live in poverty, starvation and squalor, leading people astray or breaking the Universal Laws of Harmony and Divine Love, there are people who do these things, and these people are part of us.

You and I are affected profoundly by other peoples' behavior because we are all One. So instead of judging people, saying they are bad, disassociating ourselves from them and hating them, we need to say, *"How can I help to lift up that other facet of myself and assist in transforming that behavior?"*

By focusing our attention on other people's negative behavior, talking badly about them, criticizing them and being angry with them, we are actually empowering the very thing we are upset about.

If, however, we go within to the deepest recesses of our hearts and ask our God Selves how we can assist in a positive way to dissipate the negativity and correct the negative behavior, we will receive the answers we are seeking. *"Ask and you shall receive. Knock and the door will be opened."*

We have each been preparing for aeons to be instruments of God during this critical time. Our God Selves have been patiently waiting and will joyously respond to our heart's call.

The statement *"As I Am lifted up, ALL life is lifted up with me"* is a Divine Truth. For lifetimes we have been learning how to cope with the type of negativity that is now surfacing on

Earth. We have all of the knowledge, skill, talent, courage and strength we need to succeed in this Divine Mission.

We must be eternally vigilant and take the time to consciously choose how we allow the negative things to affect us. We cannot control everything that is happening, but we have absolute control over how we respond to each experience. If we become angry and filled with hate or choose to broadcast our indignation to the world, we will feed and intensify the problem. If, instead, we detach from the anger and invoke the Light of God into the situation, we will transmute the negativity and perceive positive ways to handle the problem.

When we ask our God Selves to intervene, we are shown new solutions to old problems, and we will learn new ways of dealing with old challenges that will make our lives easier and happier.

If other people are involved in negative situations, we must ask their God Selves to take control of their actions. Then we should invoke the Light of God to create an environment so the God Self of that person can get through to them to guide them in a more positive direction.

This is not a complicated process; it just takes discipline, consistency and determination on our part. Becoming furious and outraged is a very normal reflex response when we hear about the atrocities people are inflicting on each other. The problem is that those feelings don't help the situation.

We must pay attention, and we must learn to identify the negativity manifesting in our lives and in the world in a conscious but detached manner. Then we will be free to instantly invoke the Light of God into the situation.

We can easily invoke the Light of God by affirming:

I Am an instrument of God.

I Am a force of the Violet Flame instantly transmuting the negativity associated with this situation.

I Am invoking the God Selves of all of those involved to take full dominion of their lives NOW.

I KNOW my consistent, positive response will change the

course of history and the direction of the world!

Here is another positive invocation we can use to dissipate the negativity surfacing on Earth. Whenever we are confronted with a negative thought, word, action, feeling, person, place, condition or thing either in our own lives or in the world, we can assist in transmuting it by decreeing with deep feeling:

Through the Power of God pulsating in my heart,
I invoke the Light of God into this situation.

I Am One with all life, and I understand that as
I Am lifted up, ALL life is lifted up with me.

Beloved Father-Mother God, transmute into
Divine Light every electron of energy associated with
this situation.

Transmute the cause, core, effect, record and memory of
this situation back into its original Divine Intent.

I ask my God Presence, the God Presence of every
person involved and the God Presence of ALL Humanity
to take full command of our
thoughts, words, actions and feelings NOW.
Empower every soul with the Truth of Oneness and
reverence for ALL life.

Guide and direct us so that we will each recognize the
error of our ways, and help us to take the necessary steps to
create a new reality based on Divine Love and Harmony.

* I Am a force of the Violet Flame of God's Limitless
Transmutation more powerful than any
human miscreation.

(Repeat 3 times from *)

This activity of Light is being victoriously
accomplished even as I speak.

*The Light of God is now increasing through me and ALL
Humanity with every breath I take.*

*The Light of God is ALWAYS Victorious, and
I Am that Light!*

And so it is, Beloved I Am.

Chapter 2

Chapter 2

PROSPERITY   IS   THE   KEY   TO   PEACE

In the beginning, our God Parents gave us everything we needed to easily sustain our physical bodies during our Earthly sojourn. We were given the Light of the Sun, fresh air, water, food and materials from which to build shelters and make clothing for ourselves. The Divine Intent was for our physical needs to be taken care of so that we could focus on using our gift of free will to learn to cocreate the patterns of perfection from the Causal Body of God on Earth.

It was never the Divine Plan that we struggle from morning until night in mundane jobs just to put food on the table and supply the needs of our physical bodies. This, in fact, is a gross distortion of the Divine Plan, and it is a cumbersome distraction from our purpose and reason for being in this school of learning.

After the "fall," we lost awareness of our Divine Heritage and the fact that we are Children of God. We descended into denser and denser frequencies of our own human miscreations, and our God Selves were unable to communicate with us. To compensate for that void in our lives, we developed our fragmented human egos. We gave away our power to this mutated aspect of ourselves and allowed it to manipulate us into believing that our physical bodies are who we are and that the physical plane is our only reality.

With that distorted perception, we started believing in lack and limitation. We forgot that we are cocreating this reality and that the unformed primal Light that comprises every particle of life in the physical plane is limitless. We forgot about the abundance of God, and we started fearing for our very survival. We became afraid that there was not going to be enough of the necessities of life for everyone to live in comfort and peace.

We began hoarding the things we needed to sustain our

physical bodies, which blocked the flow of God's limitless abundance. As our fear-based thoughts and feelings reflected on the elemental substance of the Earth, we started experiencing inclement weather conditions, which resulted in floods, droughts, famines, plagues and pestilence. When that happened, we were catapulted into a vicious circle. The more we hoarded the things we needed to survive, the less the necessities of life were made available to us and the more afraid we became.

We developed a consciousness of greed and selfishness that we believed was necessary in order to survive. We started fighting with each other over land, food, water and material things. Eventually we created a monetary system to barter for the very things God had freely given to each of us. As the confusion and chaos built in momentum, our human egos coerced us into believing that whatever we needed to do to survive was appropriate, even if it meant lying, stealing, cheating or killing.

We clearly see the evidence of that tragic situation everywhere we look. Practically every malady manifesting on Earth can be traced back to the fear-based consciousness of lack and limitation. This is true whether we are talking about the corruption, violence and moral depravity in governments, the military, financial institutions, corporations, the medical, insurance and pharmaceutical industries, religious organizations, educational institutions, profit and nonprofit organizations or the private sector and individuals.

Our ego-based fear for survival infuses Humanity with a willingness to do whatever it takes to get what we want. For aeons of time, people have continually acted out of the distorted perception of lack and limitation. As a result of this illusion, people everywhere are writhing in the pain and suffering our human egos perpetuated by entrapping us in poverty consciousness.

It is time for us to take back the power our human egos have usurped from us, and it is time for us to give our God Selves full dominion of our lives. We have the ability to reclaim our Divine Heritage and to restore the limitless flow of God's abundance. *Never has it been more important for us to do so.*

As the Light of God increases on Earth and the negativity that conflicts with that Light is pushed to the surface to be transmuted and healed, we are seeing the global economy reel on the shifting sands of corruption and greed. From outer appearances, it looks like the economy is headed for total collapse but, in fact, *this is only the darkness before the dawn.*

The purging that is taking place in the economic world is a necessary part of the healing process. The old-age archetypes of greed, selfishness, corruption and moral depravity are being exposed and shattered in order to clear the way for the new archetypes of limitless abundance. Those who are willing to attain their wealth by harming another part of life are doomed to failure. Whether they are hurting people or polluting the Earth, their nefarious efforts are being exposed in the radiant Light of Divine Truth.

The dog-eat-dog, looking-out-for-number-one selfishness that has been so prevalent over the years cannot be sustained once the new archetypes of limitless abundance are in place. This is the time that has been prophesied when *"All that is hidden must now be revealed."* The clandestine schemes of deception and dishonesty that have trapped the multitudes in a web of poverty and fear will no longer be concealed in a cloak of darkness. The elite few who hoard the wealth of the world while millions live in hunger, disease and squalor will no longer succeed in their self-obsessed ventures.

Poverty is a human miscreation, and it was never intended to be part of our Divine Plan. The distorted patterns of lack and limitation are an illusion which we created and that we are sustaining through our thoughts, words, feelings, actions and beliefs.

The new archetypes of limitless abundance are based on the Divine Truth that *God is our supply*, not outer world circumstances. Our natural heritage is the continual God supply of all good things. When we remember this Truth, we open our hearts up once again to the limitless flow of God's abundance.

This unique moment will be recorded in the Golden Book of Life as the time in which the Era of Eternal Peace and Limitless Abundance was permanently established on Earth. Just imagine, you and I are physically present to cocreate the events that will lift this planet and all her life into the Light of Eternal Peace and Limitless Abundance.

Reclaiming Limitless Abundance

In order for us to reclaim our natural Birthright of God's limitless abundance, we need to clear our relationship with money. Since we have chosen to live in a system that uses money as our source of exchange, we need to eliminate our fear of it and realize that money is just a source of energy—*period*. It is not some awesome entity that comes into our lives to wield its power over us and rule our destinies. It is only because of our fear for survival that we have allowed money to have that kind of control over us.

First of all, we must eliminate poverty consciousness and start functioning with prosperity consciousness. Instead of worrying all of the time about not having enough money, we need to focus on our gratitude for the money we do have. Gratitude is a magnet that brings more of what we are grateful for into our lives.

Every time we spend a penny of our money, whether it is to buy groceries, pay our bills, for entertainment or whatever, we should bless it with gratitude for the service it is providing to us. Then we should let it go freely, *knowing* that money is just *a source of energy* and, like ALL energy, it will go out, expand and return to us for more service.

If we send our money forth grudgingly, bemoaning the high cost of living, fearing we won't have enough to cover our expenses, hating to spend it on the necessities of life, we will automatically block the flow of God's abundance.

The process of developing prosperity consciousness does not mean going out and charging unnecessary things and getting ourselves deeper in debt by spending money we don't have. It does mean, however, that we recognize money is providing a service to us that we should accept with gratitude and appreciation.

As we move forward at warp speed, it is crucial for us to remember that we are responsible for cocreating our own prosperity. We must perpetually ask ourselves, *"Is what I Am thinking, saying, feeling or doing adding to my prosperity and prosperity consciousness, or am I blocking my prosperity with poverty consciousness?"*

If what we are expressing is reflecting poverty consciousness, then we must ask ourselves, *"What do I need to change in order to express prosperity consciousness and open up to God's flow of abundance right now?"* It is imperative that we hold tenaciously to our positive visions, and energize them daily with our affirmations and the focus of our attention. We must be deliberate about our wealth. Through persistence, confidence and acceptance, we will open our hearts to the God supply of all good things.

A Vital Factor in Receiving God's Abundance

The ebb and flow of life, which is so clearly demonstrated in the Law of the Circle, is a critical factor in order for us to receive God's flow of limitless abundance. There are many expressions that describe the ebb and flow of our lifeforce: inbreath and outbreath, radiation and magnetization, giving and receiving, cause and effect, action and reaction, involution and evolution. In order for us to receive a continual flow of God's limitless abundance, the ebb and flow of our gift of life must be *balanced*. If we are receiving more lifeforce than we are sending out, or vice versa, an imbalance is created that blocks the flow.

When we volunteered to embody on Earth, we agreed that we would cooperate with the Universal Law of the Circle and maintain the balance of our lifeforce. Our God Parents agreed to provide what we would need to sustain our physical bodies and the electronic Light substance that beats our hearts and enables us to live, move, breathe, think and have our Being in the physical plane.

In return, we agreed that we would balance our gift of life by using our lifeforce to expand the borders of the Kingdom of Heaven on Earth. We agreed that we would observe the patterns of perfection in the Causal Body of God and then combine those patterns to create previously unknown expressions of Divinity.

When we fell into the abyss of our own human miscreations, we forgot about the contracts we made with God. Even though we were still receiving and using all of the gifts our God Parents were providing for us, we were not giving anything back in return. We were not balancing the gift of life with love and appreciation. That self-centered behavior blocked the flow of God's abundance.

Once our supply was blocked, we fell into the pattern of struggling every day just to make enough money to pay for the things we needed to sustain our physical bodies. Those were the same things that God had already given to us for free. When we expend our time, energy and money to pay for what God has already provided, it is like not giving anything back at all.

As a result, we were cast into the throes of poverty.

This perplexing condition is the cause of poverty, and it is the reason for the financial situations that are affecting the global economy now. The good news is that we created this problem, and we have the power to do something about it. *We have the ability to renew our contracts with God and to change our direction.*

All we have to do to renew our contract with God is to begin doing what we agreed to do in the first place. This means that we need to balance the gifts of life we receive and benefit from every day by giving something back in return. This may sound complicated, but it is actually very simple.

Anything we do to improve the quality of life on Earth expands the borders of Divinity. There are as many ways to open up to the flow of God's abundance as there are people on the planet devising ways to balance their gift of life by sharing their love and appreciation.

Increasing Our Cash Flow

If we specifically want to increase the abundance of *money* in our lives, however, there is a very specific process we must follow. We use money as our means of exchange, so in order for us to attain prosperity and become financially free, we need to increase our flow of money. Remember, like attracts like. What we send out in the form of energy expands and returns to us. Money is energy. *In order for us to attract more money into our lives, we need to send out money.*

We are all sending out money to pay for our bodily needs. The problem is God has already provided those needs to us for free, so that money doesn't count as our gift of appreciation. In order to increase our cash flow, we must give money back to support things over and above what God has already given to us for free.

The spiritual key to increasing our cash flow is for us to give a portion of our money away to people who will use it to assist in cocreating Heaven on Earth. We can accomplish this by giving money to people, institutions, organizations, charities, spiritual groups, religious groups, corporations, human- or animal-rights groups, environmental groups, human endeavors associated with science, medicine, research, alternative fuels and energy sources, the arts, education, sustainable development, global peace, justice or any other person, place, condition or thing that we know is working with reverence for ALL life and a genuine desire to cocreate the wonders of Heaven on Earth.

The general consensus is that if we will give as little as *ten percent* of our income back to God in appreciation for our gift of life, we will open up to such an influx of money that we won't be able to handle it all.

The attitude and consciousness with which we give our money away is critical to our success. Our money must be freely given away with no strings attached. We cannot expect anything in return from the people or places we give our money to other than for them to use the money for the highest good of all concerned and *to improve the quality of life on the planet*. However, once we give our money away, it is important for us to acknowledge and accept that the money will expand and return to us through God's supply of all good things.

The reason we need to consciously claim the return of our money is because we have forgotten that money is a form of energy which should have been going out and returning to us all along. We have just been blocking that natural process with our poverty consciousness.

Through the distorted perception of our human egos, we have developed the expectation that money goes out but that it never comes back. By claiming our Divine Birthright and decreeing to accept God's limitless flow of abundance, we reprogram ourselves to expect prosperity. We can start by claiming a tenfold return of our gift, but, in Truth, there is no limit to the return we can expect. When we state the following decree with deep feeling, we affirm our gift of love and appreciation and claim God's flow of abundance on the return current.

Prosperity Decree

I Am giving ($100.00)   back to God as a gift of Love in appreciation for my gift of Life.

I expect and accept that this money is blessing all life and increasing tenfold   ($1,000.00)   on its return to me with the highest good of all concerned.

Once we give our love and appreciation back to God in the form of money and claim our tenfold return, it is important for us to *consciously expect* to receive an increase of money. We must not limit God by trying to figure out where the money will come from; we just need to be open and receptive to every single avenue of return.

Every time we receive unexpected money, for example, if someone buys something for us or pays for something that we thought we were going to have to pay for ourselves, we should accept that is God's abundance flowing back into our lives. If things we need are on sale or if our bills are less than we thought they were going to be, that is our gift of money coming back to us. If someone gives us an item that we thought we were going to have to purchase or we get a raise or a higher paying job, we are receiving God's abundance. If someone finally pays an old debt that we thought was lost forever or we receive a bigger refund than we were expecting on our income tax return, we should acknowledge the money is part of our returning abundance.

The more we adjust to the constant flow of giving and receiving our money in love and appreciation for our gift of life, the sooner the limitless abundance of God will be an ever-present state of Being and a tangible presence in our lives.

Reaching the Critical Mass of Prosperity Consciousness

Because of the urgency of the hour, we are receiving more assistance from the Heavenly Realms than ever before. To assist us in reaching the critical mass of prosperity consciousness, we are receiving unprecedented gifts from our Father-Mother God. One of the gifts is a unique frequency of the Violet Flame that is specifically designed to transmute the thoughts, words, actions and feelings we have expressed in the past that are vibrating with poverty consciousness.

When we invoke that Violet Flame, it flows through our Heart Flame and is stamped with our own unique, electronic pattern. The Violet Flame then flows out into the Universe and magnetizes to itself every electron of precious life energy we have ever misqualified with poverty consciousness. The Violet Flame instantly transmutes these distorted patterns back into

Light so they will no longer manifest as poverty in our Earthly experiences.

The following is a powerful visualization that has been given to us by the Legions of Light to help us receive the maximum benefit from this Violet Flame.

Transmuting Poverty Consciousness

To participate in this activity of Light, sit comfortably in your chair with your arms and legs uncrossed, your spine as straight as possible. Rest your hands gently in your lap with your palms facing upward.

Breathe in deeply, and as you exhale, let all of the tension of the day just drop away. Feel yourself become completely relaxed. Your mind is activated, and the cobwebs of confusion, doubt and fear are swept away. You are mentally alert and vibrantly aware. You are enveloped in a forcefield of invincible protection, which prevents anything that is not of the Light from distracting you or interfering with this sacred moment.

Feel the deep, inner glow of peace and well-being. Experience the joy of expectancy and enthusiasm. Accept the Divine Truth that *you are the Open Door that no one can shut.*

Now participate in this visualization with the full power of your attention. This visualization is stated in the first person so each of us will experience it personally.

Beloved Presence of God blazing in my heart, I accept and *know* that you have taken command of my physical, etheric, mental and emotional bodies. My bodies are now rising in vibration as they integrate with your radiant Presence. My awareness is increasing, and I clearly hear your *"still, small voice within."* I experience your exquisite vibrations, and I Am flooded with Light. My consciousness is open and receptive to your pure, spiritual energy. You respond to my every call for assistance. From my new level of awareness, I now know *you are in me, and I Am in you. I clearly remember I Am YOU.*

I Am a Being of Radiant Light!
I Am One with the energy and vibration

that is the all-encompassing Presence of God.
I Am One with the Divine Love
that fills the Universe with the glory of Itself.
I Am One with every particle of life.
I AM One with the Divine Plan for Planet Earth.
I Am One with the limitless flow
of God's abundance.
I Am that I Am.

A reactivation and initiation into multidimensional aware-ness is occurring within me, and I Am lifted up, closer in vibra-tion to the very Heart of God. The pre-encoded memories that were imprinted deep within my cellular patterns aeons ago are activated. These patterns reveal my Divine Plan, my purpose and reason for Being. I Am experiencing a great soaring and awakening as I remember my Divine Heritage.

I Am now stepping through the doorway into multidimen-sional reality. Here I Am empowered with even more rarefied frequencies of Divinity. Moment to moment, this radiant Light is awakening within me previously untapped levels of wisdom and illumination. I easily grasp each Divine Thought and Idea. As I do, avenues of opportunity unfold before me. I feel a sense of elation as each opportunity presents itself. I joyously seize the Divine Opportunities, and I feel a greater sense of self-worth and accomplishment than ever before. My life is pulsating with a sense of meaning and warmth.

I Am now lifted higher into the Realms of Perfection...and now higher...and now higher.

In this realm, I easily release and let go of attachments and behavior patterns that do not support my highest good. I re-lease all patterns that reflect a consciousness less than prosper-ity. I recognize *this is the moment of my new beginning.*

I now have the absolute ability to create prosperity con-sciousness, and I do so easily and joyously.

I Am experiencing my true integrity.
I Am trustworthy and honest.
I Am an expression of Divine Truth.
I Am worthy and deserving of prosperity, and
I Am able to transform every aspect of my life now.

Change is manifesting in my life through Divine Grace

and Love. As each aspect that needs changing surfaces before me, I easily love it free and forgive myself for my perceived transgression.

I know I Am a Child of God, and I deserve to be loved and forgiven. As the changes take place, I Am experiencing a sense of inner calm, patience and silence.

I Am in the Divine Flow of my true God Reality. I Am One with the Infinite Intelligence within me, and I Am *always* able to make correct choices. I love myself unconditionally, and I Am grateful for this opportunity to change. In deep humility and gratitude, I accept this merciful opportunity.

The Divine Power to sustain these changes is continually flowing through me, and from this moment forth, I choose to create a life of prosperity and that which supports my highest good.

Once again I Am lifted higher into the Realms of Perfection...and now higher...and now higher.

I focus on the sacred essence of my Holy Breath. I realize that with every *inbreath,* I extend in consciousness through my eternal journey into Infinity to the source of never-ending perfection. With every *outbreath*, I magnetize the full momentum of that perfection and radiate its blessings forth to all life evolving on Earth.

My inbreath is the open portal to the Pure Land of Boundless Splendor and Infinite Light, and my outbreath is the source of all Divine Blessings for Humanity and the planet. I understand now that the Divine Gifts being presented to Humanity from the Legions of Light serving this sweet Earth will be drawn into the world of form on the Holy Breath.

I consecrate and dedicate myself to be the Open Door for these sacred gifts of Light.

Father-Mother God, make me an instrument of your limitless abundance. I Am the flaming Hands of God, now made manifest in the physical plane of Earth.

I Am ready to transmute every electron of energy I have ever released in any existence or dimension that is vibrating with a frequency less than God's limitless flow of abundance, prosperity, opulence, the supply of all good things and my eternal financial freedom.

I Am enveloped in an invincible forcefield of protection

and eternal peace. I Am able to review my life as an objective observer. I ask my God Self to push to the surface of my conscious mind every experience I have ever had, both known and unknown, that is in any way preventing me from attaining prosperity.

As these experiences begin to surface, I breathe in deeply, and on the Holy Breath, I pierce into the heart of the Violet Flame. I absorb the most powerful frequency of the Violet Flame I can endure, and I breathe it in, through and around all of the energy returning to me now to be loved free.

The sacred Violet Flame instantly transmutes the negative thoughts, words, actions, feelings, beliefs and memories that are blocking my eternal financial freedom. Every electron of poverty or poverty consciousness, as well as every electron reflecting lack or limitation of any kind, is being transformed back into its original perfection.

My God Self now expands this activity of Light and reaches back through the Ages of time to magnetize into the Violet Flame every electron of poverty consciousness that is stamped with my individual electronic pattern. These records and memories flow effortlessly into the Violet Flame, and I Am able to release them without pain or fear. I feel the buoyant joy of my newfound freedom.

As I slowly inbreathe, I continue to reach deeper into the sacred Violet Flame. As I slowly exhale, this unprecedented gift from God floods the physical plane of Earth with its Divine Essence.

I now affirm with deep feeling and a true inner knowing:

I Am a force of the Violet Flame
more powerful than anything less than prosperity.

I realize I Am able to transmute, through the power of this sacred gift, the mass consciousness of poverty. All records and memories of Humanity's abuse of the substance of money now flow into the Violet Flame.

Under the direction of my God Self and the entire Company of Heaven, every electron of poverty consciousness that has ever been released by any part of life, in any existence or dimension, both known and unknown, is surfacing for transmutation by the Violet Flame.

As each electron enters the Violet Flame, it is instantly trans-

muted—cause, core, effect, record and memory—back into the
frequencies of prosperity and God's limitless abundance.

I Am a force of the Violet Flame
more powerful than anything less than prosperity.

I Am a force of the Violet Flame
more powerful than anything less than prosperity.

I Am a force of the Violet Flame
more powerful than anything less than prosperity.

I Am Free! I Am Free! I Am Free!
I Am eternally, financially FREE!

It is done! And, so it is!

I accept, through the Presence of God pulsating in my heart,
that this sacred activity of Light will be maintained, eternally
self-sustained, increased with every breath I take daily and
hourly, moment to moment, the maximum that Cosmic Law
will allow until all life belonging to or serving the Earth at this
time is wholly Ascended and FREE!

Our Prosperity is
the Greatest Need of the Hour

Awakening Humanity is reaching up in energy, vibration
and consciousness as never before, and we are tapping into the
patterns of perfection from the Causal Body of God that are
now flowing into the mental stratum of Earth. These patterns
contain effective and viable solutions for all of the maladies
occurring on the planet. They are pulsating with the Divine Ideas
from the Heart and Mind of God that will help us to cocreate
successful ways to feed the hungry, heal the sick, house the
homeless and bring abundance to the poverty stricken.

By reaching into the Causal Body of God, we will learn
how to rid the Earth of pollution, develop clean and sustainable
energy sources, establish global peace and tolerance, bring happiness and joy to the desperate and hopeless, educate the un-
educated and enlighten the unaware. We will also learn rever-

ence for life, mutual respect and acceptance, harmonious cooperation and how to develop a win-win consciousness that will
support the highest good for all life evolving here. The Causal
Body of God contains every wondrous thing we can imagine or
envision to assist us in cocreating Heaven on Earth.

If we are to implement the new, innovative ideas and bring
them into physical manifestation, *we must attain our financial
freedom.* Awakening souls must have financial support in order
to develop the technology and the systems that will enable us
to bring the new ideas into tangible reality. According to the
Legions of Light who are assisting us from the Heavenly
Realms:

*"The greatest need of the hour is for awakening Light-
workers to attain financial freedom so that you can be
FREE to fulfill your individual Divine Plans and quickly
implement the viable solutions for the world's problems
that are flowing into your conscious minds from the
Causal Body of God."*

Our skills, talents, awareness, wisdom, knowledge,
strength and courage are urgently needed NOW. It is imperative that we stop distracting ourselves from fulfilling our Divine Plans by struggling from morning until
night just to sustain our physical bodies. Our financial
freedom will allow us to respond to the inner promptings
of our hearts, and God's limitless abundance will free us
up to go and do whatever our God Selves guide us to do
in service to Humanity and Mother Earth.

The time for us to fulfill what we have come to Earth
to do is NOW! The Earth's Ascension process is being
accelerated, and the moment when we will reach critical
mass is nearer than it appears. The Spiritual Hierarchy is
assisting us to attain financial freedom in the shortest
amount of time possible.

Through unprecedented Divine Intervention, a matrix of
Light has been created above the planet that is magnetizing the
Golden Light of God's Eternal Peace and Limitless Abundance
into the atmosphere of Earth. The matrix was created in 1992
shortly after the Earth began the initial impulse of her ascent up
the Spiral of Evolution into the 4th Dimension. This powerful
forcefield has been energized and sustained by dedicated Light-

workers all over the world, and it has been building in power and momentum daily and hourly. Now it is time for this force-field of prosperity to be lifted into the 5th Dimension.

The 5th-Dimensional matrix for God's Eternal Peace and Limitless Abundance is empowered through the following visualization, which is stated in the first person so that we will each experience it personally.

The Gift of Divine Intervention

I Am now lifted up in consciousness into the Realms of Perfection. I pass over the Highway of Light that bridges Heaven and Earth. I enter the Pure Land of Boundless Splendor and Infinite Light that radiates in the atmosphere of Earth, and *I KNOW I AM ONE WITH GOD.*

All the Light Beings evolving on Earth are joining me in consciousness in this octave of pure joy. I know I Am One with every part of life. As one unified voice, we send forth a clarion call into the Universe invoking our illumined brothers and sisters to come and help us in our moment of transformation. The Cosmic Tone reverberates through all dimensions, and the response comes from every corner of the Cosmos. Legions of Divine Beings descend into the atmosphere of Earth and take their strategic positions. They stand shoulder to shoulder, forming a tremendous circle above the Earth.

As one breath, one heartbeat, one energy and vibration of perfection, they breathe in the *Golden Light of Eternal Peace and Limitless Abundance* from the core of Creation. It is the most glorious, scintillating color of gold I have ever seen. As these resplendent Beings absorb the essence of this Divine Gift into their Heart Flames, they become filled with Golden Light.

Now, in perfect synchronicity, they each exhale a Golden Ray of Light into the center of the circle. As the Golden Rays merge, they form a brilliant Sun. The Sun is the forcefield within which the 5th-Dimensional Matrix of Eternal Peace and Limitless Abundance is held.

The matrix is a scintillating Golden Pyramid of Light, and within its base is a shimmering Lotus Blossom. As the Lotus Blossom pulsates, it sends concentric circles of Golden Light charged with Eternal Peace and Limitless Abundance into the atmosphere of Earth.

In order for Humanity to receive the blessings of this Golden

Light, it must be drawn though the Heart Flames of souls embodied on Earth. I volunteer to be an Open Door through which this Divine Gift of Peace and Abundance will continually flow.

My Heart Flame begins expanding. I experience a beautiful blue Flame blazing through my left-brain hemisphere and the left side of my body. This is the masculine polarity of God, and it is qualified with Divine Will, Authority, Power and Protection.

I now experience a beautiful pink Flame blazing through my right-brain hemisphere and the right side of my body. This is the feminine polarity of God, and it is qualified with Divine Love, Adoration and Reverence for All Life.

As the masculine and feminine polarities of God are balanced within me, they give birth to the sunshine yellow Flame of God—the Son/Daughter of God—the Christ Light of Divine Wisdom, Understanding, Illumination and Enlightenment.

I Am now enveloped in my victorious, Threefold Flame,
and I Am an Open Door for the Golden Flame of
Eternal Peace and Limitless Abundance!

As I breathe in deeply, I magnetize into my Heart Flame a replica of the Golden Pyramid and Lotus Blossom from the luminous matrix pulsating above the Earth. The replica creates a permanent, magnetic forcefield in my heart that draws the blessings of the Golden Flame of Eternal Peace and Limitless Abundance into the physical plane of Earth.

I breathe in once again, and as I exhale, a cascading fountain of Golden Light pours through my Heart Center. The sacred Light of Peace and Abundance floods the planet and flows into the hands of every awakening soul, every activity of Light and every conscious person who will use this gift of prosperity to improve the quality of life on Earth.

Through this gift, the substance of money becomes tangibly available and flows continually into my hands and the hands of every person who is receiving the ideas and viable solutions from the Causal Body of God that will solve the problems and maladies existing on Earth. Money flows easily and effortlessly into the hands and use of all on the planet who are operating from a consciousness of reverence for ALL life.

As the Golden Light of Eternal Peace and Limitless Abundance reaches its furthest point of destination in the world of form, it begins its return journey back to the source. It flows back to my Heart Flame and brings the limitless flow of money and the God supply of all good things into my life. As I receive it into my heart, I affirm:

Through the Power of God blazing in my heart and the hearts of ALL Humanity, I receive the Golden Light of Eternal Peace and Limitless Abundance.

In deep humility and gratitude, I accept God's Eternal Peace and Limitless Abundance as a tangible presence in my life.

On the wings of this Divine Light, I Ascend into the Realms of Truth. From this higher perspective, I have the clear inner knowing that GOD IS MY SUPPLY!

I relinquish now, in the name of God, all of the power I have ever given to lack and limitation through my thoughts, words, actions and feelings.

I relinquish now, in the name of God, all of the beliefs I have ever had that are based in poverty consciousness.

I consecrate and dedicate my very life to be the Open Door through which the Golden Light of Eternal Peace and Limitless Abundance will flow to bless me, my family, friends, coworkers and ALL Humanity.

As I breathe, think, speak, feel and act, the Presence of God within me perpetually expands the Golden Light of Eternal Peace and Limitless Abundance to all life evolving on Earth.

I now breathe in deeply and return my consciousness to the room. I become aware of my physical body and gently move my hands and feet.

I Am a multidimensional Being of Light, and I abide at once in both the Pure Land of Boundless Splendor and Infinite Light and on Earth.

I realize that each time I participate in this visualization, the sacred gifts of Eternal Peace and Limitless Abundance build in momentum and effectiveness.

Moment by moment the transformation is taking place, and new matrixes and archetypes for peace and abundance are being secured. A higher consciousness is awakening within Humanity, and reverence for life, mutual respect and a heart desire to always seek the highest good for all concerned is becoming the order of the new Cosmic Day.

My life now reflects my permanent financial freedom. From this moment forth, everything I need to fulfill my Divine Plan is always available to me.

The Universal Laws "Ask and you shall receive" and "Knock and the door will be opened" are instantly manifest.

I feel the buoyancy and elation of my newfound freedom. The Company of Heaven rejoices with me as I reclaim my Divine Birthright of Eternal Peace and Limitless Abundance.

* I Am! I Am! I Am! The eternally sustained manifestation of God's limitless supply of money and every good thing I require to assist me in my service to the Light, NOW made manifest and sustained by Holy Grace.

(Repeat 3 times from *)

It is done! And so it is!

During a powerful activation of the Golden Christ Grid that took place on April 13, 2002, the Legions of Light accelerated the matrix of the Golden Pyramid and Lotus Blossom into the frequencies of the *5th Dimension.*

The 5th-Dimensional frequencies of the Golden Light of Eternal Peace and Limitless Abundance must now be anchored in the physical plane through the Heart Flames of souls who are embodied on Earth. In other words, God needs a body!

We are being asked to redouble our efforts and to increase our affirmations and visualizations as we empower this *5th-*

Dimensional matrix.

When the matrix was originally created in 1992, we were asked by the Spiritual Hierarchy to produce an audio cassette tape of a guided visualization that would sustain and empower the flow of Eternal Peace and Limitless Abundance on Earth. When Lightworkers all over the world are empowering and energizing a thoughtform in exactly the same way by listening to the same tape, the effect is exponential and extremely powerful. Whereas, if each Lightworker is creating a different vision of the thoughtform, our collective efforts are fragmented and not nearly as effective.

Tens of thousands of people have used the tape titled *"The Gift To Reclaim Your Prosperity"* to empower the matrix of Eternal Peace and Limitless Abundance for all Humanity. Now, the Spiritual Hierarchy is asking Lightworkers to use the tape to energize the new *5th-Dimensional* frequencies of this resplendent forcefield into the physical plane.

THE DIVINE INTENT IS TO ASSIST EACH AWAKENING SOUL TO ATTAIN HIS OR HER FINANCIAL FREEDOM IN THE FASTEST TIME POSSIBLE.

For those of you who already have the tape, please listen to it with the KNOWING that this forcefield is now vibrating with *5th-Dimensional* frequencies of the Golden Light of Eternal Peace and Limitless Abundance.

If you do not have a copy of the tape and you would like to purchase one, they are available. To order the tape, please send in the order form on page **327** or contact us through the information in the front of this book.

We also have a very informative prosperity booklet available that has a beautiful color picture of the Pyramid and Lotus Blossom Matrix on the cover, which will help us each envision that powerful gift of Light. The booklet is titled *"It Is Time For YOU To Be Financially Free."* If you would like to order the booklet, you may do so by sending in the order form on page **325** or by contacting us through the information in the front of this book.

Thank You!

The Lightworkers at the New Age Study of Humanity's Purpose have dedicated our lives to making the life-transforming information pouring forth from the Realms of Illumined Truth readily available to everyone who is interested. This information is a sacred gift from the Spiritual Hierarchy, given at this time to assist Humanity in our awakening process. These are wondrous but very challenging times, and the assistance we are being given from the Heavenly Realms in the way of guidance, encouragement and practical tools helps immeasurably.

In order to make this information available to everyone, since 1980 we have presented FREE seminars and workshops in the United States of America and various other parts of the world. Gratefully, we have been able to continue this ongoing service to Humanity because of financial donations from generous people who are willing to help us with this vitally important facet of the Divine Plan.

The New Age Study of Humanity's Purpose, Inc. is a non-profit, educational organization. We have a 501 (c) 3 tax deductible status for contributions and financial donations. We are very grateful for all of the contributions that have been given to us thus far and for the contributions that will be given to us in the future to help us continue this work.

As One Unified Heart, we at the
New Age Study of Humanity's Purpose
invoke our Father-Mother God and the entire Company
of Heaven to increase the precious Financial Gifts
you give to us
one thousand-times one thousandfold
as they flow back to YOU.

God Bless You for your service to the Light!

May the perpetual flow of
God's Limitless Abundance
expand daily and hourly as it tangibly
manifests in YOUR life
and the lives of ALL Humanity.

Chapter 3

Chapter 3

The Illusion of "Good and Evil"

The painful events of September 11, 2001, evoked an outpouring of love, generosity and unity beyond anything the United States of America or the world had ever experienced. It also evoked a level of fear and insecurity that temporarily shattered our comfort zones and changed our way of life. The fear caused some people to demand immediate retaliation and war. The love, however, caused people to open their hearts and reach out to the family of Humanity in nurturing, helpful ways.

People have reevaluated their lives and determined what is really important to them. As a result, they are reconnecting with their spiritual roots and awakening to the Truth of who they are and why they are here.

Our God Selves are taking advantage of the moment, and they are catapulting us forward into new levels of awareness. The misperceptions of our fragmented human egos are being exposed in the blazing Light of Illumined Truth. This process is always a little disconcerting and scary. When it happens, the belief systems that we have trusted to be stable and true crumble before our very eyes, and new concepts that seem conflicting and unfamiliar begin to filter into our conscious minds.

One of the greatest misperceptions of our human egos is the notion that the polarities of God are good and evil. Our egos have coerced us into believing that since God is all there is, "evil" must have been created by God and, therefore, must be part of God's plan.

We know that polarities must be balanced in order for harmony to exist in the physical plane so, through the eyes of our egos, we look at the *human miscreations* existing in our lives and just accept them as polarities we must adjust to and learn to live with. We believe that the polarities of God are: love—hate, peace—war, health—disease, prosperity—poverty, happiness—grief, etcetera. Our egos have convinced us that both polarities are necessary and that we cannot experience one without the other. Unfortunately, *this is the most erroneous and destructive belief system we can have*. As long as we believe that the natural polarity of peace is war, we will continue to perpetuate war. As long as we believe that the natural polarity of prosperity is poverty, we will cocreate poverty. War is not the *polarity* of peace; it is a grossly, mutated human miscreation—the *opposite* of peace. Poverty is not the *polarity* of prosperity; it is a grossly, mutated human miscreation—the *opposite* of prosperity. Humanly-created mutations or opposites are entirely different from the natural polarities of God.

During this unique time of awakening, our fragmented human egos are being given an opportunity to be transformed into Light, but they don't believe that they will survive the process. Consequently, they are fighting tooth and nail to cling to their painful, limited, obsolete realities. Most of them have been so traumatized by the Earthly experiences we have gone through that they are afraid to trust. They think it is better to face the pain we know rather than risk the unknown. Even though our egos are miserable, at least what we are going through is familiar to them, and they know what to expect.

That distorted thinking is wreaking havoc all over the world and creating the confusion and chaos that we are witnessing daily through the media. It is time for us to lift our heads above the misinformation and disinformation being propagated by our fragmented human egos. It is time for each of us to tap into our own Divine Guidance.

If we step back and observe the events unfolding on the planet, we will realize that what we are witnessing is a metaphor for Humanity's awakening. The metaphor reflects the struggle that is occurring within each of us as our God Selves strive to lift our human egos into the Light and regain control of our physical, etheric, mental and emotional bodies.

In Truth, God does not release one electron of precious life energy that is less than the harmony and love of God. Therefore, *anything* that conflicts with the limitless perfection of God, for example: pain, suffering, poverty, war, hatred, prejudice, intolerance, corruption, violence, abuse of power, greed, selfishness, disease, aging, death as we know it or any other expression of "evil," is a distorted *human miscreation*. These miscreations were created through Humanity's free will choices and the misuse of our creative faculties of thought and feeling, *NOT BY GOD*. It is true that we use our gift of life and the electronic substance from God to create these distorted mutations, but *we* created them—not God. They have nothing whatsoever to do with the polarities of God, and we certainly do not have to experience these gross miscreations in order to experience the polarities of God.

The Polarities of God

The polarities of our Father-Mother God are *NOT* good and evil. The polarities of God are the *masculine polarity* of Divine Will, Authority, Power, the Outbreath, Radiation and Activity of our Father God and the *feminine polarity* of Divine Love, Adoration, Reverence for Life, the Inbreath, Magnetization and Cohesive Stillness of our Mother God.

It is true that in order for something to manifest and be sustained in a *physical reality,* both polarities of God must be present, but, as you can see, the polarities are not good and evil or positive and negative. The polarities of our Father-Mother God are: Power—Love, Will—Adoration, Outbreath—Inbreath, Radiation—Magnetization, Activity—Stillness.

Prior to the fall, these polarities were perfectly balanced within each of us. The masculine polarity of our Father God activated our left-brain hemispheres—our rational, logical minds. It then radiated out through the power center of our Throat Chakras. The feminine polarity of our Mother God activated our right-brain hemispheres—our intuitive, creative minds. It then radiated out through the love center of our Heart Chakras.

When our right- and left-brain hemispheres were equally balanced, our spiritual brain centers—the pituitary, pineal, hypothalamus glands and the ganglionic centers at the base of our brains—were activated. They functioned at full capacity and held open the center of enlightenment, our Crown Chakras.

With our Crown Chakras of Enlightenment opened to full breadth, our God Selves were able to maintain control of our Earthly vehicles. Our power was always balanced with love and reverence for life, and our gift of free will was used as God intended it to be used. We used our lifeforce to cocreate the patterns of perfection from the Causal Body of God on Earth, and we demonstrated the Universal Law *"As above, so below."* Day by day, we learned to become cocreators with our God Parents.

During our evolutionary process, something dramatically shifted, and everything changed. There are myriad, diverse and conflicting scenarios describing just what happened, but for our purposes here, I am just going to say that, tragically, there came a point in time when the men and women evolving on Earth chose to use our free will to create mutated patterns of imperfection that conflicted with the Causal Body of God.

Once we started using our free will to distort our gift of life with negative thoughts and feelings, we began to experience pain and suffering for the very first time. Our reflex response was to close our Heart Chakras so the negative experiences we were creating wouldn't hurt so much. When we closed our hearts, we blocked the portal through which the Divine Love of our Mother God entered the physical plane. That tragic event forced Her to withdraw from the Earth. Her Light diminished to a mere fraction of its former power, and the trickle of our Mother God's polarity that remained was barely enough to sustain brain consciousness.

Without the full lifeforce of our Mother God's polarity, our right brains became almost dormant, which caused our spiritual brain centers to atrophy and our Crown Chakras to close. Humanity was gradually reduced to using only ten percent of our brain capacity. As time went by, we descended into the chaotic frequencies of our own human miscreations, which short-circuited our communications with our God Selves. When that occurred, we became desperate. To fill the void left by our lack of communication with our God Selves, we created our fragmented, fear-based human egos.

Eventually, we forgot about our God Selves, and we began accepting our limited human egos as the totality of who we are. Through the distorted perception of our egos, we decided that the physical plane of Earth must be the only reality that exists. That caused us to give full control of our Earthly bodies to our egos. Our egos, in turn, determined that since the physical plane and our physical bodies are all that exist, our purpose and reason for being must be to use our bodies to gratify our physical senses. With that notion, we were catapulted into a quagmire of compulsive, obsessive greed and excesses.

We began using the power of our Throat Chakras without the love of our Heart Chakras or the enlightenment of our Crown Chakras. Without enlightenment and love, we started abusing and misusing our power. When we embodied as males, we abused our power by becoming aggressive, violent and domineering. When we embodied as females, we abused our power by being passive, subservient and allowing ourselves to be dominated.

That imbalance and abuse of power has been reflected in relationships between men and women throughout history. To this very day, we see how diversely men and women are treated in the various world religions, in political situations, in the business world, in families and marriages and in every other field of endeavor.

Now we are standing on the threshold of opportunity for the greatest shift of consciousness ever attempted in the whole of Creation. In order for Humanity to awaken in time to change our course of direction so that we will succeed in this wondrous adventure, the Divine Love of our Mother God must return to Earth, and the feminine polarity of God must become a balanced, tangible presence in our lives.

We must open the door and pave the way, so our Mother God can reclaim Her rightful authority within our Heart Chakras. She must likewise reclaim our right-brain hemispheres, so that our spiritual brain centers and our Crown Chakras of Enlightenment will be restored to their full Divine Potential, thus birthing our Solar Christ Presence, who are the true representatives of our God Selves in the physical plane.

The use of power within every man, woman and child must now be balanced with love, reverence for life and enlightenment. It is imperative for this vital healing to occur within every evolving soul whether we are in male or female bodies at this time. This healing will allow our God Selves to, once again, become the guiding Light of our Earthly experiences.

Chapter 4

Chapter 4

LOVING OUR HUMAN EGOS INTO THE LIGHT

Our human egos know that once the love of our Mother God is balanced within us, they will no longer be able to control and manipulate us through fear. They understand that their reign will be over, and they are terrified.

Our egos realize that when the Divine Authority, Will and Power of our Father God and the Divine Love, Adoration and Reverence for Life of our Mother God are brought into perfect balance, NOTH-ING can prevent the opening of our Crown Chakras of Enlightenment and the rebirth of our Solar Christ Presence—God Selves.

Once our God Selves reclaim our Earthly vehicles, the only option our egos will have is to move into the Light. This is a merciful gift of Divine Grace, but it is beyond our egos' comprehension. Consequently, they are doing everything they can to suppress the feminine polarity of Divine Love and to prevent our Mother God from opening the Stargates of our hearts. Our egos will not succeed, however, and when our they are loved into the Light, we will experience the transformation of our lives, both individually and collectively.

The world religions and the prophecies of old have all indicated that there will be a time when Humanity will experience a shift of consciousness and deliberately change our course of direction. Even though the terminology varies and the scenarios differ, the end result is the same. The prophecies all proclaim that during this auspicious time, Humanity will stop our self-destructive behavior and join together to cocreate a life-promoting world of peace and abundance—Heaven on Earth. This is not just a fantasy; it will be the natural result of the transformation of our egos and the return of our Mother God.

Fortunately, as we are lifted into the Light, our egos are lifted up with us. Then through patience and persistence, our egos will start trusting our God Selves. Once that occurs, they will gladly relinquish their control.

The following visualization has been given to us by the Company of Heaven to accelerate the process of transforming our Earthly bodies and lifting our egos into the Light.

I Am Creating My Solar Light Bodies

Through the Power of God blazing in my heart, I invoke the energy, vibration and consciousness of my God Presence to take full dominion of my physical, etheric, mental and emotional bodies. From this day forth, I consecrate my Earthly bodies to limitless physical perfection.

I invoke Beloved Helios and Vesta, the representatives of our Father-Mother God from our physical Sun; Alpha and Omega, the representatives of our Father-Mother God from our Central Sun; Elohae and Eloha, the representatives of our Father-Mother God from our Great Central Sun; El and Ela, the representatives of our Father-Mother from our Great, Great Central Sun.

I invoke the Beings of the Air Element, the Beings of the Water Element, the Beings of the Earth Element, the Beings of the Fire Element, the Beings of the Ether Element and my Body Elemental.

Blessed Ones, come forth now, and assist me in transforming my vehicles into expressions of Light. As of this moment, I Am entering my Solar Light Bodies of limitless physical perfection.

First, I see my glorious *Solar Etheric Vehicle* embodying the soul of my Divine Plan. This vehicle sets the tone or vibration of all energies entering the world of form through my emotional, mental and physical bodies.

Under the Law of Karma, Humanity had little chance of experiencing true health, youth or beauty in our physical bodies. Now, however, my 5th-Dimensional Solar Christ Presence takes command, and the Law of the Divine Plan supersedes the Law of Karma. Within my Solar Etheric Vehicle, God declares to all obsolete karmic patterns, *"Stand aside for the Solar Christ Presence and the formation of the Solar Light Bodies."* Thus, all energy from my I Am Presence now passing into my physical vehicles will only pass through the pulsating perfection patterns of my Divine Plan. The patterns of misuse within my etheric vehicle dissolve. All imperfect energy is now handled perfectly by my Solar Christ Self. Negativity no longer sets the tone of reality in my flesh. It is instantly transmuted through Divine Love. In my Solar Etheric Vehicle, only the patterns of energy associated with the Divine Plan enter into form.

I feel my Solar Etheric Vehicle baptized with the sacred Air Element, sealing my etheric body in a scintillating forcefield of the Divine Plan. I accept now that all energy reaching my outer world *comes straight out of my Divine Plan!* Only memories of absolute perfection functioning on all realms are within my Solar Etheric Vehicle. This vehicle is now outpicturing my magnificent Causal Body, the aura of my glorious I Am Presence through my flesh form. My Causal Body is one of my Cosmic Vehicles. It is a Celestial Forcefield containing all the Divine experiences, expertise, strengths, talents, virtues and excellence I have built into my God Presence since my first breath as a Cosmic Being.   *(pause)*

My *Solar Emotional Vehicle* now comes into view, pulsating with the Divine Love and Harmony of God. This is my most powerful vehicle baptized with the sacred Water Element. As my God Presence steps forth and claims this vehicle, my emotional body is transformed into the *feeling nature* of the Cosmic Holy Spirit. Thus, within my elemental presence on Earth is generated a Cosmic Forcefield that *will encompass the world in my heart of Divine Love.* My Divine Heart is holding the love nature for the planet, ensuring soul growth for all life everywhere. My Divine Love will ensure that all life will enter the glorious realms of Spiritual Freedom.

I have always known that *love reigns supreme*, and now this shall become a *tangible reality* rather than a wishful thought. I know, *with certainty*, that within this all-encompassing heart of Divine Love, my human ego finally lets go, slipping into its eternal resting place, literally going into a deep, deep sleep in the arms of Holy Spirit. It is like a fitful child who is letting go of its resistance to the Divine Plan and falling asleep in the arms of its unconditionally loving parent.

My ego is transformed by love, scientifically, psychologically, physiologically and spiritually transformed. It is inbreathed and absorbed into the fullness of my Solar Christ Presence/I Am Presence/Causal Body/White Fire Being through my Solar Emotional Body. As this occurs, my feeling world becomes God's feeling world, filled with the glorious qualities of Divine Being—Cosmic Love expressing in all its many facets. *(pause)*

My *Solar Physical Vehicle* now comes into view. It is a magnificent Solar Christ Being. It enters each cell of my physical body through the Light of my own glorious God Self. My Body Elemental has waited for centuries anticipating my return to Christ Consciousness. Every cell joyously accepts this Divine Light Body. I feel the baptism of my physical body with the sacred Earth Element now expressing its optimal Solar Frequencies.

I Am now composed of Solar Cells. I Am absorbing the Light of the Infinite Universe into the Solar Atoms that form each cell. I Am the Cosmic River of Solar Light from the Heart of God cascading in from my Solar Christ Presence/I Am Presence/Causal Body/White Fire Being. *I Am the Solar Christ of the Physical Realm* inbreathing, absorbing, expanding and projecting the fullness of my Divine Plan into my flesh vehicle.

Not only does each cell become a Solar Cell made up of Solar Atoms, each swirling with dazzling, multicolored Solar Energies, but the cells now combine their energies with each other in *a newly emerging Divine Alchemy within my Body of Light, generating unexplored levels of limitless physical perfection, health, beauty, abundance, joy and pleasure.*

My Solar Physical Vehicle is *only responsive to Divine Input* coming from the Infinite Realms of Light within Solar Atoms, from the Realms of Harmony within the other Solar Elemental Vehicles (Solar Mind, Solar Feelings, Solar Ethers) and the Eternal Realms of Light of my Solar Christ Presence/I Am Presence/Causal Body/White Fire Being.

My transformed, physical vehicle will never again accept karma dictating the reality of its physical functioning. Rather, I Am as the *Solar Christ of the Physical Realm* now functioning within my Solar Light Body, *managing all returning energy perfectly.* The old purpose of the flesh vehicle as the "repository of karmic lessons never learned" *has been transmuted forever!* I accept this and live in my Solar Light Body, deeply enjoying the Divine Alchemy continually expanding within it. It was created to experience the deep joy and abiding pleasure of living within Limitless Physical Perfection. I explore this and clear this path for all Humanity.   *(pause)*

Now, I turn to Divine Mind. My *Solar Mental Vehicle*, now baptized with the sacred Fire Element, blazes like a great Sun of

Light beginning as a halo around my head but eventually encompassing all of my form until I Am a *Sun*. Divine Mind receives fire life from the Heart of God. Only the Fire Breath of The Almighty now activates my mind with all Divine Thoughts, Ideas, Concepts, Imagination and *all aspects of Divine Mind beyond Imagination*. All of this is steadily anchoring now in my outer consciousness.

Slowly but surely I become aware of this, beginning as a soft, effulgent Light filling my mind. It leads me past imagination (my hopes and dreams of a future Divinity) into the *ever-present moment* of Divine Enlightenment, Illumination and Cosmic Wisdom.

All the layers of human thought (conscious, subconscious, unconscious mind) derived from my lower ego now slowly dissolve into this Light setting up an entirely new, Divine process of assimilating information. Now everything is seen as energy, vibration and consciousness, whether coming from my daily life or that reaching me from dimensions beyond. I watch for this in my meditations and in my awakened life. I Am prepared for a new mind and accept it as it happens, for *my acceptance is the Open Door*. It will begin subtly with no wrenching changes. *But it is happening!* It is getting stronger, and I Ascend with the Earth into all of her Divine Harmony and Perfection. *(pause)*

My Solar Light Bodies are now sealed in the Flame of the Immaculate Concept, and the Flame of Harmony has set the Divine Tone and Pattern for each of my Solar Vehicles. The Cosmic Flame of Harmony realigns the manifestation of Elemental Life on Earth with all Elemental existence everywhere present! The conditions necessary for passage safely and harmoniously onto the 5th-Dimensional Spiral of Evolution are now anchored and absorbed by Humanity. The Divine Plan for all life is victoriously underway, and all Elemental life sends forth its gratitude and loving adoration.

My Solar Light Bodies are building in power and momentum, and they expand daily and hourly with every breath I take.

* I Am the Resurrection and the Life of the Immaculate Concept
of Limitless Physical Perfection in my
physical, etheric, mental and emotional bodies
now made manifest
and permanently sustained by Holy Grace.
And so it is!
I Am, I Am, I Am.   *(Repeat 3 times from *)*

Chapter 5

Chapter 5

BECOMING AN INSTRUMENT OF GOD

We have volunteered to be on Earth during this critical moment to be the Heart, Head and Hands of God. Once again, we are in this schoolroom to learn how to use our creative faculties of thought and feeling to cocreate, in a physical reality, the patterns of perfection from the Causal Body of God. We have the gift of free will, and our thoughts and feelings are creative regardless of what we focus on. During this momentous time, it is imperative that we truly grasp the full meaning of this Divine Truth. By remembering this fact and acting out of this inner knowing, we can turn around what is happening on Earth and reclaim our course of direction.

Every soul evolving on Earth at this time has been preparing for aeons to cocreate a new reality on Earth during this Cosmic Moment. Through our individual life experiences, we have each developed unique skills, training, understanding and wisdom that no one else possesses in exactly the same way. Our unique abilities are vital for the salvation of this planet. It is time that we each go within to the deepest recesses of our hearts and ask our God Presence to guide and assist us in fulfilling the missions we have volunteered to accomplish. The entire Company of Heaven, Mother Earth and all life evolving on this planet are depending on each of us to remember who we are and why we are here.

For several decades, Lightworkers all over the globe have been working ceaselessly to awaken the masses and alert Humanity to the opportunities being presented to us by our Father-Mother God. We are Ascending into the 5th Dimension. The reason this is so significant is because the 5th Dimension is the octave of existence in which we will tangibly manifest our Solar Reality of Limitless Physical Perfection. It is within the 5th-Dimensional frequencies of Light that our Solar Christ Presence will take dominion of our four Earthly bodies and transform them, through Divine Alchemy, into the full perfection of our Solar Light Bodies.

In the 5th Dimension, we will reach into the Divine Mind and the Causal Body of God and tap into the Divine Ideas and viable solutions that will heal the maladies existing on Earth. It is the dimension in which we will fully claim our Divine Birthrights as Sons and Daughters of God. When that is accomplished, we will manifest a previously unknown expression of Godhood. Within the full embrace of that glorious Dimension of Solar Perfection, our options will be limitless and our potential infinite.

Before we can complete our Ascension into the 5th Dimension, we have some work to do. During the dawn of the new millennium, we were informed by the Spiritual Hierarchy that there were some resistant factions of Humanity who were in danger of not choosing to make the shift in time to Ascend with the rest of the planet. These recalcitrant souls were not only resisting their own Ascension, they were striving to prevent the Earth from moving forward in the Light as well. They were creating chaos and trying to entrap Humanity. To try to remedy the problem, our Father-Mother God, in unison with the Legions of Light from the whole of Creation, invoked the God Selves of Humanity for assistance and initiated an experiment unlike any ever attempted.

A previously unknown frequency of Divine Light that had been waiting in dormancy since the inception of the Universe was called forth from the Heart of God and activated into tangible use. This unparalleled expression of Divinity is known as the *Flame of Transfiguring Divine Love*. The Flame itself is a magnificent deep rose color with an aquamarine aura of Divine Clarity. Pulsating within the core of the Flame is an opalescent Sun of Transfiguration.

The scope and power of this Sacred Fire is monumental, actually beyond the comprehension of our finite minds. The Flame of Transfiguring Divine Love contains within its frequencies a *Divine Intelligence* that will reveal within each person's heart of hearts the erroneous information, concepts, thoughts, feelings, attitudes and fears that have perpetuated distorted belief systems and destructive behavior patterns.

For example, every heartless, depraved, mean, selfish, dishonest, abusive, corrupt, unethical, destructive, greedy, violent, ignorant, hateful thing the lower human ego manipulates a person into doing is based on *the illusion of separation, fear and the lack of reverence for life*. The Divine Intelligence within this Flame will expose these illusions in the Light of Clarity. Then, through the power of Transfiguring Divine Love, the Divine Intelligence reveals the Truth of our Oneness and our Divine Potential as Beloved Sons and Daughters of God. This is accomplished by activating the genetic codings of Divinity within our RNA/DNA structures.

When it was time for the Flame of Transfiguring Divine Love to be anchored on Earth, Lightworkers around the world volunteered to assist. With the guidance of the Spiritual Hierarchy, various activities of Light were performed to help raise vibrations and prepare Humanity for the influx of this Sacred Fire.

When all was in readiness, the Mighty Elohim, the Builders of Form, created a resplendent rose brazier that was lowered into the atmosphere of Earth in the southwestern portion of the United States of America. The stamen of the rose brazier was secured in the vicinity of Tucson, Arizona, and the rest of the rose expanded to envelop the entire state.

When everything was in place, the Flame of Transfiguring Divine Love was projected from the Heart of God into the Heart Flames of volunteer Lightworkers and anchored into the rose brazier. This occurred during the fifteenth celebration of Harmonic Convergence in August 2001. After the Flame was securely anchored, the brazier was lowered into the center of the Earth. The Flame then merged with the heart of Beloved Mother Earth and expanded out through the entire Crystal Grid System.

On August 17, 2001, the Flame of Transfiguring Divine Love blazed through the Crystal Grid System and was anchored in the spark of Divinity blazing in the heart of every man, woman and child. That miraculous event completed the healing of Humanity's ancient wounded hearts and further opened our heart of hearts to receive the love of our Mother God.

After that activity of Light was victoriously accomplished, the Divine Authority, Will and Power of our Father God returned to Earth. This is the Light of God that was distorted aeons ago when we fell from Grace, closed our Heart Chakras and started using the power center in our Throat Chakras without the balance of Divine Love.

As the Divine Authority, Will and Power of our Father God pierced into every electron of life on Earth, the abuse of power Humanity has expressed since the fall aeons ago was pushed to the surface to be healed and transmuted into Light. What we experienced on September 11, 2001, clearly reflected that abuse of power, and much of what we are experiencing now is reflecting that abuse as well. These are the last desperate attempts to block Earth's Ascension in the Light by the fallen souls who are still in embodiment. They are confused and afraid, and they are vehemently struggling to maintain control.

The awakening of these fallen souls is the last phase of healing that has to occur in order for ALL Humanity to make the shift into the 5th Dimension with the rest of our Solar System. Needless to say, these souls are not in a frame of mind to negotiate or listen to the words of the Lightworkers revealing the Oneness of all life. The Legions of Light in the Realms of Truth have said that the last, best hope of reaching the closed minds and hearts of these wayward souls is through the Flame of Transfiguring Divine Love.

Our responsibility as Lightworkers is to be ever-vigilant instruments of God and to unceasingly invoke the God Presence of every person on Earth to take full dominion of their thoughts, words, actions and feelings. We must invoke the Flame of Transfiguring Divine Love that has been anchored in every Heart Flame and ask that the Divine Intelligence within the Flame reveal to each soul the erroneous, destructive beliefs that are inciting hatred, violence and lack of reverence for life.

We must remember and KNOW that as instruments of God we are the Open Doors that no one can shut. We are the Light of the world, and *our time is at hand.* This is the moment we have been preparing for through thousands of lifetimes. This is the moment when this sweet Earth and all her life are being given an unprecedented opportunity to Ascend up the Spiral of Evolution into the 5th-Dimensional frequencies of Limitless Physical Perfection. We are standing on the threshold of the greatest shift in consciousness ever manifest in the whole of Creation. And *we*, as instruments of God, are the key to the success of this Divine Mission.

Communication networks around the world are being flooded with valid information as well as misinformation and disinformation. During this unprecedented time, it is imperative that we use the full capacity of our Divine, Discerning Intelligence to evaluate *everything* that comes across our path.

We must take whatever we see, hear, read or experience into the deepest recesses of our hearts, and blaze the Flame of Illumined Truth through it. Then we must command our manipulative, lower human egos into the Light, and ask our God Selves to reveal any Truth that is contained within the information or message we received. We must ask for everything that is not Truth to be clearly exposed to us as well. As the Heart, Head and Hands of God during this defining moment of Earth's Transfiguration and Ascension, it is vital that we stay on purpose. We must not be mislead by the myriad distractions that are being projected onto the screen of life by the forces of imbalance.

Any of the scenarios that indicate the "plan" is for someone else to miraculously intervene in our lives and save us in spite of ourselves and our free will is a deception. It is true that we are receiving more assistance from the Legions of Light in the Heavenly Realms than ever before, but *we* are responsible for cocreating the perfection of Heaven on Earth ourselves. Each of us individually must make the personal decision as to whether or not we are going to voluntarily do what is necessary in order to Ascend up the Spiral of Evolution with the Planet Earth and the rest of Humanity. No one outside of ourselves can do that for us. Our God Selves know this. That is exactly why we agreed to go through countless lifetimes of preparation in order to be capable of fulfilling the mission we have embarked upon in this lifetime.

The reason the prophets and seers of ancient times foretold of the coming Golden Age of Eternal Peace and Prosperity is because they witnessed what life on Earth will be like in the 5th-Dimensional Realms of Limitless Physical Perfection. The 5th Dimension vibrates with a frequency of Light that transcends the discord and maladies we are experiencing on Earth. The mutated frequencies of disease, poverty, war, corruption, greed, hatred, suffering, pain, violence, death as we know it and every other human miscreation cannot be sustained in the 5th Dimension.

Since the dawn of the new millennium, a very elaborate Divine Plan has been unfolding step by step. The plan is helping us prepare for the moment when the Earth and all her life will receive the patterns of perfection from the Causal Body of God that will result in the tangible manifestation of Heaven on Earth.

The Spiritual Hierarchy is beseeching us to listen to the inner promptings of our hearts. Every awakening Lightworker has been prepared to assist at some level in the fulfillment of this very important phase of the Divine Plan. It is time for us to respond with courage, trust, willingness and confidence. We must not allow our manipulative human egos to prevent us from becoming instruments of God by bombarding us with thoughts of lack, limitation, insecurity, failure consciousness, unworthiness or any of the other ploys our egos use to prevent us from accomplishing our Divine Missions.

Our God Selves are what science calls our superconscious minds. Through our superconscious minds we are one with the Divine Heart and Mind of God. Through that level of consciousness, we clearly understand the Divine Principles governing this Earthly school of learning, and we know the urgent need of the hour. Our God Selves realize that all life is interrelated and that if the family of Humanity is going to survive, the Human Race has to come together as one unified force of Divine Love, Harmony and Balance.

Our God Selves also know that every evolving soul is going through a unique learning experience on Earth and that our various races, religions, creeds, beliefs, cultures, nationalities and lifestyles are part of that learning experience. Our human egos have manipulated us into creating gross mutations of those learning experiences and much of what we are expressing through our diversities is distorted. When our God Selves take control of our Earthly bodies, however, we will revel in the beauty and wonder of our uniqueness, and we will joyously honor each other and enjoy our differences.

When our God Selves are governing our individual and collective lives, we will understand that through our diversities, we can learn and grow at a greatly accelerated pace. Since our God Selves know the full significance of the Oneness of all life, they know that only by working toward the highest good of all concerned in every facet of life will we succeed in accomplishing the Divine Plan. Only by creating win-win situations for everyone involved will there be Eternal Peace and Limitless Abundance on Earth.

When our God Selves are governing the planet, they will easily reach into the Causal Body of God and tap into the viable solutions for every problem manifesting on Earth.

I know that when we observe what is taking place in the world, it seems as if it will be in the far-distant future before Humanity's God Selves will finally be governing the planet, but that is not true. Actually, there are literally millions of awakening Lightworkers who, at this very moment, listen and respond to the Divine Directives of their God Selves.

We must stop allowing our human egos to manipulate us into believing that we don't have any power because we are just one small soul out of billions. That misinformation is designed to prevent us from trusting our God Selves and from becoming instruments of God.

In Truth, we are each magnificent, multifaceted, multidimensional reflections of our Father-Mother God. We are radiant Suns expressing ALL of the various frequencies of Divinity pulsating in the Causal Body of God. We are Gods and Goddesses standing on the threshold of the greatest leap in consciousness ever experienced in any System of Worlds.

When we join together with other Lightworkers who also have the Divine Intent of serving as instruments of God and as surrogates on behalf of Humanity, our God Selves project through our Heart Flames the full power and momentum of our Sun. The intensity of that Light is unfathomable.

When our individual Sun blends with the Suns of other Lightworkers, our Light expands exponentially, and the Light of a *thousand* Suns is projected through our Heart Flames into the physical plane. That influx of Light will assist greatly in accomplishing the Divine Plan and awakening the rest of Humanity. We must never underestimate ourselves. We are wondrous Children of God, and ALL that our Father-Mother God has is ours.

The following sacred blessings, affirmations, visualizations and meditations have been given to us by the Company of Heaven to help each of us become empowered instruments of God. They are stated in the first person so that we will each experience these gifts personally and tangibly. At the same time, we should KNOW that there are thousands of Lightworkers empowering these gifts with us. Every time we participate in these activities of Light, we are reaching higher and higher into the frequencies of the 5th Dimension and becoming empowered instruments of God.

Consecration by Archangel Raphael

I am sitting comfortably in my chair or lying down, whichever feels better to me at this moment. My arms and legs are uncrossed, and my spine is as straight as possible. Through the power of God blazing in my heart, I command my human ego into the Light and ask my God Self to take full dominion of my physical, etheric, mental and emotional bodies. My heart is open and my mind is alert, yet I am completely relaxed. With every breath I take, my God Self integrates further into my bodies at a cellular level.

I hear a voice speaking in the deepest recesses of my heart ...and I *listen*.

The Divine Words reverberating in my heart remind me that I Am an instrument of God and that I have come to Earth during this critical moment to be the Heart, Head and Hands of God in the physical world of form...I *remember*.

The remembrance stirs within me the inner knowing that I have been preparing for aeons of time for this Divine Mission. Deep within I know that I have all of the wisdom, strength, skill, knowledge, talent and ability I need to succeed God Victoriously...I have the *courage* to act.

Now I hear the Voice of God calling me to a higher octave of Divine Service...I *respond* with willingness and enthusiasm.

The Voice of God reveals to me that due to the urgency of the hour a contingency plan for the Earth has been set into motion, and my assistance is acutely needed in order for the plan to succeed...I joyously agree to *serve*.

The Voice of God speaking within my heart reveals that the time is short and that I Am needed as a surrogate in this unprecedented Divine Plan to serve as an instrument of God on behalf of ALL Humanity...in deep humility and compassion, I *volunteer*.

Suddenly, I feel myself spiralling up a scintillating shaft of Light. In an instant, I Am standing before the august Presence of Beloved Archangel Raphael, the Angel of Consecration. Light is pouring forth from his Being, and he appears to be standing in the center of a radiant Emerald Green Sun.

Archangel Raphael beckons me, and I move closer to his luminous Presence. He raises his hands and invokes the Emerald Flame of Consecration from the heart of the omniscient, omnipotent, omnipresent Cosmic I AM—All That Is.

The Emerald Green Flame of Consecration pours forth from the heart of the Cosmic I AM and flows into Archangel Raphael's Crown Chakra, then down into his heart. The Flame merges with the Divinity in his heart and expands out into his hands. His hands become blazing Emerald Green Suns of Consecration.

Archangel Raphael places his radiant hands upon my brow and decrees:

"I Consecrate your mind to be One with the Divine Mind of God."

He places his fiery hands upon my heart and decrees:

"I Consecrate your heart to be the Open Door through which God's Infinite Divine Love and Limitless Abundance will flow to bless you and all life. Always hold your heart open, even in the face of adversity."

Archangel Raphael then places his hands upon my eyes and decrees:

"I Consecrate your eyes to perceive the Truth and to recognize perfection in all things."

He places his hands upon my ears and decrees:

"I Consecrate your ears to hear the still, small voice of God within for guidance and illumination. Truly listen to and hear all those who communicate with you."

Archangel Raphael then places his blazing hands upon my lips and decrees:

"I Consecrate your lips to express only Truth and to communicate clearly, openly and honestly whenever you speak."

He places his hands upon my nose and decrees:

"I Consecrate your nostrils to breathe in the Holy Breath of the Holy Spirit. The Breath of the Holy Spirit will now revitalize, rejuvenate and heal your bodies with every breath you take."

Archangel Raphael places his hands upon my hands and decrees:

"I Consecrate your hands to bless and heal all that you touch."

He places his hands upon my feet and decrees:

"I Consecrate your feet so that as you continue your Earthly sojourn, you will walk the Path of Light. As you fulfill your Divine Plan, you reach your highest potential as an instrument of God."

Then Archangel Raphael decrees:

"In the name of the Cosmic I AM, All That Is, I decree that this Consecration has been victoriously fulfilled."

From the very deepest recesses of my heart, I affirm:

"In deep humility and gratitude, I accept my Divine Mission as an instrument of God. From this moment forth, I Consecrate my every breath to be the Open Door for the Light of God, the Door which no one can shut."

In an instant I am back on Earth. My newly Consecrated vehicles are open and receptive to the Divine Directives of God. I experience a new level of inner knowing, and I understand my mission with a new clarity.

There is an awakening taking place within my Heart Flame. I Am recognizing my responsibility for the conditions existing in my life and on Earth. I remember deep within that, through the Universal Law of Attraction, I am a cocreator of the physical plane.

My thoughts, words, actions and feelings are projected onto the atomic substance of physical matter, and they manifest in physical form. As my gift of life flows through me, it picks up the vibrations of my consciousness and then expresses those vibrations in visible form, experiences and circumstances. In other words, what I think about, what I put my feelings and energy into, I bring into form.

Because of the confusion I have experienced in the past, I have given power to physical matter. I have allowed the distorted manifestation of physical matter to become my reality, when, in Truth, it is only an illusion created by my beliefs, thoughts, words, actions and feelings. I now realize with my new level of understanding and clarity, that physical matter is nothing more than a mass of atomic energy controlled by my consciousness. Never does matter control consciousness.

My world reflects my human consciousness. In the past, I have set about trying to change the physical conditions in my world instead of changing my consciousness. Those conditions are only the reflection of my consciousness. Trying to change physical conditions without changing my consciousness is like trying to change the reflection in a mirror without changing the object causing the reflection. It is a futile effort.

Now, through my sacred Consecration, I Am becoming One with my own Divinity. My consciousness is beginning to rise. My transformation is occurring subtly and deeply at an atomic, cellular level. The seed of awareness is growing within me. It is blazing like a Sun and radiating forth rays of Light.

My Heart Flame is expanding, and the Flame of Transfiguring Divine Love which is cradled in the Divinity of my heart is expanding as well. This is a magnificent rose colored Flame with an aquamarine aura of Clarity. Pulsating in the heart of that Flame is a resplendent, opalescent Sun of Transfiguration.

The Flame of Transfiguring Divine Love in my heart is now expanding and connecting with the same Flame blazing in the hearts of every man, woman and child on Earth. This activity of Light is creating a powerful forcefield around the planet, an actual network of Light, a planetary grid system of Transfiguring Divine Love.

The collective radiance of this network of Light is the most powerful force on the planet. It has created a bridge of Light that spans the abyss from the lowest octaves of human suffering and consciousness into the highest Realms of Illumined Truth and Limitless Physical Perfection. This is the Bridge to Freedom over which the recalcitrant souls who are resisting their own awakening and their Ascension in the 5th Dimension will now be able to safely and quickly travel once they consciously choose the Path of Light.

With my Heart Flame united with the Heart Flames of every person on the planet and my Light pulsating throughout the planetary grid system of Transfiguring Divine Love, I realize that I am now being presented with unparalleled opportunities to be an instrument of God.

I weave my gifts, talents, skills, knowledge, strength,
courage, compassion and love into the tapestry of the
Divine Plan for Mother Earth.

I respond to my heart's call to action.

I Consecrate my very life to being the greatest
force of good I can be on this planet.

I Consecrate my thoughts, words, actions and feelings to make a
positive difference every day.

By focusing my attention, I empower the
following Divine Truths:

I Am One with ALL Life.

I Am Limitless Abundance.

I Am the Harmony of my true Being.

My ability to love is infinite.

I Am vibrantly healthy and eternally youthful.

I Am a Peace-Commanding Presence.

*The actions I take improve my family, my job, my community, my
city, my country and the world.*

I have a healing touch.

I Am One with the Angelic and the Nature Kingdoms.

I Am Transfiguring my life.

Toning the Sacred Name of God

An ancient, sacred name for God is HU. The word HU-man

reflects HU-manity's Divinity. I will now increase the flow of God's Light into my Being on the Sound Ray by toning HU—the sacred name of God.

I inbreathe deeply, and on the outbreath, I tone aloud the word HU slowly and steadily until I have expended my breath. I will repeat this tone 12 times, each time lifting my energy, vibration and consciousness to a higher frequency of God's Light on the reverberation of my own voice. I begin now.

I breathe in slowly and deeply.
I exhale slowly while toning the sacred word HU.

(Repeat the Toning Breath 12 times)

The Light of God is now reverberating through every fiber of my Being.

God's Protective Universal Light

I thank you Father-Mother God for revealing to me your protective, Universal Light. Within this Light is complete protection from ALL *destructive forces*.

The Holy Spirit permeates me in this Light and wherever I *Will* the Light to descend.

God's White Light of Protection now floods through me and bathes all life on Earth.   *(pause)*

I thank you Father-Mother God for filling me with your protective Fire of Love. Within this Love is complete protection from ALL *destructive thoughts and feelings*.

Divine Consciousness is lifted up in me in this Love and wherever I Will this Love to be inflamed.

God's rose, aquamarine and opalescent Light of Transfiguring Divine Love now floods through me and bathes all life on Earth. *(pause)*

I thank you, Father-Mother God, that you are in me and I Am in you. Through me, your Will is sent forth on the wings of power, and your purpose is accomplished on Earth as it is in Heaven.

Through me, your Light and Love and Power are manifest to ALL of the Sons and Daughters of Humanity.

God's Deep Purple and Golden Light of Divine Will, Love, Power, Wisdom and Purpose now floods through me and bathes all life on Earth.   *(pause)*

Affirmation as an Instrument of God

As an instrument of God I have come to set right the vibratory action of all energy and substance in my world and in all the world.

I Am the sacred Hands of God moving through all life.

I Am instantly reestablishing Divinity wherever the Light of God is applied.

I invite, invoke, focus, concentrate, manifest and sustain the Light of God on Earth with every breath I take.

I Am a director of God's Light. I Am humble before Its magnificent Presence, and I Am grateful to unleash Its Power on Earth.

* I Am the Light of God flowing through my Heart Flame loving all life FREE!

(Repeat 3 times from *)

Invoking the Holy Spirit

I now invoke the Holy Spirit to purify, illumine and transfigure my four lower bodies, so that they are fitting vehicles serving their purpose on this planet through which I, as an instrument of God, Am a focus of the Light of my Father-Mother God.

My Light is daily and hourly increasing until I Am One with my God Self working through the flesh in this embodiment to further serve the supreme Source, the animating principle of life I Am throughout Infinity.

I Am the Fire Breath of the Almighty, and I consciously enter the Flaming Presence of the Holy Spirit. The Holy Breath of the Holy Spirit now flows through me in a constant, rhythmic pulsation.

From this focus of Transfiguring Divine Love, I invoke a ray of Light from the heart of the Holy Spirit into the feeling world of every person on the planet. This ray of Light infuses the feeling nature of every Human Being on Earth with the Power and Grace of the Holy Spirit.

Now, through the full authority of the Presence of God blazing in every human heart, I make this call to the Celestial Giver of All Life, the Cosmic I AM—All That Is. May the electronic substance of the Universe, the lifeforce of Humanity, be invincibly charged with perfection's Flame in action. As it passes through Humanity's vehicles, which are the Open Doors to its expression in the physical world, the electronic Light will now remain within an invincible armor of Transfiguring Divine Love, emitting perfection, but allowing none of the discord of the lower vehicles to change the vibratory action, color or sound of its comforting presence. I accept this done with full power in God's most Holy name I Am.

The Golden Holy Breath

Now, to further prepare myself to be a clear and powerful instrument of God, I Am going to do the Golden Holy Breath exercise.

During this breathing exercise, I slowly breathe in as much air as my lungs will hold. As I inbreathe, I feel the air press down through the trunk of my body into my lungs, my arms and hands, my legs and feet and up through the top of my head.

I hold the breath as long as I comfortably can. While the breath is in my body, I visualize the added lifeforce, the prana, within the air. It is the pure, deep-golden color of Peace. As I hold the Golden Breath in my body, it is energizing, healing, transforming, rejuvenating and transfiguring my physical, etheric, mental and emotional bodies.

Then I exhale slowly and deliberately. I feel the breath leaving the tips of my ears and the inside of my scalp first. Then I draw it up from my toes and through the calves of my legs, through the trunk of my body and back into my lungs, and then gently, but steadily, I exhale it outward until there is not a remaining ounce of air within my body. I rest for a moment, and then I repeat the Golden Breath three more times.

Golden Light of Peace Affirmation

Now, with the Golden Light of Peace permeating every cell of my body I affirm:

I Am the Open Door for the Divine Rays of Cosmic Peace from the Great, Great Central Sun. I Am Eternal Peace now established in the heart centers of ALL Humanity.

I Am the Golden Light of Eternal Peace pervading all life. I Am claiming every cell, atom and electron of this sweet Earth and all her life into the Heart of Peace.

I Am Eternal Peace, reflecting Humanity's victory now in all experiences.

I Am in the world, but as an instrument of God, I dwell in the consciousness of the Peace of the Great Solar Quiet. I Am enfolded in God's Eternal Peace, and I radiate that Golden Essence to all life on Earth.

I Am Peace. I Am Peace. I Am Peace.

I now behold the entire planet enfolded in the Golden Light of Peace. The pink essence of Divine Love is joyously crowning every electron of that Peace.

From this day and this moment forward, every thought, word, action or feeling I express is qualified with Divine Peace, and the Golden Flame of Peace is blazing through my Heart Flame to bless all life.

Affirmation of My True Being

I now seal these activities of Light and the gifts and blessings given to me from On High by affirming the reality of my true Being:

I Am a Being of Flame, and I Am its Light.
I Am part of an activity reacquainting all Human Beings
*   with their Flame and their Light.*

I Am the Flame that is the vibration of the Godhead. I Am the Flame that is the cohesive Divine Love which holds the Sun and Stars in place. I Am the Flame whose power projects Light Rays from the Sun. I Am the Flame which fills all the Universe with the glory of Itself.

I Am the Flame, the animating principle of life. Wherever I Am, there is God Activity. I Am the Alpha and the Omega of Creation. I Am the beginning, and I Am the end of manifestation, all externalization, for I Am the Flame which is the Source of all and into which all returns.

The Flame which I Am is a power. The Flame which I Am is a substance. The Flame which I Am is the all of everything: energy, vibration and consciousness in action, ever fulfilling the Divine Plan of Creation. The Flame which I Am shall restore the Planet Earth and set her free eternally.

The Flame which I Am is a 5th-Dimensional activity. The Flame which I Am is the Higher Law of God come to assert its full dominion over all the lesser laws of the 3rd-Dimensional world of Humanity. It is master over every vibration less than itself. It is all-loving, all-knowing and all-powerful, and I Am that Flame in action amongst Humanity.

Within the Flame which I Am is every good and perfect thing, every thought and feeling my God Parents have ever had for the blessing of their Creation. This perfection is externalized as Light. Within the Flame is the seed of all things, and within the Light is the full manifestation of all things. I Am the Flame, and I Am its Light.

The Flame which I Am is available like air or water. It is everywhere present, available to those who perceive it and accept it. This is my reason for Being—the Flame and the Light embodied in a form acceptable to Humanity. I Am the Flame, again reaching the withering souls of the Human Race, filling them with Light, the substance of myself—my Holy Self. I Am embodied for this reason and no other.

For I Am part of an activity designed to reacquaint every man, woman and child with their Flame and their Light.

I Am a Being of Flame, and I Am Its Light.

I Am the Flame of Life.
I Am an instrument of God.

I Am that I Am.

The information and meditations in this chapter are available on a cassette tape titled "*Becoming An Instrument of God.*" If you would like to order the tape, please see page **329** or contact us through the information at the front of the book.

Chapter 6

82   HOME

Chapter 6

THE NEW TECHNOLOGY OF THE VIOLET FLAME

Since the dawn of the new millennium, the Earth has officially moved from the forcefield of Pisces into the full embrace of Aquarius, thus empowering every facet of life with the Seventh Solar Aspect of Deity. This aspect of Deity pulsates with the Divine Qualities of the Violet Flame, which include Spiritual Freedom, Limitless Physical Perfection, Transmutation, Mercy, Compassion, Forgiveness, Freedom, Liberty, Justice, Victory, Opportunity, Invocation, Divine Ceremony and Divine Technology.

It is time for the next phase of the Divine Plan, and our 5th-Dimensional Solar Christ Presence are standing in readiness, waiting to receive the new frequencies of Divine Technology within the Violet Flame.

With all of the miraculous changes that have taken place over the past several years, Humanity, en masse, has raised up in energy, vibration and consciousness. We are now able to withstand *higher* frequencies of the Violet Flame. These frequencies are pouring forth from the core of Creation and will greatly assist in transforming our Earthly bodies and our Earthly experiences into the perfection of Heaven on Earth, right here and right now.

The guidelines and instructions on how to utilize the Divine Technology within the Violet Flame are being given to Humanity by the Beings of Light in the Realms of Illumined Truth. These guidelines will allow each of us to easily and effectively utilize the inconceivably powerful new technology.

Our Solar Christ Presence are now integrating at a cellular level into our Earthly vehicles. As this occurs, our physical, etheric, mental and emotional bodies are being infused with the 5th-Dimensional frequencies of our Solar Light Bodies. Daily and hourly we are gradually being lifted up into the frequencies of Limitless Physical Perfection.

Even though our Solar Christ Presence are still in the embryonic stage of development, they are Beings of Light beyond our comprehension. They have the ability to receive and assimilate information and frequencies of Light from the Divine Heart and Mind of God that will move us forward in our process of self-mastery more rapidly than we ever dreamed possible.

Our Solar Christ Presence also have the ability to penetrate into all dimensions and all levels of consciousness in the Realms of Perfection. They can then bring back to our conscious minds the Sacred Knowledge and Wisdom of the Ages. In order to bypass the resistance and scepticism of our lower human egos, we must know and trust that a powerful part of our Divine Consciousness is *truly* in control now, and this facet of our Being has the ability to transcend all of the interference of our human egos.

The new technology of the Violet Flame is so miraculous, so incredible and yet so simple that it is hard for our egos to believe it can possibly be true. The Truth of the matter is, however, that it is not only true, it is a technique that has always been available to us and that we just lost awareness of after the fall. With the new technology of the Violet Flame, we are merely remembering what we have forgotten and reclaiming our Divine Birthright of self-empowerment.

The ancient Hermetic teachings that were brought to the world through the Greek philosopher Hermes express the Divine Truth *"As above, so below."* Even though Humanity has often misconstrued the true meaning of these words, they reflect the Universal Law that governs this planet.

"As above, so below" reflects the original Divine Intent for the schoolroom of Earth. Contained within those simple words is the sacred knowing that the Earth is designed to reflect ALL of the perfection contained within the Causal Body of God and the Realms of Limitless Physical Perfection.

After the fall, our human egos observed the humanly miscreated negativity and discord manifesting on Earth and misinterpreted the statement *"As above, so below"* to mean that the negativity on Earth must also exist in the realms above. That erroneous perception caused our egos to come to the destructive conclusion that all of the discord, pain and suffering on Earth must have been created by God and, therefore, must be God's Will.

Now, everything is changing at warp speed, and our Divine Faculties are being restored. We are lifting up in consciousness, and we are beginning to perceive the Truth contained within the Universal Law "*As above, so below.*" We are realizing that even though we have misused our gift of free will and created mutated patterns of imperfection that are not present in the Causal Body of God, we have the absolute ability to transmute those patterns of discord and reclaim the Divine Plan which is for Humanity to create Heaven on Earth.

The Flame of the Immaculate Concept

During this unprecedented Cosmic Moment of Beloved Mother Earth's rebirth, we are receiving a unique form of assistance from On High that has never before been given to any evolving planet. That assistance involves a newly created and Divinely Empowered frequency of the Flame of the Immaculate Concept.

First of all, we must understand that the Flame of the Immaculate Concept is an aspect of the Sacred Fire from the very Heart and Mind of God that holds and energizes the Divine Blueprints for ALL of the patterns of perfection in the Causal Body of God.

The Flame of the Immaculate Concept is a resplendent, Madonna-blue Flame with an iridescent, Mother-of-Pearl radiance. When Humanity fell from Grace and no longer magnetized the patterns of perfection from the Causal Body of God into our Earthly experiences, the Flame of the Immaculate Concept was withdrawn from the physical plane. Our Father-Mother God directed that Sacred Fire to return to the Great, Great Silence until a future time when Humanity would awaken and reclaim the original Divine Plan for this planet.

On October 29, 1980, after literally thousands of lifetimes of dedicated, selfless service by myriad Beings of Light both in and out of embodiment, the consciousness of Humanity had shifted enough to warrant the return of the Flame of the Immaculate Concept.

In a sublime Ceremony of Light, a tremendous crystalline lotus blossom brazier was lowered into the physical plane of Earth by the Elohim. Then, under the direction of Beloved Alpha and Omega, the Flame of the Immaculate Concept was breathed forth from the Great, Great Silence and anchored in the brazier. The Flame was then projected into the center of the Earth and anchored in the Sun of Even Pressure that pulsates there.

For over two decades, this Sacred Fire has been energizing and sustaining every harmonious and loving thought, word, action and feeling that awakening Humanity has expressed. If we will reflect for a moment on the shift of consciousness and the astounding spiritual awakening that has taken place over the last twenty-plus years, we will clearly see what an incredible gift of assistance the Flame of the Immaculate Concept has been to all life on Earth.

After the awesome activities of Light accomplished during the past two decades, Humanity was given another gift of assistance from the Flame of the Immaculate Concept. On October 29, 2000, the twentieth anniversary of the return of the Flame of the Immaculate Concept, another glorious Divine Ceremony took place under the direction of our God Parents from the *Great, Great Central Sun*. For the past few years, these incredible Beings of Light have been ever-so-gently infusing the Earth with the highest frequencies of Light we have ever been able to endure. These magnificent expressions of our Father-Mother God have always vibrated at a frequency beyond the octave we could glimpse from even our highest level of consciousness. Consequently, even though we knew of their existence, we were never able to reach up high enough to hear the tonal frequencies of their names.

With the quantum shifts of vibration that have taken place on the planet over the past few years, we have reached into the frequencies that allow us to experience the Divine Heart and Mind of our Father-Mother God in the Great, Great Central Sun. This has opened new pathways of communication and created new opportunities for Humanity to soar in consciousness into higher Realms of Illumined Truth.

During the Divine Ceremony on October 29, 2000, our God Parents from the Great, Great Central Sun projected their luminious Presence into the atmosphere of Earth and took their strategic positions at the north and south poles. Beloved El, the masculine aspect of our Father God, stood at the north pole, and Beloved Ela, the feminine aspect of our Mother God, stood at the south pole.

After assuming their positions, they directed Legions of Galactic Solar Archangels who had joined them from their Regal Court to traverse the planet. A magnificent Archangel entered the aura of every person evolving on Earth.

The Galactic Solar Archangels then breathed the Twelve Solar Aspects of Deity from the Great, Great Central Sun into Humanity's Twelve Solar Chakras.

When that step of preparation was complete, Beloved El and Ela drew mighty pillars of Light up from the center of the Earth and into their Heart Flames. They then raised their arms above their heads and projected the pillars of Light through their Crown Chakras and fingertips into the hearts of our God Parents in the physical Sun, Beloved Helios and Vesta. Once Helios and Vesta anchored the Light in their Heart Flames, the Light continued to ascend into the hearts of our God Parents in the Central Sun, Beloved Alpha and Omega. The Light then ascended into the hearts of our God Parents in the Great Central Sun, Beloved Elohae and Eloha. Finally, the Light ascended through all dimensions of existence into the heart of the omnipresent, omniscient, omnipotent Cosmic I AM where it was securely anchored in the heart of All That Is.

Beloved El and Ela then sounded a Cosmic Tone that reverberated in perfect harmony with the Celestial Keynote of the Cosmic I AM. For an instant, time and space ceased to exist, and the senses of the Solar Christ Presence of Humanity were filled with the Music of the Spheres. Exquisitely beautiful and indescribably unique sacred geometric patterns of Light, color and sound filled the Universe, and a plethora of celestial sensations overwhelmed the feelings and minds of our God Selves.

Through a higher level of Divine Consciousness, we knew that we were tangibly experiencing the Causal Body of God in all of its resplendent glory. From that level of awareness, we understood that the myriad patterns of perfection blazing within God's Causal Body are now infinitely available to ALL Humanity.

After the Earth and all life evolving upon her were bathed

in the wonder of that celestial experience, Beloved El and Ela invoked a previously unknown frequency of the Flame of the Immaculate Concept from the core of Creation. The sacred Flame flowed through the newly-created pillars of Light into the center of the Earth. Wave upon wave of new frequencies of the Madonna-blue Flame with its scintillating Mother-of-Pearl radiance poured into the Sun of Even Pressure and blazed out through the Crystal Grid System to engulf every particle of life.

The Galactic Solar Archangels standing in the aura of each soul assisted each person to integrate the higher frequencies of the Flame of the Immaculate Concept, and a brand new octave of Divinity was created on Earth. This newly-created and Divinely Empowered Flame of the Immaculate Concept is now pulsating in, through and around every electron of precious life energy. It is available to assist each and every one of us in our Ascension process. All we have to do is ask for its Divine Intervention in our lives.

The new Flame of the Immaculate Concept will help Humanity to utilize the new technology of the Violet Flame and greatly accelerate our Transfiguration into the Light.

Using the New Technology of the Violet Flame

We began experiencing the initial frequencies of the Violet Flame from the forcefield of Aquarius during the latter part of the 1800s. At that time, the Beings of Light in the Realms of Illumined Truth started informing Humanity about the wonders of the sacred Violet Fire. Due to the fragile state we were in at the time and our human ego's limited ability to comprehend Divine Truths, the Ascended Masters taught us only about the most gentle frequencies of the Violet Flame. Those frequencies reverberated with the Divine Qualities of Mercy, Transmutation, Forgiveness, Compassion, Freedom, Invocation, Rhythm, Divine Justice and Divine Ceremony.

For over one hundred years, selfless Lightworkers have used these gifts of the Violet Flame to transmute the effluvia of the world and the mass karma of fallen Humanity. They have also used the Violet Flame to transmute the human miscreations they personally created in present and past experiences. The results have been life transforming and the Violet Flame has been a major factor in accelerating the awakening that is now taking place on Earth.

With the birth of our 5th-Dimensional Solar Christ Presence and the restoration of our spiritual faculties*, we are finally in a position to learn about the advanced technology of the Violet Flame. This technology is associated with 5th-Dimensional *Solar* frequencies of Light. In order for us to use these frequencies safely, they must first be drawn through our Solar Christ Presence who will step down the vibrations, if necessary, for our highest good at any given moment.

We can experience a limited demonstration of how this technology works by observing how our computers download and install new programs and by witnessing how they scan for problems and viruses and delete old programs. Even though we have developed elaborate computer systems on Earth, our technology is infantile compared to the incredible technology existing in the 5th Dimension.

To begin using the new technology of the Violet Flame, we invoke the various aspects of our Father-Mother God, from Suns beyond Suns, and the multidimensional aspects of our own Divinity. After we have completed the initial invocation, we simply decide what programs we want to experience from the Causal Body of God and ask our Solar Christ Presence to download them. The downloading occurs instantly and automatically, very similar to what occurs when we put a disc with a new program on it into our computer.

After the programs are downloaded, our Solar Christ Selves use the technology of the Solar Violet Flame to *scan* all of our records, memories, belief systems, fears, blocks, etcetera, from all time frames and dimensions both known and unknown. Any thoughts, words, actions or feelings that we have ever expressed that conflict with the new programs are identified and *deleted*. This means that there is no energy, vibration, record or memory remaining in our physical, etheric, mental or emotional bodies that will block or interfere with the new programs. We still have the gift of free will, of course, so we can recreate our fears, blocks and resistance if we choose to focus on them, but once the programs have been downloaded and the scanning has been completed, the old programs no longer exist no matter how long we have been dealing with them.

After a program is downloaded, our Solar Christ Presence

* *See Part 2 for details.*

will *automatically* update it everyday and scan all levels of our consciousness for thoughts, words, actions or feelings that we may have recreated that conflict with the new program. Those things will then be instantly deleted. If we choose to, we can download the programs more than once to help convince our conscious minds of the Truth of this Divine Technology. Then it is up to each of us to accept our new reality and to live out of that new paradigm. The more we accept the reality of this process, the faster the new programs will reflect in our life experiences.

As you can see, the hardest part of using this technology is overcoming the scepticism of our human egos and accepting the Divine Truth that this new technology is available to us and that it is actually that easy to use. More than anything else, this process involves an adjustment in our level of trust and our acceptance.

It helps to remember that this process is being accomplished by the Divine Technology in the 5th-Dimensional Solar Violet Flame and our Solar Christ Presence. Our lower human egos with all of their fears and frailties have nothing whatsoever to do with it. This process may seem too miraculous and too good to be true, but it is part of the original Divine Plan and a process that we were *always* supposed to have available to us. We only lost access to this advanced, spiritual technology when we fell into the abyss of our human miscreations.

The programs can be downloaded individually or grouped together, and they can be general or specific. For instance, we can download an overall program for vibrant health, or we can download a program for the health of an area of our body that we specifically name such as our heart or lungs, bones, joints, skin, etcetera. We can download both types of programs if we want to; there is no limit to the number of programs or the variety of programs we can download. The patterns of perfection in the Causal Body of God are limitless.

We also have the ability to download programs for our families, loved ones, friends and all Humanity. All we have to do is invoke their Solar Christ Presence and ask that the program be downloaded according to their Divine Plans.

The Downloading Process

Here is an example of the process of downloading programs from the Causal Body of God using the new technology of the Violet Flame. I am including an invocation and some universal programs that most people are interested in. I will also demonstrate how we can invoke the new technology for our families, friends and all of Humanity.

To begin, we invoke the multidimensional aspects of our Father-Mother God, the various aspects of our own Divinity and the Sacred Fire. This must be done prior to downloading any program to be sure that we are downloading programs exclusively through our 5th-Dimensional Solar Christ Presence and not our human egos. This is easily accomplished through the following Invocation.

Invocation

Through the Presence of God I Am...
I invoke the omniscient, omnipresent, omnipotent
Cosmic I AM—All That Is.

I invoke the aspects of my Father-Mother God from the
Great, Great Central Sun, Beloved El and Ela.

I invoke the aspects of my Father-Mother God from the
Great Central Sun, Beloved Elohae and Eloha.

I invoke the aspects of my Father-Mother God from the
Central Sun, Beloved Alpha and Omega.

I invoke the aspects of my Father-Mother God from the
physical Sun, Beloved Helios and Vesta.

I now invoke ALL of the aspects of my own
Divinity and my own Being:

My White Fire Being,
My Solar Causal Body,
My I Am Presence,
My Solar Christ Presence,

My Body Elemental,
My human ego and my subconscious mind.

I invoke the full-gathered momentum
of the Flame of the Immaculate Concept.

And I invoke the full-gathered momentum
of the 5th-Dimensional Solar Violet Flame.

(Optional for Family, Friends and Humanity)

I invoke the Solar Christ Presence and all of the Divine
aspects of each member of my family, my friends and
the entire family of Humanity.

Blessed Ones, download the following programs
according to each person's highest good and
individual Divine Plan.

~Begin Downloading the Programs~

Beloved Solar Christ Presence, download now the
programs from the Causal Body of God for the
limitless flow of God's Abundance, Opulence,
Financial Freedom and the God-Supply of
ALL good things.   (pause)

The programs are successfully downloaded, and my
Solar Christ Presence now scans through all facets of
my Being and deletes anything that conflicts
with these programs.   (pause)

Beloved Solar Christ Presence, download now the
programs from the Causal Body of God for Eternal
Youth, Vibrant Health, Radiant Beauty and Slim, Firm,
Flawless Form.   (pause)

The programs are successfully downloaded, and my
Solar Christ Presence now scans through all facets of
my Being and deletes anything that conflicts
with these programs.   (pause)

*Beloved Solar Christ Presence, download now the
programs from the Causal Body of God for
Perfect Health Habits, Perfect Eating and Drinking
Habits, Perfect Exercise Habits, Perfect Work Habits,
Perfect Relaxation and Recreation Habits,
Perfect Spiritual Devotion, Meditation and
Contemplation Habits.* (pause)

*The programs are successfully downloaded, and my
Solar Christ Presence now scans through all facets of
my Being and deletes anything that conflicts
with these programs.* (pause)

*Beloved Solar Christ Presence, download now the
programs from the Causal Body of God for Divine
Family Life, Loving Relationships, Adoration, Divine
Love, Divine Sexuality, True Understanding, Clear and
Effective Communication, Open-Heart Sharing,
Oneness, and the Unification of
the Family of Humanity.* (pause)

*The programs are successfully downloaded, and my
Solar Christ Presence now scans through all facets of
my Being and deletes anything that conflicts
with these programs.* (pause)

*Beloved Solar Christ Presence, download now the
programs from the Causal Body of God for
Eternal Peace, Harmony, Balance and
Reverence for ALL Life.* (pause)

*The programs are successfully downloaded, and my
Solar Christ Presence now scans through all facets of
my Being and deletes anything that conflicts
with these programs.* (pause)

*Beloved Solar Christ Presence, download now the
programs from the Causal Body of God for
Self-Empowerment, Success, Fulfillment,
Divine Purpose, a Rewarding Career,
Self-Esteem, Spiritual Development,*

Enlightenment, Divine Consciousness
and Divine Perception.   (pause)

The programs are successfully downloaded, and my
Solar Christ Presence now scans through all facets of
my Being and deletes anything that conflicts
with these programs.   (pause)

Beloved Solar Christ Presence, download now the
programs from the Causal Body of God for
the Conscious Perception and the Open-Heart and
Open-Mind Telepathic Communication with
the entire Company of Heaven and the
Angelic and Elemental Kingdoms.   (pause)

The programs are successfully downloaded, and my
Solar Christ Presence now scans through all facets of
my Being and deletes anything that conflicts
with these programs.   (pause)

Beloved Solar Christ Presence, download now the
programs from the Causal Body of God for
Inspired Creativity through Music,
Singing, Sound, Toning, Dance, Movement,
Art and Education.   (pause)

The programs are successfully downloaded, and my
Solar Christ Presence now scans through all facets of
my Being and deletes anything that conflicts
with these programs.   (pause)

Beloved Solar Christ Presence, download now the
programs from the Causal Body of God for
Laughter, Joy, Playfulness, Fun,
Self-expression, Elation, Enthusiasm, Bliss,
Ecstasy, Wonder and Awe.   (pause)

The programs are successfully downloaded, and my
Solar Christ Presence now scans through all facets of
my Being and deletes anything that conflicts
with these programs.   (pause)

*Beloved Solar Christ Presence, download now the
programs from the Causal Body of God for
the physical manifestation of
Heaven on Earth.*   (pause)

*The programs are successfully downloaded, and my
Solar Christ Presence now scans through all facets of
my Being and deletes anything that conflicts
with these programs.*   (pause)

~Sealing Affirmation~

*I now ACCEPT and KNOW through every fiber of my
Being that these programs from the
Causal Body of God have been
successfully downloaded.*

*I also ACCEPT and KNOW that my
Solar Christ Presence will automatically update these
programs every single day and continually delete
anything in my consciousness that conflicts
with these programs.*

In deep Humility, Love and Gratitude, I Decree

*"It is done. And so it is.
Beloved I Am, Beloved I Am, Beloved I Am."*

The information and meditations in this chapter are available on a cassette tape titled "*The New Technology of the Violet Flame.*" If you would like to order the tape, please see page **331** or contact us through the information at the front of the book.

Chapter 7

Chapter 7

CHANGES IN OUR PHYSICAL BODIES

In every single nanosecond, the vibratory rate of our bodies is being increased by our God Selves the maximum we can withstand without physical harm. This is causing some stress and some unusual sensations. Sometimes this process makes us feel more nervous or irritable. Other times we feel like we are getting the flu; we feel achy and feverish. On some occasions, we may feel lightheaded or disoriented and a little out of touch with ourselves.

It is also very common to retain water during this increase of Light. Water is a conductor of electricity. As more Light enters each cell in our bodies, our God Selves direct our Body Elementals to hold onto the water, so our cells can absorb more Light without damage. Regardless of how this acceleration is affecting each of us personally, these symptoms are only temporary and will soon pass.

If you feel you are physically ill, I certainly encourage you to see your doctor. If nothing is physically wrong, then you will have peace of mind knowing that you are not crazy, you are merely Ascending into the Light.

If we consciously raise our vibratory rate, we will experience less discomfort during the Ascension process we are going through. The fastest and most effective way to raise our vibrations is through buoyant, joyous energy. Laughter, playfulness, fun, uplifting experiences, elation, bliss, wonder, ecstasy and love are all avenues to higher vibrations. Beautiful music, being in nature, meditation, harmonious interaction with loved ones, peaceful relaxation and being in tune with the Infinite are also powerful ways of raising our vibrations.

Pure, living (raw), organic foods are an important part of this Ascension process as well. Fruits, vegetables, nuts, seeds, sprouted grains and pure water should be our main staples. The less cooked, dead, devitalized food we eat, the higher and Lighter our vibrations will be.

We must also monitor our thoughts, words, actions and, most of all, feelings. Eighty percent of our energy is expressed through our feelings. The other twenty percent is used to express our thoughts, words and actions. Just imagine how much faster our Ascension process will be when we discipline ourselves to release *only* harmonious, peaceful, loving, happy, joy-filled energy every moment of every day.

Unfortunately, we are so used to letting our feelings control us that the concept of controlling our feelings often seems like an impossible feat, but that is an illusion. Since we are the creators of the circumstances in our lives, we have the free will to determine how we are going to let various situations affect us emotionally.

We usually give our power of choice away to our egos. When something negative happens, we often respond as if we are saying, *"Here are my emotions. Go ahead and mess up my life."* Instead, we should carefully evaluate the situation at hand and say to ourselves, *"I have a choice as to how I am going to allow this to affect me. I can get angry and blow my top, or I can take a deep breath and calmly look for viable solutions and a positive response."*

When we are used to letting everything that comes along push our buttons, it takes real discipline to think before reacting, but the rewards will be well worth the effort. If eighty percent of the energy we expend every day is charged with negative emotions, this Ascension process will be excruciating for us, truly, a living hell.

The bottom line is the Planet Earth and Humanity are Ascending up the Spiral of Evolution. How effortless or how difficult the process will be is up to us. We can utilize the information that is pouring forth from the Realms of Truth and Ascend in harmony and joy, or we can be dragged kicking and screaming into the Light by our God Selves. Either way, we are moving into the Light—period. The process has already begun, and WE HAVE PASSED THE POINT OF NO RETURN!

You and I, as awakening Light Beings, have taken sacred vows within the heart of our Father-Mother God. We made a commitment to be the clearest instruments of God we are capable of being. It is time for us to walk our talk. It is time for us to be tangible examples of how glorious this Ascension process can be. We have the free-will choice to renege on our vows and to stay in the illusion and struggle of our lower human egos, but if we do, it will be a tragedy of unfathomable proportions.

We are powerful beyond our wildest imaginations, and our ability to make a profoundly significant difference in what is happening on Earth at this time is staggering. All we have to do is remember who we are and where we have come from. I am not referring to the specifics of particular lifetimes, I am talking about who we are at the very core of our Beings within the deepest recesses of our Divine Blueprints. We are Sons and Daughters of God empowered with the full potential of our Beloved God Parents.

Never in the history of time has it been more important for us to know and live that Truth. Never, since we were first breathed forth from the Heart of God, have we had a more urgent need or greater opportunity to be of service to all life evolving on this sweet Earth.

Millions and millions of people are being overwhelmed by the labor pains of Earth's birth into the 5th Dimension. They have no conscious knowledge of what is going on or how they can ease their pain. They are experiencing grief, hopelessness, terror and rage. They are acting out of that space and greatly exacerbating their problems.

The Lightworkers are aware of what is happening, and we have knowledge of the wonderful tools God has given to us to help shift our realities from pain and limitation to Heaven on Earth. Yet we still struggle with life's challenges. Imagine how desperate we would feel if we were going through our experiences without knowing about God's Divine Plan and the assistance we are receiving from On High. Imagine how hard it would be if we just accepted the things we see on television or read in the newspaper as our reality.

In our vows, we volunteered to be our brother's and sister's keepers. We promised to hold the Light for them until they could lift up in consciousness and perceive the Light for themselves. This is an awesome responsibility, but it is the most rewarding thing we will ever do. It just takes the full power of our focused attention and the full momentum of Divine Love blazing in our hearts.

Lighting Our Path

*Oh, Father-Mother God, I invoke the full momentum of Your
Divine Light and the Light of the Company of Heaven.
Powers of Light! Powers of Light! Powers of Light!
Come forth NOW!*

*In deep humility and profound gratitude, I consecrate every
facet of my Being to be the Open Door that no one can shut.*

*In Divine Truth, I accept my reality as a Beloved Child of
God. I Am a Cup, a Holy Grail, through which the Light of
God will pour to lift ALL life on Earth into the blissful
octaves of Heaven on Earth.*

Through the Presence of God, I Am, blazing in my heart:

I Am One with the Divine Heart and Mind of God.

I Am One with the God Presence of all Humanity.

I Am One with the Elemental Kingdom and Mother Earth.

I Am One with the Angelic Kingdom.

I Am One with all Beings of Light throughout Infinity.

*Now as one heartbeat, one breath, one voice and one
consciousness of pure Divine Love, ALL life on Earth is lifted
up into the embrace of limitless physical perfection and the
supreme harmony of Heaven on Earth!*

*Every man, woman and child is awakening to the Truth that
they are Beloved Sons and Daughters of God. Each person
now clearly remembers that all life is interconnected,
interrelated and interdependent. A renewed sense of reverence for ALL life stirs in each Heart Flame, and
the Stargate of every heart opens to full breadth.*

*As the Divine Love of God flows through each person's
Heart Flame, their lives are transformed.*

*Humanity, en masse, begins to create a
New Heaven and a New Earth.*

All traces of pain and suffering are transmuted into Light.

Every concept of lack and limitation ceases to exist.

*People everywhere perceive and acknowledge the Divinity
blazing in the heart of each person.*

Humanity, at last, realizes that all life is Divine.

*This new perception inspires every person to feel and express
only love and mutual respect for every part of life.*

*The collective thoughts and feelings of all Humanity are now
expressing the perfection of Heaven on Earth, the physical
plane is transfigured and transformed.*

*The body of Mother Earth is restored to a verdant
Paradise of Splendor and Light.*

*The life of every living Being is filled with Love, Joy, Happi-
ness, Prosperity, Fulfillment, Enlightenment, Eternal Peace,
Harmony, Balance, Spiritual Wisdom and every other
Divine Quality of our Father-Mother God.*

*Mother Earth dons her seamless garment of Light and As-
cends into the full expression of her new Solar Reality.*

The Heavens rejoice, and our Father-Mother God responds

"Welcome HOME."

It is done. And so it is.

I Am, I Am, I Am.

Chapter 8

Chapter 8

CREATING A PLANETARY FORCEFIELD OF UNCONDITIONAL DIVINE LOVE

Together we have the ability to create a unified forcefield of Unconditional Divine Love. This forcefield will be far more powerful in its impact on Humanity's global consciousness than any of the other humanly-generated forcefields of energy perpetuating the serious problems facing us on this planet. It is a Universal Law that if the inner conditions or forces within Humanity's global consciousness are transformed through Love, the outer conditions of the world will proceed to reflect the Divine Plan for the Earth.

The Divine Plan for the Earth is a living, active, all powerful forcefield that will produce perfection if not interfered with through lower, human free will. In the Heavenly Realms, the Beings of Light work purely and precisely with the great Forces of Cause knowing full well that the effects will take care of themselves. Most of us are currently trying to manage "effects" in our lives rather than focusing on the "cause," which will truly change the situation from within.

To ensure the transformation of inner conditions for Humanity and the Earth, together we will create a forcefield of Unconditional Divine Love. Centered within unity consciousness, our collective spiritual ability will empower each of us to accomplish this Divine Plan.

~Visualization~

The electronic pattern for this forcefield is a magnetic Heart of Pure Divine Love enfolding Planet Earth. This crystalline-pink Heart, formed through Humanity's unified consciousness, magnetically attracts the energy, vibration and consciousness from every Ascended level of Being in the Universe into our planetary cause of manifesting the Era of Eternal Peace and Abundance.

Seven magnificent, Solar Archangels of pure Divine Love now descend into the atmosphere of Earth from the electronic belt around the Great, Great Central Sun. They joyously take their strategic positions around this planet to assist us in this activity of Light. The Solar Archangels are stationed at the four cardinal points around the planet, as well as above, below and directly within the center of the Earth.

These Beings are now conducting a symphony of Love ensouling and interpenetrating our Beloved Earth. Each Lightworker is a power point of Light unified in consciousness with every other Lightworker inbreathing, absorbing, expanding and projecting this forcefield throughout Humanity, the Nature and Elemental Kingdoms, the Angelic Kingdoms and the entire atmosphere of Earth.

The God Presence within every Lightworker is the Open Door for this resplendent Light. The God Presence of each soul is the doing, the doer and the deed.

As we experience the manifestation of this forcefield of Unconditional Divine Love, we see the deep colors of Love, smell the fragrance of Love and hear the Cosmic Tones and moving melodies of Love. Through this activity, we are truly Love in action, collectively changing the core vibration of the primal Light substance, which has gone into the present conditions on Earth.

We are the CAUSE of this magnetic forcefield of Love anchored on Earth. Through this activity of Light, we are setting in place the basic spiritual forces of Divine Love over which Humanity will Ascend out of our long exile in darkness into the Realms of Light.

As we unify in consciousness with the Kingdoms of Earth and the Realms of Heaven, we create an Open Door to explore and rediscover the great Family of God in which we will find complete support for the fulfillment of our Divine Plans.

This is what the magnetic forcefield of Divine Love will attract to each of us personally if we live within it. We will be raised into a profound reawakening of supreme Love consciousness—to become again the Masters of Love we have always been and truly are here and now.

For the greatest success, we must recognize ourselves as Beings of Love, accepting responsibility for Loving this sweet Earth and all her life free. We are One with this blessed planet, and the planet is One with us.

The seven Solar Archangels are now projecting their luminous presences to surround each of us in a Cosmic Forcefield of Divine Love. This forcefield is anchored to the north, south, east and west of us as well as above, below and directly within the Divinity of our hearts.

We are now a planetary forcefield of Unconditional Divine Love. The Love of God is now thriving on Earth through us. We each feel the Heart of Love healing the primal Light substance of our four lower bodies and all the physical, etheric, mental and emotional spheres of Earth.

Together we are changing the inner conditions for the entire planet, and we are setting this Earth on a new planetary course of Divine Love. We feel complete unity with ALL Life as we inbreathe, absorb, expand and project this forcefield into every aspect of Humanity's day-to-day functioning on the Holy Breath:

~Breathing Statement~

(Inbreathing Slowly)

I Am inbreathing and absorbing the healing power of Unconditional Divine Love into Humanity's global consciousness.

(Exhaling Slowly)

I Am expanding and projecting the healing power of Unconditional Divine Love into Humanity's global consciousness.

(Continue the Holy Breath for five minutes.
Repeat several times a day.)

We accept that this forcefield of Unconditional Divine Love is manifest now and forever through God's Holy Grace.
It is done, and so it is. Beloved I Am.

Chapter 9

Chapter 9

THE EARTH'S 500-YEAR PERIOD OF GRACE

The United States of America has a very important role to play in the unfolding Divine Plan. This is an extremely complex plan, and it has been a work-in-progress for the past 500 years. In order to understand how America's role is related to the events now taking place on the planet, I am going to share some background information with you that was given to Humanity by the Beings of Light in the Realms of Truth.

Approximately 500 years ago, during a time when Humanity was writhing in the pain and suffering from our own human miscreations, the Cosmic I AM—All That Is—issued a Divine Edict that caught by surprise the Legions of Light from our Solar System. The edict decreed that it was time for a Cosmic Inbreath in which the *whole of Creation* would be breathed into a higher state of evolution. That meant that it was time for the Suns and planets in the System of Alpha and Omega to Ascend up the Spiral of Evolution into the *5th Dimension*.

When a Solar System is created, the Suns and planets are breathed out from the heart of the Cosmic I AM into physical manifestation. This is the involutionary process our scientists refer to as "the Big Bang."

As the Suns and planets evolve, they are breathed back into the heart of God. This evolutionary process occurs in increments over billions of years as the Solar System gradually Ascends, dimension by dimension, up the Spiral of Evolution.

When it is time for a Cosmic Inbreath, any souls evolving in that system who are not capable of making the shift onto the next Spiral of Evolution are left behind. This sad situation only happens when the souls' negative behavior patterns have created such discordant frequencies of vibration in their physical bodies that moving into the higher dimension would cause them to perish.

When the recalcitrant souls are left behind, they experience what is referred to in the Bible as the *second death*. Their physical substance and lifeforce are returned to the Central Sun for repolarization, and their primal Light is eventually used for future systems. Nothing is ever totally lost, but those souls lose their individual identity as that particular Child of God. This is the most tragic thing that can happen to any evolving Being.

Millions of years ago, the Cosmic I AM sent forth the edict for the Solar System of Alpha and Omega to Ascend up the Spiral of Evolution from the 3rd Dimension into the 4th Dimension. At that time, the Earth was reflecting the perfection of the Garden of Eden referred to in the allegory of Adam and Eve. Unfortunately, on some of the other planets in this system, there were souls who had chosen to use their free will to create patterns of discord and negativity. These souls were not going to be able to make the shift, and they were destined to be left behind.

To try and avoid that tragedy, the souls evolving on Earth volunteered to remain in the 3rd Dimension. In an unprecedented act of compassion and love, the children of Earth asked Alpha and Omega if the laggard souls could be transferred to this planet, so they could try to help them. The hope was, since the Earth was not bogged down with negativity, the people here would be able to assist the laggard souls to regain their direction. That way, their fallen sisters and brothers from the other planets would not have to experience the second death.

Never in the whole of Creation had an act of love that monumental or a sacrifice that great been made by the Children of God. Never had an experiment of that nature even been attempted. Our very purpose and reason for being is to become cocreators with our Father-Mother God, consequently, whenever we come up with new, innovative ideas, especially ones that involve great outpourings of love, special dispensations are granted, and new Divine Plans are set into motion.

Alpha and Omega agreed to allow the laggard souls one more opportunity to reclaim their course of direction. The Solar Logos of our physical Sun, Helios and Vesta, agreed to sustain the Earth in the 3rd Dimension until she could catch up with the rest of the Solar System.

Once the decision was made, a Cosmic Tone rang through

the Universe, and in an instant, the 12 Suns and the remaining 143 planets in the System of Alpha and Omega Ascended into the 4th Dimension. The laggard souls were instantaneously transferred to the inner planes surrounding the Earth. They entered the various schools of learning and began preparing for physical embodiment on Earth through the natural process of birth.

The reason it appears as though the other planets in our Solar System cannot sustain life is because we are viewing them with our 3rd-Dimensional eyes and instruments. Those planets are in the 4th Dimension, and they vibrate with frequencies that are beyond our physical sight. The only thing our instruments and cameras can detect is the very densest residue of physical matter associated with each planet.

The "Fall"

There is an expression that states, *"We don't know what we don't know."* Never was that statement more accurate than in the situation involving the laggard souls. The Sons and Daughters of God evolving on Earth had never experienced anything like the negativity that was created by the laggard souls. When they selflessly volunteered to help them, they really had no idea what they were getting themselves into.

At first it seemed as if the experiment was working. When the laggards were infants, their families were able to easily transmute their returning negative energy with the Violet Flame. As they grew up, however, and more and more of their karmic liabilities flooded the planet, the innocent children of Earth were stunned and overwhelmed by the pain and suffering. Instead of being able to transmute the horrendous negativity into Light, the souls on Earth ended up getting trapped in poverty, lack, limitation, disease, violence and hatred. As this situation progressed, they fell into the abyss of their own human miscreations, and the Earth fell off of the Spiral of Evolution onto what is called the Wheel of Karma, where we have been struggling for what seems like an eternity.

Women have carried the burden of the fall because it is said that Eve ate the apple and broke the commandment of God by *"partaking of the tree of knowledge of good and evil."* Well, the story of Adam and Eve is symbolic, not literal. The reason it is said that Eve ate the apple is because it was the love nature within the men and women on Earth, *the feminine polarity of our Mother God*, that caused them to have the compassion to volunteer to take on the laggard souls. That compassionate act of Divine Love brought a sea of negativity to Earth beyond what they were capable of handling. Tragically, that situation caused the fall.

A Universal Cosmic Inbreath

Even though every Solar System evolves at its own pace, every several billion years or so something unusual takes place. The Cosmic I AM evaluates the need of the hour and ultimately determines that it is time for ALL Creation to Ascend into the next evolutionary experience. During that rare moment, all life in the body of God, ready or not, is inbreathed into a new level of Godhood. That Cosmic Inbreath was announced 500 years ago and caught off guard the Legions of Light in the System of Alpha and Omega.

The edict revealed that the Cosmic Inbreath had already been delayed for thousands of years while the Universe waited for Earth to claim her position on the Spiral of the 4th Dimension. Alpha and Omega were told that the evolutionary shift had been postponed for too long, and the Universe could no longer wait for the Earth to try to regain her course of direction.

Since the Earth had gotten into her terrible plight through the greatest act of selfless Divine Love ever manifested in the history of time, no one wanted to give up on her. Over the Ages unprecedented assistance had been given from On High to try and awaken Humanity, but it was to no avail. Humanity kept sinking deeper and deeper into the abyss of our own humanly-created pain and suffering.

When the Cosmic Edict was issued 500 years ago, the Legions of Light from the System of Alpha and Omega realized that the Earth and the billions of souls evolving upon her were destined to go through the second death. They sent forth a heartfelt call to the Universe pleading for assistance. An overwhelming response came from Galaxies beyond Galaxies and Suns beyond Suns. Our Father-Mother God said that never before had that much Light and love been offered to save one small planet. A Cosmic Dispensation was implemented, and a 500-

year period of Grace was granted.

During that time, the Earth and the souls evolving upon her would have to make *two* dimensional shifts. Not only did we have to shift in energy, vibration and consciousness effectively enough to Ascend onto the Spiral of the 4th Dimension, we had to be ready to shift onto the Spiral of the 5th Dimension with the rest of our Solar System as well. Never had a planet that had fallen to the depths of discord the Earth was experiencing been given an opportunity to Ascend through two dimensional shifts in such a short period of time.

The prospects of our succeeding in such a monumental task were not good. Humanity had not been able to raise our heads above the mud puddle of our own miscreations for hundreds of thousands of years. The chance of us accomplishing that feat in only 500 years was almost nonexistent.

The Legions of Light throughout the Universe volunteered to assist us the maximum that Cosmic Law would allow. Several plans involving superhuman Divine Intervention were set into motion, and the unprecedented experiment began.

The first facet of the Divine Plan was to pave the way for the return of our Mother God, which would activate Humanity's creative right-brain hemispheres and awaken our spiritual brain centers. In order for this to be accomplished, the portal for the feminine polarity of our Mother God, which pulsates through the Andes Mountains near Lake Titicaca in Bolivia, had to be opened to full breadth. The masculine polarity of our Father God enters the Earth through the Himalayan Mountains in the area of Tibet, and it was necessary for that portal to be balanced with the love of our Mother God.

During the fall, when we closed our Heart Chakras, our Mother God's Light was withdrawn from the Earth. That caused the Light flowing through our right-brain hemispheres and the portal in South America to be reduced to a mere trickle of its original intensity. The remaining Light was barely enough to maintain brain consciousness. Our brain capacity deteriorated to just ten percent of its original potential. That tragic flaw caused us to lose contact with our God Selves, and it created the illusion that we are separated from God.

In order to begin reopening the portal in South America, Humanity needed to hold the focus of our attention on our Mother God. Approximately 500 years ago, an aspect of our

Mother God, known as the Virgin of Guadalupe, began appearing in Mexico to a peasant named Juan Diego. As word of the apparition swept like wildfire throughout Mexico and South America, literally millions of people turned the focus of their attention to the Divine Mother. Gradually the portal began to open, and the Light of our Mother God began to bathe the planet once again.

The second facet of the Divine Plan was designed to expand the activation of Humanity's creative right-brain hemispheres. The Legions of Light from the Realms of Illumined Truth flooded the mental stratum of Earth with new archetypes for culture and a civilized existence. As awakening souls reached up in consciousness, a new level of creativity began to filter into the hearts and minds of Humanity, and the Renaissance was born.

Five hundred years ago a literary and artistic movement began that was stimulated by the study of classical literature, art, dance and music. The movement began in Florence, Italy, and spread throughout Europe, signaling the end of the Dark Ages and the beginning of modern history. The Renaissance inspired civil liberty and a new internal order of culture and political development.

It was a time of Enlightenment and a crucial stage in the liberation of the human mind from superstition and error. Individualism and self-empowerment rose up in the hearts of Humanity. In the midst of unrivaled, barbaric darkness, the Renaissance birthed a civilization of a higher order.

In addition to awakening our spiritual brain centers and our creative right-brain hemispheres, it was clear to the Legions of Light that if Humanity was going to make the shift in time to Ascend up the Spiral of Evolution with the rest of our Solar System, we needed to have new archetypes to follow in reference to our relationships with each other. Those archetypes needed to demonstrate the family of Humanity living together in an environment that honors both the Earth and all of Humanity's unique diversities: a model of freedom, prosperity, equality, happiness, peace, love and liberty, a model of a New World, a model of Heaven on Earth.

As that concept began reverberating through the ethers 500 years ago, Christopher Columbus, began to receive the Divine Inspiration to search for the New World.

Christopher Columbus was one of the embodiments of St. Germain. I know there is a lot of negativity projected onto Christopher Columbus because of the atrocities inflicted on the indigenous peoples of the Americas by his crew and the Europeans who followed him to America. The Spiritual Hierarchy has revealed additional information about that situation, and they said it is very important for us to understand the greater picture.

When Christopher Columbus received the Divine Inspiration to cross the seas in search of new routes for trade and prosperity, nobody really believed he could survive. Consequently, he was only allowed to take prison inmates and demented souls from mental institutions to accompany him on his journey. When that motley crew arrived in the New World without the restraints of laws and discipline, they reverted to their basest instincts and destructive behavior patterns. In spite of that tragedy, Christopher Columbus's facet of the Divine Plan was accomplished God Victoriously.

St. Germain is a Son of Freedom, and he is an exponent of the Violet Flame. During his mission as Christopher Columbus, his flotilla was magnetized into the largest forcefield of the Violet Flame on Earth. That forcefield pulsates as a tremendous portal of Light that envelopes Florida, Cuba, the Dominican Republic and the Caribbean Islands.

When Christopher Columbus first set foot on land in Santo Domingo, the Violet Flame was anchored in his Heart Flame. He then traveled to Florida, and when he set foot on that land, the Violet Flame of Spiritual Freedom, Liberty, Justice, Opportunity, Forgiveness and Victory ignited the entire land mass that would become the United States of America. As the Flame spread throughout the land, the archetypes for the New World were imprinted on every electron of precious life energy.

The indigenous peoples of North America knew that they were preparing for a race of God-conscious souls who would one day come and inhabit the land. The plan was for these souls to model the love and harmony of the family of Humanity the way God originally intended. They would be the I AM RACE— men and women comprised of all races, all nationalities, all religions, all cultures and all lifestyles living together in mutual love, respect, reverence, harmony, prosperity, cooperation, honor, peace and happiness.

AMERICA is an anagram for the I AM RACE!

When Christopher Columbus returned home, the word spread, and people throughout Europe who were longing for freedom from oppression and freedom of religion responded to their hearts' call. They began flocking in droves to the New World.

Unfortunately, once they arrived in the New World, their fear-based human egos got the upper hand. Greed and selfishness overpowered the original Divine Intent of this country, and people lost the concept of Oneness and reverence for life. They began falling into the dysfunctional behavior patterns of hatred, prejudice, corruption, lack, limitation, war and all of the other expressions of human frailty.

In spite of the antics and the treachery of Humanity's human egos, through the Grace of God, our founding Fathers were able to tap into the original archetypes of the Divine Plan for the United States of America. They perceived the plan effectively enough to express it in our sacred documents. The Constitution of the United States of America, the Bill of Rights and our Declaration of Independence all state our purpose and reason for being as a nation. Even though we have fallen far from fulfilling the original Divine Plan for this country, the archetypes are firmly established and have been waiting in dormancy for the moment when they will be victoriously activated. Contrary to outer appearances, WE HAVE REACHED THAT MOMENT.

Americans, en masse, are now awakening and striving to reclaim the original Divine Intent for this nation. This is the moment we have been preparing for, the moment when we will remember who we are and why we are here. Together, we will fulfill the Divine Plan for this sacred land in all of its splendor and glory.

This does not mean America will be a military superpower wielding our authority and might over every other country to manipulate people into doing things our way. That is the antithesis of America's Divine Plan. Our Divine Plan is to be the microcosm of the macrocosm of Heaven on Earth. The intent of the New World is to demonstrate how people from every country, every religion, every culture, every lifestyle, every creed and belief system can live together in harmony and love. We are to show the world how very diverse people can live together with honor and respect for each other while enjoying and revering our various appearances, cultures, beliefs, foods, music and unique ways of doing things.

The vision is for every American to reach our highest potential as a Son or Daughter of God while assisting our fellow Human Beings all over the world to do the same. We are to help Humanity live lives of abundance, health, peace and freedom while always being cognizant of working for the highest good of all concerned. By our example, we are to unify the world and lift the consciousness of all evolving souls. Through compassion, a win-win attitude, and a reverence for all life, we will create a new level of trust and caring amongst all the peoples of the world.

This can, and will, be accomplished without harming one another or any other part of life. We already have everything we need within us to accomplish this mighty feat. Our God Selves are ready to take command of our thoughts, words, actions and feelings. All we need to do is accept that Divine Truth, and release our fear-based egos into the Light. We have the absolute ability to do this, and the entire Company of Heaven is standing by to help us. *"Ask and you shall receive. Knock and the Door will be opened."*

We have been preparing for this moment for thousands of years and, at long last, OUR TIME IS AT HAND!

Once Christopher Columbus' mission was accomplished, the Legions of Light assisting the Earth evaluated the need of the hour. They clearly perceived that Humanity's lower human egos had great potential to mess things up in the New World, so they came up with another plan to try and curtail that problem.

The plan was to show Humanity, through Divinely Inspired prophecies, the dire events that might happen if we insisted on letting our human egos control our lives. Then, hopefully, we would be motivated to change our behavior patterns.

As that plan filtered into the ethers, a man in France responded to the call and volunteered to transcribe the prophecies. Approximately 500 years ago, Michel de Nostredame, known to us as Nostradamas, began transcribing his famous Quatrains. He stated that the predicted events were an indication of where Humanity was headed if we didn't change our direction.

A fulfilled negative prophecy is a failed prophecy. The *only* reason negative prophecies are ever given through Divine Inspiration is so that we will observe the potential results of our destructive actions and put forth the effort to avert the prophecy.

Nostradamas gave his prophecies of the holocaust nuclear war that was to occur at the end of the 1990s in order to warn the New World—United States of America—of our potential demise. The prophesies indicated that if we did not change our direction and heal the atrocities we were perpetrating on Humanity and the Earth through our greed and selfishness, ninety percent of life evolving on this planet would be destroyed.

On the other hand, the prophecies revealed that if Humanity changed our course of direction and stopped wreaking havoc on Beloved Mother Earth and our fellow Human Beings, we would reclaim our original Divine Plan and fulfill our mission of modeling the I Am Race and the harmony of Heaven on Earth for the rest of the world.

Even with all of those critically important facets of the Divine Plan in place, the Legions of Light were not at all confident that the masses of Humanity could make the shift in time to Ascend into the 5th Dimension with the rest of our Solar System. So, once again, a clarion call went out to the Universe asking for assistance. This time an even more powerful response came forth from the Company of Heaven. Tremendous Beings of Light, from realms and dimensions of perfection beyond anything we have ever experienced, volunteered to embody on Earth to help raise Humanity's collective consciousness. These Beings are simply our brothers and sisters who evolved long before us. They are like college professors compared to our being kindergarten students.

Initially, our Father-Mother God gave only a few of the illumined Beings permission to embody on Earth. This was a unique experiment that had never been attempted before, and our God Parents wanted to be sure that these selfless Beings of Light would not be overwhelmed by the negativity existing on this planet.

For 400 years, these magnificent Beings of Light were allowed to embody on Earth. One by one they came in through the natural process of birth and received the band of forgetfulness just like the rest of Humanity. Most of these Beings came and anchored their Light without anyone in the outer world recognizing their presence. Then, in the latter part of the 1800s, the Spiritual Hierarchy reevaluated the situation and determined that the experiment was succeeding beyond all expectations. At that time, our Father-Mother God lifted the floodgates and gave permission for literally millions of the highly-evolved Beings to embody on Earth.

Over the past one hundred years, these souls have embodied on Earth by the millions. They have embodied in every corner of the world and into every conceivable walk of life and Earthly situation. They are well aware of the Universal Law *"As I Am lifted up, all life is lifted up with me."* Consequently, they have volunteered to delve into the depths of human suffering and despair in order to lift those fallen energies into the Light.

It is due to the tremendous influx of these Beings of Light that the Earth has experienced such a huge population explosion over the past century. From outer appearances, it looks as if this increase in population will take us down the tubes, but nothing could be further from the Truth. If there was the slightest chance that this large influx of souls would cause more harm than good, the experiment would never have been allowed. When the shift is complete, these souls will return to their original homes, and the Earth will continue her evolutionary journey as planned.

These souls are now awakening in vast numbers all over the world. They are beginning to remember who they are and why they are here. They are the major catalyst for the tremendous shift of consciousness that is taking place on Earth, and they are responsible for the unprecedented advancement in technology we have experienced in the short span of 100 years.

Just observe what Humanity has "discovered" in the past century. During the latter part of the 1800s, we discovered electricity and invented the light bulb, the telephone and the first combustion engine. In the span of 100 years, we have made quantum leaps in the technology of computers, fiber optics, fax machines, medicine, space travel and myriad other mind-boggling achievements. Normal human evolution cannot possibly explain the accelerated achievements Humanity has made in the past 100 years.

We have experienced this incredible shift of consciousness because the Beings who have embodied on Earth to assist us are able to reach into the Realms of Illumined Truth and tap the patterns of perfection in the Causal Body of God in ways that fallen Humanity could not.

I want to strongly emphasize the fact that these Beings were given permission to embody on Earth on the condition that they would blend into mainstream Humanity and teach us through example. They will not be identified in any way, and when they remember who they are and why they are here, they will hold that information in their hearts as a sacred trust and not discuss it with anyone.

The Truth is, it does not matter one iota if we are one of the illumined Beings from higher realms who have come to help the people evolving on Earth or if we are one of the souls on Earth who volunteered to take on our fallen sisters and brothers, or if we are one of the fallen souls from the other planets who has awakened and reclaimed the path of Light. All that matters is that we know that we are all One, and it is time for us to fulfill our Divine Potential as stewards of the Earth.

For 500 years, this multifaceted, multidimensional Divine Plan unfolded step by step. Humanity's human egos threw monkey wrenches into the project whenever they had the chance, but in spite of their malevolent efforts, the Light of God prevailed.

At last, in 1987 the Earth and all her life reached a frequency of energy, vibration and consciousness that allowed us to begin our ascent off the Wheel of Karma and onto the Spiral of the 4th Dimension.

In 1987, an opportunity known as Harmonic Convergence began to filter into the consciousness of awakening Lightworkers. People around the world responded to the inner promptings of their hearts and traveled to sacred sites on the planet by the hundreds of thousands. Whether they were consciously aware of it or not, people were being inspired by their God Selves and the Company of Heaven to line up along the acupuncture points and meridians of the Crystal Grid System of Earth.

During a three-day period, August 15-17, 1987, the Light of God poured through the collective Heart Flames of Lightworkers around the world and activated the Earth's Crystal Grid System to its original Divine Potential. That activation allowed God's Light to expand exponentially through all life.

The Legions of Light revealed to us that the entire activation process would take 25 years. They told us that the first five years would be the most tumultuous, and then there would be a shift of vibration that would move us a quantum leap up the Spiral of Evolution. They said that from that point on, the Divine Plan would unfold at a greatly accelerated pace.

The shift the Light Beings were referring to was called *"Moving through the Doorway of the 11:11."* It involved a unique six-month Doorway of Opportunity that was opened during the powerful Solar Eclipse on July 11, 1991, and built in power and momentum until January 11, 1992.

On January 11, 1992, the Light of God that had been building in momentum for six months blazed through the Crystal Grid System and lifted this sweet Earth and all her life onto the initial impulse of the Spiral of the 4th Dimension.

Once we successfully began our ascent up the Spiral of the 4th Dimension, the Company of Heaven revealed to us that there were two critical things that had to be accomplished in order for us to make the shift onto the Spiral of the 5th Dimension.

The first was for Humanity to heal the schism that we had created with the Elemental Kingdom. There are three lifeforms evolving on Earth: the Human Kingdom, the Angelic Kingdom and the Elemental Kingdom. All three lifeforms consist of intelligent Beings who are evolving according to God's Plan with different purposes and reasons for being.

The Human Kingdom consists of the Sons and Daughters of God who are in this physical plane to learn to use our free will and our creative faculties of thought and feeling to become cocreators with our Father-Mother God. The Divine Intent of our learning experience is for us to learn to cocreate new, expressions of Divinity in order to expand the borders of the Kingdom of Heaven on Earth.

The Angelic Kingdom consists of Beings of Light who are entrusted with the feeling nature of God and who are empowered to guide and protect the Sons and Daughters of God during our Earthly sojourn.

The Elemental Kingdom consists of intelligent Beings who are trained to draw the unformed, primal Light substance from the core of Creation and hold it in fixed patterns to create a physical reality and the physical bodies for the Sons and Daughters of God to use while we are evolving on Earth.

The Elemental Kingdom is the intelligent lifeforce we associate with the Nature Kingdom and the elements on Earth such as the earth, air, water, fire and ether. The Elemental Kingdom provides the substance for our physical bodies and the bodies of the plants and animals as well.

The original Divine Plan was for these three kingdoms to work together and to remain consciously aware of each other during our Earthly experience. Prior to the "fall," Humanity walked and talked with the Angels and the Elementals in perfect harmony and balance while we each fulfilled our missions and evolved side by side.

When Humanity fell into the abyss of our human miscreations and developed our fragmented human egos, we lost awareness of the fact that the Earth is a living, breathing organism and that the substance of Earth is alive and intelligent. Instead, we came to the erroneous and devastating conclusion that the Earth is a dead, inanimate object that we can use and abuse as we will, for our own personal gain.

We developed a very distorted perception about the plants, animals, minerals, water, fire and air. Our human egos talked us into believing that these Beings of the Nature Kingdom are here merely for our pleasure and entertainment. Through the arrogance, greed, selfishness and fear of our human egos, we lost the concept of reverence for ALL life. The atrocities and pollution we have inflicted on this planet and her various lifeforms are a dire testament to that sad fact.

As a result of our arrogance and our blatant abuse of the Elemental Kingdom, Humanity created a tremendous schism that has resulted in the Elemental Kingdom's all-out rebellion against us. The horrendous effects of that rebellion manifest on Earth as extreme weather conditions, earthquakes, volcanos, tornados, hurricanes, tidal waves, droughts, floods, famine, wildfires, plagues, pestilence, disease, ozone depletion, death and dying as we know it and myriad other painful experiences.

As time went on, the more we ignored the signs and continued to pollute the Earth for our own selfish intent, the worse the effects of the rebellion became. Eventually, this war between Humanity and the Elemental Kingdom brought the Earth to the very brink of extinction.

In 1992, after we began our ascent up the Spiral of the 4th Dimension, enough of Humanity had finally awakened to attempt making amends with the Elemental Kingdom for the atrocities Human Beings had inflicted on them over aeons of time. A plan that had been unfolding for several decades was now ready to be implemented in full force.

When individual souls first began to awaken around the world, one of the things that registered in our conscious minds was the fact that through the outrageous behavior of our greedy, obsessive human egos, we had brought the Earth to the brink of her destruction. That shocking realization motivated Lightworkers everywhere to seek viable solutions to heal the Earth.

Individuals and groups began seeking out the wisdom and knowledge of the indigenous peoples of the world who had not lost the awareness of the intelligent lifeforce within the Elemental Kingdom.

Gratefully, the indigenous peoples opened their hearts to the awakening Lightworkers and agreed to teach us how to commune with the Elementals. Through sacred ceremonies of love and forgiveness, the Light of God was projected forth to flood the Elemental Kingdom.

The Elemental Kingdom began to cautiously observe the Lightworkers' efforts and, at first, very skeptically watched and wondered. It was obvious that we had burst asunder every bit of trust the Elementals had for us and that trust was not going to be restored easily. Fortunately, the awakening souls realized the extreme degree of abuse we had inflicted upon the Elementals and continued to persevere in their healing efforts.

Ever so slowly, the Elementals began to trust the sincere desire of the Lightworkers to heal the separation. They began to understand that Humanity was asking for another chance to reclaim our responsibility as stewards of the Earth.

The sincere desire to heal and reunite, arising in the hearts of Humanity and the Elementals, drew the attention of the Company of Heaven. The awakening Lightworkers invoked assistance from On High, and a plan was set into motion that was designed to permanently heal the schism between Humanity and the Elementals. It was a plan designed to *avert* the cataclysmic Earth changes that the prophets and seers of old had predicted.

A clarion call rang through the Universe and activated within the hearts and minds of Humanity the need to set aside our petty differences and come together as a unified force with the common goal of healing the Earth.

People already aligned with the environment began to redouble their efforts. A Divine Blueprint for an outer-world activity of Light began to form in the ethers. The blueprint filtered into the consciousness of world leaders and lay people alike. The organization that symbolizes global unification, the United Nations, chose to accept the responsibility of organizing this event, and the very first Earth Summit began to manifest.

I know there is a lot of negative information floating around regarding the United Nations. This organization, however, is like the United States of America in that the original Divine Intent and the original archetypes for the United Nations contain patterns of perfection that are specifically designed to heal the maladies of separation on Earth in a way that will reflect the highest good of all concerned. Regardless of how far either the USA or the UN may be from demonstrating their full Divine Potential, their blueprints are still viable and are destined to be activated very soon.

The United Nations Conference on Environment and Development (UNCED)—the First Earth Summit—was held in Rio de Janeiro, Brazil, June 1-14, 1992. This event was organized to demonstrate to the Elemental Kingdom the fact that Humanity was indeed sorry for the abuse we had inflicted upon the Earth and ALL her life and that we were finally ready to accept our responsibility as stewards of this planet.

For the first time ever, 176 world leaders, each representing the entire population of their individual countries, and over 40,000 non-governmental organizations from around the world came together for one unified cause: the healing of the Earth. This sacred gathering was the outer-world demonstration the Elemental Kingdom had been waiting for to clearly prove that Humanity was, at long last, worthy of their trust.

On June 1, 1992, the Lightworkers gathered at the Earth

Summit created a tremendous Chalice of Light through the Cup of our collective consciousness. The Chalice formed an open portal between Heaven and Earth, and as the events of the summit progressed, day after day, the Light of God's Love and Forgiveness bathed all life on Earth.

Daily and hourly the Light built in momentum, reaching a tremendous crescendo on June 7, 1992, during the midpoint of the Earth Summit. It was not by chance that day fell on Pentecost Sunday, the day celebrated as the Day of the Baptism of the Holy Spirit. The Holy Spirit is actually our Mother God, the Holy Comforter and the exponent of the Love of God. She is also the Divine Presence who sustains and nurtures the Elemental Kingdom. That is why we refer to *Mother* Earth and *Mother* Nature. On that holy day, activities of Light took place that enabled us to anchor powerful frequencies of Divine Love into the heart of Mother Earth. It was, truly, a baptism of the Holy Spirit.

Through that gift of Divine Love, the God Selves of ALL Humanity and the Beings of the Elemental Kingdom were able to reach into the higher realms of consciousness. A miraculous healing took place, and the schism between Humanity and the Elemental Kingdom was permanently healed. Humanity's self-inflicted separation from the Elementals was eliminated, and a New Covenant was formed between the Sons and Daughters of God and the Beings of the Elements.

In the New Covenant, the Elemental Kingdom promised to cooperate with Humanity and to purge and purify the body of Mother Earth in a way that will result in as little loss of human life as possible.

In the New Covenant, Humanity promised to stop polluting and desecrating the Earth by educating and informing the polluters that the Earth is a living, breathing Being of Light that must be honored and revered in order to survive. We promised to work tenaciously toward shifting the consciousness of Humanity by teaching the masses the Divine Truth that we are ALL One. We promised to become proactive in Earth's healing process, and we promised to remind each soul of the urgent need for each of us to develop a deep reverence for ALL life.

Through the miracle of the New Covenant, the cataclysmic Earth changes that had been predicted by the prophets were *averted,* and a new, harmonious plan for planetary transformation was initiated.

The final day of the Earth Summit was June 14, 1992. It was the Full Moon of Gemini, which is celebrated as the Festival of the Goodwill of Humanity. There was also a magnificent Lunar Eclipse that night.

Within the embrace of the Lunar Eclipse, 250,000 people gathered on the beaches in Rio de Janeiro. Through an awesome light and sound show with music and dancing, the patterns of perfection from the First Earth Summit were permanently anchored in the heart of Mother Earth. With incredible joy and expectation, Humanity and the Elemental Kingdom embarked on a joint venture to restore this sweet Earth to the perfection of Heaven on Earth.

Evidence of the New Covenant
Weather Changes in the 1990s

There was a dramatic increase in the frequency and severity of natural disasters in the 1990s, but mercifully, they involved relatively little loss of life. Here are a few of the statistics:

* Natural disasters in the form of earthquakes, tornados, volcanos, floods, hurricanes, landslides and wildfires affected more than a billion people in the last five years of the 1990s.

* One third of all natural disasters in the 20th century occurred in the 1990s.

* Normally there are 700 natural disasters per decade. In the 1990s, there were over 2,400. That is more than three times the average, and they were more severe than usual.

* Nine out of ten of the most deadly natural disasters in recorded history occurred in the 1990s.

* Floods affected 130 million people a year in the 1990s. That is a 700 percent increase over the floods in the 1970s.

* Six times as many hurricanes and tornados affected people in the 1990s as in the 1970s.

* Four times as many people were affected by landslides in the 1990s as in the 1970s.

* From 1960 to 1989, there was only one year when the USA had 1,000 or more tornados. Since 1990, we had at least 1,000 every year.

Once the schism between Humanity and the Elemental Kingdom was healed, it was necessary for us to prepare for the second facet of the plan. For the next eight years, myriad Activities of Light took place on Earth that were orchestrated through the unified efforts of awakening Humanity and the Legions of Light in the Realms of Perfection. These events were designed to lift the consciousness of Humanity and increase the Light of God on Earth.

Day by day, as the Light increased, the patterns of human miscreation were pushed to the surface to be healed and transmuted into Light. From outer appearances, it seemed as though things on the planet were getting worse but, in fact, we were merely going through our healing crisis.

With the dawn of the new millennium, we officially moved into the full embrace of the forcefield of Aquarius, and through the increased frequencies of the Violet Flame and the Seventh Solar Aspect of Deity, the Earth was catapulted forward a quantum leap into the Light.

During the Grand Planetary Alignment that took place the first week of May 2000, the Solar Christ Presence of every man, woman and child evolving on Earth was birthed within each person's Heart Flame. That higher aspect of our own Divinity is now integrating daily and hourly into our Earthly vehicles, and we are finally ready to accomplish the second critical facet of the Divine Plan.

The second thing Humanity must accomplish in order to Ascend up the Spiral of the 5th Dimension with the rest of our Solar System is to heal the schisms in our relationships with each other. This includes the schisms between races, nations, religions, cultures, genders, creeds, economic groups, political factions, belief systems, age groups and people, in general. Obviously, our work is cut out for us.

It is the destiny of the United States of America to demonstrate to the world the family of Humanity expressing our full

Divine Potential. Those of us abiding in this country have made a commitment, through our God Selves, to model the archetypes for the New World to the rest of the planet.

The Legions of Light are well aware of the resistance of our human egos, and they continually try to set up safeguards to guide us in the right direction. They cannot interfere with our free will, but they can assist in creating opportunities to inspire us to make better choices. They are asking now,

"Are you going to cling to the old, ego-based habits of fear and greed that got you into this situation in the first place, or are you going to lift up in consciousness, open your hearts and soar into your full Divine Potential as Sons and Daughters of God"?

The choice is up to us. These Beings of Light have been serving us selflessly during our 500-year period of Grace. Now they would dearly love for us to make the choice to cocreate the wonders of Heaven on Earth easily and painlessly. In order to do that, we must move into the full experience of our Oneness with ALL life. That may sound like a monumental task, but a slight shift of consciousness is all that is necessary for our God Selves to take full dominion of our lives.

It is time for those of us in the United States of America, and those of us in every other country in the world who are awakening to the Divine Plan, to become proactive in implementing and living what we know to be true. It is time for us to model the Truth of who we are as Beloved Sons and Daughters of God.

In addition to being *God in Action* every day of our lives, our greatest responsibility is to support and encourage those souls who are beginning to awaken. We must share the Truth about the opportunities at hand and help them to understand what we can all do to assist in this healing process. This doesn't mean standing on our soap boxes or preaching to people who are not interested. It means lovingly and graciously presenting the Truth that is pouring forth from the Realms of Perfection in a nonthreatening, non-judgmental way. It means giving a drink from our Cup to those people who come to us thirsting for Divine Wisdom and those seeking nourishment for their souls.

We have been preparing for lifetimes to serve as instruments of God on Earth during this very moment. We are succeeding in our mission, and nothing is going to stop the Earth from Ascending into the Light. No outer-world event will be able to block our forward progress, no matter how dire things may look. The day of the human egos' rule is over. If you have any doubt about that, please keep reading.

In part two of this book, the Spiritual Hierarchy asked me to share the details of some of the life-transforming events that have occurred on Earth since the culmination of our 500-year period of Grace. This information is being given to encourage, support, inspire and motivate us to *"keep on keeping on"* during THE FINAL STAGES OF OUR ASCENSION INTO THE 5TH DIMENSION.

These miraculous events confirm that the Divine Plan is working God Victoriously, and that the Earth and ALL her life are going to Ascend up the 5th-Dimensional Spiral of Evolution with the rest of our Solar System. Our Victory is assured, but OUR WORK IS FAR FROM OVER.

The reason the Company of Heaven assures us that we are going to make it is because of the incredible success of the activities of Light that have been documented in part two of this book and because they are able to perceive the depth of the Lightworker's commitment to keep fulfilling our Divine Missions in the face of all adversity.

Part 2

PART 2

THE   UNFOLDING   DIVINE   PLAN

The unfolding Divine Plan is being cocreated by awakened Lightworkers, the God Selves of all Humanity, the Legions of Light in the Realms of Illumined Truth and the multidimensional aspects of our Father-Mother God.

In part two of this book, I share information about some of the incredible events that have taken place over the past few years to accelerate Mother Earth's Ascension up the Spiral of Evolution. It is important for each of us to understand that Earth's Ascension process includes all life existing on this planet. Every one of us has been preparing for aeons of time to assist during this unprecedented experiment. *Every* person's part of the plan is essential, and no facet of the Divine Plan is any more important or significant than another. The events I have included in this book represent only a fraction of the myriad activities of Light taking place.

Over thirty years ago, the Spiritual Hierarchy asked me if I would be willing to document the activities of Light taking place on Earth and transcribe the information pouring forth from the Realms of Illumined Truth in order to assist Humanity in the awakening process. In deep humility, wonder and awe, I accepted that sacred opportunity. I am only a scribe. This information is readily available to anyone who is willing to reconnect with his or her God Self and reach up in consciousness into the Realms of Light.

As you read this information and learn of the miraculous activities that have taken place, know that your God Self participated in these events. This is true whether you were consciously aware of the events or not. Pay attention to the dates, and you will often remember eventful things that took place in your life during these Cosmic Moments.

This sacred information is being shared with you now to prove to you, beyond a shadow of a doubt, that in spite of outer-world appearances, we are succeeding in reclaiming Earth's Divine Birthright and cocreating Heaven On Mother Earth—HOME.

Allow the wonder of the events recorded here to resonate in the deepest recesses of your heart. This information is a gift from On High to give us all the courage, strength and self-confidence to "*keep on keeping on*" even in the face of the adversities manifesting in our lives and in the world.

We are walking through the last vestiges of our painful pasts, and we are receiving more assistance from the Heavenly Realms than ever before in the history of time. We are standing on the threshold of the greatest shift of consciousness ever attempted in the whole of Creation. This shift will result in our eternal liberation, freedom, peace, prosperity, happiness and Ascension into the Light.

Our challenges are intense because those of us who are awakening first have volunteered to serve as surrogates on behalf of our sisters and brothers in the family of Humanity who have not, as yet, awakened. We have agreed to be the Open Doors for the Light of God. And we have agreed to transmute the negativity that is surfacing to be healed and transformed into Light.

We have been preparing for aeons of time to be the Heart, Head and Hands of God in the physical plane during this unprecedented experiment, and now—OUR TIME IS AT HAND.

The Spiritual Hierarchy of the Piscean Age

The Spiritual Hierarchy who have served so selflessly during the past 2,000 years are coming to the forefront to assist in bringing the Piscean Age to fruition. They are also ushering in the Age of Aquarius—the Permanent Golden Age of Spiritual Freedom, Eternal Peace and Limitless Abundance. These selfless servants of God are being joined by the Spiritual Hierarchy associated with all of the past Ages and the entire Company of Heaven.

Jesus The Christ, Mother Mary, Archangel Gabriel, Saint John the Beloved, Saint Paul (also known as Hilarion) and Saint Joseph (also known as St. Germain) have been working ceaselessly during the Piscean Age to pave the way for the removal of Humanity's Bands of Forgetfulness. The Divine Intent is that we return to *Christ Consciousness:* the state of enlightenment we enjoyed prior to the "fall."

For clarity, I would like to explain that *The Christ* is the state of enlightened consciousness every Child of God was invested with at the time of our inception. We only lost Christ Consciousness when our Crown Chakras closed, and we were cut off from our God Selves. The major focus of Jesus' mission was to model for Humanity the enlightened consciousness of The Christ and to demonstrate the Path of Divine Love that every Human Being must return to in order to regain Christ Consciousness. Jesus said, *"These things I do you shall also do, and greater things than these shall you do."*

During this wondrous, Cosmic Moment, it is imperative that we set aside the preconceived opinions that promote prejudice, separation and competition amongst the world religions. The unfolding Divine Plan is designed to include ALL life evolving on Earth, and our God Selves know that. It is only our fear-based human egos who are confused and misunderstand what is happening. We must transcend our limited beliefs and our tunnel vision. It is vital that we accept our Oneness. *Harmony in diversity is our greatest strength.*

Even though the Piscean Age ushered in the birth of Christianity and the Beings of Light associated with that Age have been mentioned predominantly in Christian Doctrine, their service is universal and all-encompassing. The Spiritual Hierarchy who served during the Age of Pisces work in perfect harmony with the Spiritual Hierarchy associated with every world religion and every spiritual endeavor.

The unfolding Divine Plan includes the Divine Truth and Wisdom associated with *every* religion, creed, philosophy or belief system. Needless to say, our human egos have often contaminated the original teachings of the various world religions and distorted them into manipulative dogmas for their own personal agendas, but the original, pure teachings of the world religions have always been based in Truth.

In the Piscean Age, Jesus brought to Earth the remembrance of Christ Consciousness, the Path of Divine Love and the Law of Forgiveness. That sacred knowledge was seeded into the Heart Flames of all Humanity, and it has been slowly growing in momentum. Jesus knew that Humanity was deeply immersed in the quagmire of our own human miscreations, however, and he understood that it would be a difficult process to penetrate through the dense consciousness of our human egos to reach the Spark of Divinity blazing in our hearts. He was quite aware that the process would take centuries of time and, therefore, he declared that not in his lifetime, but *when the Seventh Angel begins to sound,* there will be a *second* coming of *The Christ,* and the mystery of God will be fulfilled. Jesus revealed that during the second coming The Christ will be born again in the hearts of Humanity, and the Era of Eternal Peace and Abundance will be the order of the New Day.

Through many incredible activities of Light that have taken place over the past several decades, the second coming of The Christ—the return of Christ Consciousness to every Human Being—is slowly beginning to manifest. We are moving into the forcefield of Aquarius which vibrates with the Seventh Solar Aspect of Deity. *The Seventh Angel is beginning to sound.*

Preparing for the Seventh Angel

After Jesus' Ascension and the initial pageant for the birth of the Piscean Age was completed, the Spiritual Hierarchy began preparing for the next phase of the Divine Plan. In unison with our Father-Mother God and the Company of Heaven, Jesus and all those who served with him devised a plan to prepare the way for the Seventh Angel and the second coming of The Christ.

It was decided from On High that the land mass we now call the United States of America would be prepared to demonstrate the archetypes of the New World: Heaven on Earth. The destiny of this country was to model the microcosm of the macrocosm. The Divine Intent was for the United States of America to one day manifest the following principles for all the world to see:

The family of Humanity living in Divine Love and Harmony, expressing reverence for ALL life.

The I AM Race, comprised of all races, nationalities, religions and creeds, living as ONE nation under God.

Every person living with equality, liberty, justice and freedom with the right to pursue happiness and prosperity and the right to worship according to his or her heart's call.

To initiate that plan, our Father-Mother God issued a Divine Fiat and decreed that all of the sacred temples in the Heavenly Realms surrounding the Earth be duplicated in the atmosphere over the land that would eventually be the United States of America. Once these sacred Foci of Light were established above the land mass of

America, the Divine Qualities of each temple were anchored into the physical plane. The indigenous peoples of America absorbed the qualities of Light and accepted the responsibility of being the Keepers of the Flames for America.

The replica of the temples that pulsate above the Holy Land in Jerusalem were projected into the ethers above what is now the State of Arizona. This is a tremendous complex of temples known as the *Holy Cities of Saint John the Beloved.*

The temples of the Holy Cities are centrally located above Tucson, Arizona, and expand out like a tremendous Sun to envelop the entire state. The disciple known as John the Beloved has been the Hierarch of this Focus of Light for almost 2,000 years. He is the *Keeper of the Flame* that blazes on the altar in the *Temple of Divine Grace.*

In addition to that magnificent Temple of Light, the Holy Cities of Saint John the Beloved include:

Mother Mary's Temple
of the Immaculate Concept (Divine Blueprint).

Archangel Gabriel's Temple
of Resurrection and Ascension.

Hilarion's (Saint Paul's) Temple of Healing
through the Power of Limitless Transmutation.

Jesus The Christ's Temple
of Solar Christ Consciousness.

Lord Lanto's Temple
of Reverence for ALL Life.

And the Temple of the First Initiation
which is now the
Initiation into the Reverence for ALL Life.

All of the Beings of Light associated with the Holy Cities of John the Beloved were instrumental in bringing forth the Divine Wisdom of the Piscean Age: the Truth of Christ Consciousness, the Path of Divine Love and the Law of Forgiveness. After their missions on Earth were completed, they each selflessly volunteered to continue their work at inner levels to help Humanity prepare for the second coming of The Christ and the time when the Seventh Angel would begin to sound.

For almost 2,000 years, each man, woman and child evolving on Earth, both in and out of embodiment, has been drawn into the temples of the Holy Cities above Arizona in their finer bodies as they slept at night. They were taught about the dawning Permanent Golden Age of Spiritual Freedom, Eternal Peace and Limitless Abundance and the true meaning of the second coming of The Christ. They were taught about their Divine Birthrights as Sons and Daughters of God and their responsibility in assisting the Earth and all her life to Ascend up the Spiral of Evolution into the 4th, and now the 5th, Dimensions.

John the Beloved and all of the Beings of Light associated with the Holy Cities have worked unceasingly to help Humanity *avert* the cataclysmic prophesies foretold in Revelations and proclaimed by ancient seers from the various world religions. According to prophesy, those cataclysms were supposed to take place during these "*end times.*"

In 1980, the Lightworkers abiding in Tucson, Arizona, were asked by John the Beloved, Hilarion and Mother Mary if we would be willing to assist in magnetizing a forcefield of healing into the physical plane of Earth from the heart of the Great, Great Central Sun. The Beings of Light from the Holy Cities said that due to the tremendous success of dedicated Lightworkers all over the world, the Earth had finally reached a frequency of vibration that would sustain the new, unparalleled frequency of healing known as the *Flame of Healing through the Power of Limitless Transmutation.* In deep humility and abounding joy, we accepted that sacred opportunity.

Under the guidance of the Spiritual Hierarchy, the Lightworkers in Tucson met regularly for three years. On the Holy Breath, we magnetized the exquisite *emerald green Flame with its amethyst radiance* from the heart of the Great, Great Central Sun and anchored it into our own Heart Flames. The Beings of Light have said that the Flame of Healing through the Power of Limitless Transmutation is the most powerful frequency of healing Humanity is able to withstand at this time.

In 1983, the Spiritual Hierarchy said that the Flame had built in momentum in our hearts sufficiently to sustain it in the physical plane. They said it was time to anchor the Flame permanently in the center of the Earth.

In a Divine Ceremony, the Flame of Healing through the Power of Limitless Transmutation was anchored from the heart of the Great, Great Central Sun through a specific vortex in the foothills in Tucson, Arizona, into the Sun of Even Pressure in the center of the Earth. Once the Flame was permanently anchored into the heart of Mother Earth, it expanded out through the Crystal Grid System. Now, the Flame's emerald green and amethyst healing unguent perpetually blesses every particle of life evolving on this planet.

A few months later, in perfect Divine Order, a beautiful forty-one million dollar, five star resort was built in Tucson, Arizona, in the exact location where the Flame of Healing through the Power of Limitless Transmutation enters the Earth. In the lobby of the resort, on a square table that looks like an altar, rest seven large amethyst geodes. Loews Ventana Canyon Resort now magnetizes people from all over the world into the sacred portal of this Healing Flame. *Ventana* is a Spanish word that means *window*.

The Spiritual Hierarchy revealed to us that the effect this Healing Flame has had over the years in bringing the Piscean Age to fruition and paving the way for the Seventh Angel is unimaginable.

The End of the Piscean Age

In 1997, some very important activities of Light took place that brought the Age of Pisces to a close. During that momentous year, the Earth Ascended further up the Spiral of the 4th Dimension, and we began to experience the very first impulses of the 5th Dimension.

In our natural evolutionary process, the Earth is becoming a Sun. In 1997, through a rare Divine Alchemy, the base physical matter of Earth Ascended at an atomic, cellular level into the initial frequencies of Solar Light. This was accomplished with the assistance of the Comet Hale-Bopp, which was infused with the power of the Ascension Flame by the Company of Heaven.

When the Comet Hale-Bopp swept through the Heavens during the Vernal Equinox in 1997, its wake rippled into the densest octaves of the physical plane. This shattered the fragmented archetypes of the mental stratum and pushed them to the surface to be transmuted into Light.

A comet is *physically* nothing more than a ball of dirty ice spraying forth water and dust particles, but like everything else in the Universe, there is much more to a comet than just its 3rd-Dimensional substance. Every manifest form has a Divine Intelligence guiding it. Comets and meteors shake the ethers and break down crystallized models and archetypes that are obsolete and no longer relevant. This creates a fluid field of unmanifest potential onto which new paradigms and perfection patterns from the Divine Mind of God can be imprinted.

On March 22, 1997, which numerically equals 33, the master number that reflects Christ Consciousness, the Comet Hale-Bopp began it's approach to the Earth. Then on March 23, 1997, during a Full Moon Lunar Eclipse, the comet made its closest pass by the planet.

The Lunar Eclipse was centered in South America where the feminine polarity of God enters the planet. As the comet passed through that portal of our Mother God, Humanity's RNA/DNA genetic codes for a new karma-free Solar Reality were activated. Those genetic codes contain the Divine Blueprints for the full potential of Heaven on Earth.

After that activity, Lightworkers from all over the world traveled to a spiritual conference in Greece to participate in the next phase of the plan.

Greece is known as the cradle of modern civilization. Ages ago, the paradigms for the social systems involving science, medicine, philosophy, religion, architecture, politics and athletic achievements were birthed in Greece. It is not by chance that Saint John was given Revelations on the Isle of Patmos in Greece. It was actually Humanity's distortion of the models of civilization formed in Greece that were threatening to be our ruination.

Saint John was given Revelations to try to awaken Humanity so that we would stop our self-destructive behavior and our descent into oblivion. His prophecies revealed the destruction that would occur during these "end times" if we didn't change our course of direction.

It is important for Humanity to understand that A FULFILLED NEGATIVE PROPHECY IS A FAILED PROPHECY! The *only* reason Divine Revelations give negative prognostications is so Humanity will understand what will happen if we continue our destructive behavior. The Divine Intent of any prophecy proclaiming negative events is to inspire Humanity to change our behavior so that we will *avert* the cataclysmic devastation. It is never the Divine Intent that we just sit around and worry and wait for the catastrophes to take place.

For 2,000 years, Saint John has worked to help Humanity avert the destruction foretold in Revelations. From the Realms of Truth, he has taught us and inspired us to change the course of history. His selfless efforts have been amazingly successful! Through myriad activities of Light over the past 500 years, we have succeeded in averting the cataclysmic destruction of the Earth and the loss of the majority of life evolving here.

Paradigms for Our New Social Systems

The last time the Comet Hale-Bopp passed the Earth was 4,200 years ago during the *dawn of civilization*. At that time it shook the ethers and created the fluid field of unmanifest potential from which were formed the archetypes for modern civilization and the social systems of the New Day .

In 1997, the Comet Hale-Bopp returned and once again shook the ethers and created the fluid field onto which were imprinted the archetypes for the social systems in our *New Solar Reality* .

The spiritual conference in Greece began in Delphi on March 24, 1997, the day that is celebrated as *Archangel Gabriel's Feast Day*. Archangel Gabriel is the guardian of the Resurrection Flame, and on that sacred day, he projected the Resurrection Flame through the portals in Delphi to bless all life. The Resurrection Flame lifted Humanity into a new level of clarity and assisted in expanding the vision of Heaven on Earth.

March 25th is the day celebrated as *"The Annunciation,"* the day Archangel Gabriel revealed to Mother Mary that she would give birth to Jesus, the Avatar of the Piscean Age. It is also the day celebrated as the anniversary of Greece's freedom from oppression and independence from Turkey, which took place in 1821. On that day, the Spiritual Hierarchy flooded the mental stratum of Earth with the Divine Ideas from the Mind of God that contained the archetypes for the social systems for our new Solar Earth.

On March 26 and 27, 1997, the archetypes for the new social systems built in momentum as the God Selves of Humanity prepared to magnetize those patterns of perfection into the world of form.

On March 28, 1997, the Lightworkers attending the conference in Greece began a three-day cruise from the Port of Piraeus. We sailed through the sacred Isles of Greece on Good Friday and Holy Saturday. As the first rays of the Sun began to bathe the Earth on Easter morning, March 30th, we reached the port of Kusadasi in Turkey, which is the gateway to Ephesus.

Ephesus is the city that John the Beloved fled to with Mother Mary and Joseph of Arimathea when their lives were threatened in Jerusalem after Jesus' Ascension. John and Joseph built a home for Mother Mary high on a hill in Ephesus. Years later a small sanctuary was built on the original foundation that has drawn devoted souls for almost 2,000 years. There is a sacred healing spring next to the sanctuary and an array of beautiful vegetation. As we walked that holy ground on Easter Sunday, Mother Mary bathed all life with the Madonna-blue and crystalline-white Flame of the Immaculate Concept. The Flame flowed through the portal in Ephesus and merged with the Divine Momentum in the center of the Earth. It penetrated deep into the core of purity pulsating in every electron and accelerated the activation of the Divine Blueprints—the Immaculate Concepts—in Humanity's RNA/DNA structures.

After visiting Mother Mary's sanctuary, we went to the archeological site of Ephesus. We traced Saint Paul's footsteps as we walked the marble streets and sat in the great amphitheater where Saint Paul spoke to the Ephesians.

Saint Paul's awakening on the road to Damascus symbolically represents *"transformation in the twinkling of an eye."* As the Ascended Master Hilarion, Paul has worked diligently to prepare Humanity's consciousness for this moment of awakening. Hilarion is an exponent of the Fifth Solar Aspect of Deity, which reverberates with the Divine Qualities of Illumined Truth, Healing, Consecration, Concentration, Inner Vision and Divine Discerning Intelligence. As we walked the marble streets of Ephesus on Resurrection Morning, Hilarion breathed in the Fifth Solar Aspect of Deity and projected it into the Heart Flames of all Humanity, Elementals and Angels. The Sacred Fire blazed through the physical, etheric, mental and emotional strata of Earth and prepared all life to awaken safely in the new frequencies of Solar Light.

After our sojourn in Ephesus, we sailed the Aegean Sea to the Isle of Patmos. Patmos is where Saint John was exiled for 18 months, during which time he was given Revelations.

The Isle of Patmos is exquisite in its simplicity. As we boarded the small boats for our journey to shore, a beautiful rainbow filled the sky. Our tour guide said that it almost never rains on Patmos and that rainbows are extremely rare.

We boarded our buses for the trip to Saint John's Cave, and, interestingly, our bus driver and our tour guide were named Peter and Andrew.

The Cave of Saint John is actually where Saint John lived while he was in exile, and it is where he was given Revelations. The cave has been turned into a small sanctuary and has drawn the faithful for almost 2,000 years. As we entered that hallowed space on Easter Sunday, the music of the spheres was reverberating through the ethers, and Angels of all graded orders were singing *"Joy to the World."*

In that moment, we glimpsed the verdant splendor of Mother Earth in her seamless garment of Light. She was reflecting through all lifeforms the perfection of the New Earth blazing in her New Heaven.

As we absorbed the wonder and awe of that moment, the Heavens above Patmos opened, and the new archetypes for the social systems of the new Solar Earth flowed through the mental stratum into the God Selves of Humanity and penetrated deep into the higher consciousness of every soul.

The Spiritual Hierarchy revealed to us that on that holy day, the Piscean Age was God-Victoriously fulfilled. As the world turned its attention to the celebration of the Resurrection of The Christ, Jesus Ascended into a higher order of Divine Service. On Easter Sunday, March 30, 1997, Jesus expanded his luminous Presence to envelop the entire Galaxy of Alpha and Omega. He embraced all life in a higher frequency of Christ Consciousness as he Ascended into his new position as the *Solar Cosmic Christ for the System of Alpha and Omega.*

I don't believe it is possible for us to grasp the full magnitude of how very blessed we *all* are to be able to add our humble efforts to the glorious Divine Plan unfolding on Earth.

On March 31, 1997, the Lightworkers who had attended the conference in Greece journeyed to all parts of the world, carrying in their Heart Flames the full momentum of the activities of Light that had taken place in Greece. Some people traveled to Jerusalem, some to Egypt to journey up the Nile. Some went to Athens and others returned to their homelands.

On April 1, 1997, the Comet Hale-Bopp reached its closest passage to the Sun, its perihelion. A tremendous explosion of Light blazed through the Solar System, infinitely expanding the patterns of perfection and the archetypes for the new social systems on our new Solar Earth.

The Spiritual Hierarchy of the Piscean Age expanded the Flame of Healing through the Power of Limitless Transmutation and *transmuted* the blocks, resistance, fear and interference that were in any way hindering the anchoring of the new archetypes for the new social systems. Those patterns of perfection were securely anchored through the God Selves of all Humanity into every person's Heart Flame. Now, Humanity will await the approaching time when these Divine Ideas will flow into our conscious minds for implementation in the world of form.

The Divine Plan is very complex, and it is fun to observe outer world events that are being orchestrated from On High to support the activities of Light taking place.

One of those events involved the University of Arizona's basketball team, which won the NCAA National Basketball tournament, for the very first time, in 1997. Basketball may seem a bit frivolous in the overall scheme of things, but remember, when large numbers of people focus their attention on a particular event, the Spiritual Hierarchy, in cooperation with embodied Lightworkers, can qualify the energy and utilize it for the highest good of all concerned.

The Spiritual Hierarchy from the Holy Cities of John the Beloved, which pulsate over Arizona, were an integral part of the activities in Greece, and the Flame of Healing through the Power of Limitless Transmutation was a necessary element in assuring the success of those activities.

Tucson is a basketball town. That is probably the only event that would have held the attention of the entire population of Tucson transfixed in one-pointed consciousness from the Vernal Equinox on March 20, 1997, until the Comet Hale-Bopp passed the Sun on April 1, 1997. From Arizona's victory at the "Sweet Sixteen" basketball game on March 21 to our victory at the final game on March 31, Tucson was obsessed with basketball.

A few of us from Tucson who were attending the conference in Greece were able to watch the championship game live from our hotel rooms in Athens at 5:00 a.m. on April 1st. As the game took place, the Comet Hale-Bopp passed closest to the Sun, and the rays of the Sun expanded through the newly-formed archetypes for our new social systems. At the exact same time, almost everyone in Tucson watched the University of Arizona basketball team win the

NCAA Basketball Tournament. The focused attention of the entire city opened to full breadth the portal of the Flame of Healing through the Power of Limitless Transmutation. That Sacred Fire blazed around the Earth and transmuted the blocks, resistance, fear and interference that were attempting to hinder the anchoring of the new archetypes for our new Solar Earth.

On April 9th, 1997, a new satellite was able to take a picture of the largest Solar Flare ever captured on film. Solar Flares of that magnitude usually cause tremendous geomagnetic storms that knock out power grids and cause electrical blackouts and electrical disruptions of all kinds on Earth. Scientists were amazed that this Solar Flare had relatively little negative effect.

Now that we are vibrating with new Solar frequencies, we are much more compatible with the Sun, and we will experience fewer negative effects from Solar Flares. We will now utilize the Light from Solar Flares in a positive way to accelerate our growth into Godhood as was originally intended.

In April 1997, floods wreaked havoc in the lives of millions of people around the world. Even though the floods appeared to be tragic, they were actually a merciful act of Divine Love. Remember, in order for the Earth to Ascend into the 5th Dimension, a tremendous cleansing still needs to occur. Originally it was thought that the only way that could happen was for large continents and land masses to be submerged under the healing waters of the ocean, which would have resulted in the loss of millions of lives. Due to all of our efforts, a healing has taken place between the Human Kingdom and the Elemental Kingdom. A contingency plan has been set into motion to allow the Earth to be cleansed in a much gentler way with a minimal loss of life.

The souls who experienced the devastating floods agreed, at higher levels, to go through that experience for the sake of all Humanity and all life on Earth. Even though they may not consciously remember their vows, they provided a tremendous service of love for all of us.

During the spring of 1997, a very fascinating thing took place. One of the most important things that must occur in order for us to heal our self-inflicted separation from our God Presences is to balance our masculine and feminine polarities so that The Christ can be reborn within each of us. The sapphire blue Light of our Father God radiates through our Throat Chakras, and the crystalline pink Light of our Mother God radiates through our Heart Chakras. When these two polarities are balanced within us, we experience the birth of the Son or Daughter of God, which is Christ Consciousness or Enlightenment. The yellow-gold Light of The Christ radiates through our Crown Chakras. These three aspects of the Godhead create the Threefold Flame of Divinity within each of our hearts.

Our Threefold Flame represents the Holy Trinity:
The Father—Blue Flame
The Mother/Holy Spirit—Pink Flame
The Son/Daughter/The Christ—Yellow-Gold Flame

On April 18, 1997, astronomers reported that they found "A THIRD TAIL" trailing behind the Comet Hale-Bopp. The discovery was made on the Canary Islands by telescopes of the Isaac Newton Group.

The scientists were at a loss to explain how the tail was created. They have long known that comets have two types of tails: one made of dust which appears PINK in color and the other made of electrically-charged plasma which appears BLUE. This third tail, however, was a jet of sodium gas unlike any other seen before, and it had a YELLOW GLOW.

During the incredible activities of Light in Greece which brought the Piscean Age to fruition, Jesus The Christ Ascended into a higher order of service and became the Cosmic Solar Christ for the entire System of Alpha and Omega. Shortly thereafter, the Comet Hale-Bopp reflected the Holy Trinity—the Divine Balance of our Immortal, Victorious Threefold Flame—the vehicle for our Christ Presence. Is it possible that the celestial event we all experienced with the Comet Hale-Bopp the same event Saint John was witnessing when he wrote:

"Behold, he will come with the clouds; and every eye shall see him...all the kindred of the Earth..."

"I AM Alpha and Omega, the beginning and the ending says the Lord God, who is and who was and who is to come, the Almighty..." That is an interesting thought to contemplate isn't it?

April 22, 1997, was the Wesak Festival, the Celebration of Enlightenment and the Path of the Middle Way. This festival is acknowledged every year on the Full Moon of Taurus. In eastern religions, it is the holiest day of the year. On that special day in 1997, we also celebrated Passover and Earth Day. The blend of these sacred activities created another opportunity for the Ascension Flame associated with the Comet Hale-Bopp to lift all life another step closer to the 5th-Dimensional Spiral of Evolution.

The 5th Dimension is the octave of existence in which we will tangibly manifest our Solar Reality of Limitless Physical Perfection. It is the dimension in which our Solar Christ Presence will take full dominion of our four Earthly bodies and transform them, through Divine Alchemy, into our Solar Light Bodies. It is the dimension in which we will reach into the Divine Mind and the Causal Body of God and tap the Divine Ideas and viable solutions that will heal all of the maladies existing on Earth. It is the dimension in which we will fully claim our Divine Birthrights as Sons and Daughters of God, manifesting a previously unknown expression of Godhood. Within the full embrace of that glorious dimension of Solar Perfection, our options will be limitless and our potential infinite.

May 8, 1997, was the celebration of Gautama Buddha's Day of Enlightenment, and it was also Ascension Thursday—40 days after Jesus' Resurrection. On that day, Jesus amplified the Threefold Flame that was radiating through the Comet Hale-Bopp and the new frequencies of the Solar Cosmic Christ that were enveloping the System of Alpha and Omega. Gautama Buddha flooded the Earth with higher frequencies of Divine Consciousness and Enlightenment.

May 11, 1997, was Mother's Day, and our Mother God added Her Divine Love to the unfolding activity of Light. May 18, 1997, was Pentecost—the day of the Baptism of the Holy Spirit. On that day, the new frequencies of the Solar Cosmic Christ were permanently anchored in the core of purity of every atomic and subatomic particle of life on Earth. These empowered expressions of Godhood built in momentum for several days.

May 22, 1997, was the Gemini Full Moon—the celebration of the Festival of Goodwill for Humanity. On that sacred day, Alpha and Omega Inbreathed the Suns and planets in their System into a new octave of Divine Consciousness. All life was lifted into a more receptive and accepting state of Divine Intelligence, which will greatly enhance our ability comprehend the Truth of our own Divinity.

We experienced a Blue Moon on June 20, 1997, the second Full Moon of Gemini, which heightened the effects of Alpha and Omega's Inbreath. On June 21, 1997, we experienced our first

Solstice in our new Solar frequencies.

As we opened our hearts to the healing currents of the Solstice, we reached a turning point in our 26,000-year-orbit through the Universe. The Solstice points were aligned along the galactic equator which created a portal that increased our ability to walk the boundaries between worlds and dimensions. We were lifted further into multidimensional awareness, and we will now be able to *"see with new eyes and hear with new ears."*

Divine Intervention

We are receiving the maximum assistance from On High that Cosmic Law will allow to accelerate our Ascension process. Our Father-Mother God and the Company of Heaven want nothing more than for each of us to quickly move through this transitional period, so that we will experience the wonder and bliss of the new Solar Reality. They cannot, however, clear the final vestiges of human miscreation for us. They can only amplify our humble efforts.

Due to the urgency of the hour, and due to the sacrifices each of us made when we volunteered to delve into the depths of human suffering in order to save the Earth, a Cosmic Dispensation has been granted to every man, woman and child. Through the miracle of Divine Grace, our Father-Mother God issued a Fiat which decrees that every thought, word, action or feeling we express to accelerate the healing of *any facet* of life on Earth will be amplified *one thousandfold* by the Company of Heaven.

This *literally* means that every decree, prayer or invocation we make to improve the quality of life on Earth will have the power of 1,000 people decreeing. Every positive thought, every kind word, every compassionate act, every loving feeling will have the power of 1,000 people. Can you imagine the positive difference this will make in our lives and how it will accelerate our progress toward critical mass?

As we Ascend up the 4th-Dimensional Spiral of Evolution and begin experiencing the first impulses of the 5th Dimension, the cleansing of the Earth and the purification of our individual lives is increasing. The cleansing involves floods, earthquakes, wild fires, volcanic eruptions, tornadoes, cyclones, hurricanes, tidal waves, El Nino and other bizarre weather conditions. Yet, in the midst of all the chaos there is, mercifully, very little loss of life.

In our personal lives, we are experiencing a roller coaster of emotional trials and tribulations as our God Selves work to extricate us from the grip of our dysfunctional human egos. The gift of God's thousandfold amplification of our positive works is helping us move through our daily challenges much more quickly, and it is helping us detach from negativity so we can abide in joy. Joy is a cultivated emotion that we can deliberately and consciously create each moment of our lives. Remember, every time we strive to consciously be in joy, our efforts will be expanded one thousandfold.

Removing the Band of Forgetfulness

August 1997, was the eleventh Harmonic Convergence. The Spiritual Hierarchy told us that the greatest need of the hour was for the Bands of Forgetfulness to be removed from the brows of Humanity. The Spiritual Hierarchy revealed that removing our Bands of Forgetfulness would open the door to new levels of expanded consciousness and begin awakening the remaining 90 percent of our brain capacity.

The Divine Mind of God, the mental stratum of Earth and the mental bodies of Humanity are all associated with the *Fire Element.* In order for the Bands of Forgetfulness to be removed from Humanity's brows and for the Cosmic Fiat, which ordered the placing of the Band of Forgetfulness about the brow of each incarnating soul to be lifted, the mental stratum of Earth had to be transformed into a higher Solar frequency.

Our Father-Mother God and the Spiritual Hierarchy asked us to hold the Eleventh Annual World Congress On Illumination in Seattle, Washington. The state of Washington is directly connected to the *Ring of Fire* which expands throughout the entire Pacific Rim. The Ring of Fire is a multidimensional portal that connects the mental stratum of Earth with the Divine Mind of God.

Lightworkers from all over the world gathered in Seattle, and with the guidance of the Spiritual Hierarchy, the Elohim, the Directors of the Five Elements and the God Selves of all Humanity, we cocreated Beloved Mother Earth's *Pyramid of Ascension into Solar Consciousness*. Under the direction of the Elohim, a four-square base made from the rarefied Ether Element was formed beneath the Earth. Then four ascending triangles representing the additional four Elements: air, water, earth and fire, were created to form the pyramid around the planet.

When the pyramid was complete, our Father-Mother God

sounded a Cosmic Tone, and the Solar Light of God poured into the Ring of Fire. As the Solar Light blazed through the mental stratum of Earth, the mental bodies of Humanity were brought into alignment with the Divine Mind of God. Once that acceleration of consciousness was accomplished, *our Father-Mother God commanded the God Self of every soul to permanently remove the Band of Forgetfulness.* Our conscious minds will now be infinitely more receptive to frequencies of Divine Truth.

The Divine Intent of the removal of our Bands of Forgetfulness is to enhance only *positive* learning experiences that will accelerate our ascent into Godhood. The removal of the bands will not bring the negativity from our past lives to a conscious level. Our God Selves are protecting this process, and they are selectively projecting only the memories that will accelerate our Ascension. As we reach into the Mind of God, we will clearly perceive not only the ideas for our new Solar Reality but the methods through which we will bring those Divine Ideas into manifestation tangibly and practically in our daily lives.

This is the shift into Divine Consciousness that we have been hearing about for centuries. *Beings of Light from untold Universes have now descended through the portal of the Solstice to assist us by escorting us into new Realms of Divine Intelligence.* New doors are opening, and the collective awakening of all Humanity is creating an upward rush of Ascending consciousness that will lift all life on Earth further up the Spiral of Evolution.

As the masses of Humanity awaken and take responsibility for their own lives and their own Ascension into Godhood, our burdens will be lessened. Then we will be able to tangibly experience the wonder of this sacred moment on Earth in an atmosphere of joy and harmony.

We are now collectively Ascending into uncharted frequencies of Divine Intelligence, and world events are reflecting that Truth.

Princess Diana and Mother Teresa

On August 31, 1997, Princess Diana left the physical plane. She came to Earth with the mission of modeling the archetype of the Divine Feminine for all the world to see. In the face of incredible adversity, she was able to ascend to a focal point of regal beauty. At the time of her passing, she was the most well-known and most photographed woman on the planet. She exuded glamour and loveliness, but that was only a small facet of her purpose and reason for being. She also radiated forth the Divine Qualities of Motherhood, compassion, caring, love, empathy, understanding and wisdom. She was a nurturing, peace-commanding presence throughout the world, and she touched the hearts of all Humanity. Princess Diana received honor and respect from world leaders and suffering children alike. The Divine Love of our Mother God poured through her Heart Flame to bless all life.

Princess Diana left the physical plane in a traumatic way in order to shock us out of our complacency and awaken us to the moment at hand. With Humanity's attention focused one-pointedly on Princess Diana's grace, love and humanitarianism, our Father-Mother God flooded the Earth with new frequencies of Divine Love, Compassion and the Will to Act. The Will to Act motivated many Lightworkers to pick up the gauntlet and carry on Princess Diana's mission of bringing *reverence for ALL life* into reality.

In his song to Diana, Elton John called her "England's Rose." The rose is the symbol for Mother Mary who also reflects the archetype for the Divine Feminine and who has promised to embrace each one of us in her Motherly Love until we are wholly Ascended and free.

The words of Elton John's song confirmed Princess Diana *"had the Grace to place herself where lives were torn apart."* Humanity's love for Diana united our hearts in a way the world has never before witnessed. It literally rocked the Monarchy and proved that, *in the New World, the people will lead their leaders.*

Princess Diana's beautiful sons will carry on her joy, love and commitment, and their souls will sing, just as she planned. Prince William, whose very name reflects the WILL of the I AM, will be a Monarch who transcends separation. He, too, will demonstrate that being truly regal means *being One with all life.*

Diana reached across the chasm of human experience and grasped the hand of Mother Teresa, her counterpart in Divine Service. Mother Teresa could not have been further removed from the pomp and circumstance surrounding Princess Diana, but they became friends. Both of these incredible women knew that they were fulfilling God's Plan. Diana was buried with the Rosary that was given to her by Mother Teresa.

Together, Mother Teresa and Princess Diana modeled the full spectrum of the archetype of the Divine Feminine. Their diverse lifestyles proved that the Divine Feminine is a state of being and a consciousness of love that transcends all boundaries and all limitation. The Divine Feminine is not only the regal princess who sells her evening gowns worth millions of dollars and donates the money to those who suffer. She is also the self-sacrificing nun whose total worldly possessions consist of two simple robes, two pairs of eye glasses, two pairs of sandals, a Bible and a Rosary made of olive wood.

Mother Teresa made her transition on September 5, 1997, a 22 day. Twenty-two is the master number that reflects power on all planes and the ability to change the course of history. She left the Earth the day before Princess Diana's funeral.

On September 6th, as billions of people focused on Diana's funeral, Princess Diana and Mother Teresa were joined in the Heavenly Realms by Mother Mary and every Divine Aspect of our Mother God. Together, they embraced the Earth in a heart of Divine Love.

Diana was buried on a private island in the middle of a beautiful lake. She will perpetuate the legend of Camelot as she portrays the mystical *"Lady of the Lake"* in the mists of Avalon.

Mother Teresa was truly a paradox. She was petite and frail, yet she was astoundingly powerful and resilient. She was humble and reverent, yet she commanded the financial assistance and support of popes and kings.

Once, as she was anointing the wounds of a sick child, a reporter who was observing her said, "Mother Teresa, I wouldn't do that for one-hundred-thousand dollars." She replied, *"Neither would I. I am doing this for God."*

Another time, when several people were acknowledging Mother Teresa's accomplishments and giving her what she perceived to be undue attention, she said:

"I am merely a pencil in the hand of God, writing a love letter to the world. When you receive a love letter from someone, you don't say, 'My, wasn't that a wonderful pencil that wrote that letter.'"

Mother Teresa's funeral was held on September 13, 1997. On that day, every particle of life on Earth was permanently sealed in a new order of Divine Love and Empowerment from our Mother God.

Mother Teresa will one day be proclaimed a Saint by the Church, and her sacred order will continue to uplift the most downtrodden people. We were blessed beyond knowing to be here to witness the lives of these two beautiful souls.

The Return of the Goddess

The Divine Love of our Mother God built in momentum for *eleven* days following Mother Teresa's transition. On September 16, 1997, during a very unique Full Moon Lunar Eclipse, the Moon made its closest passage to the Earth and bathed the southern hemisphere with powerful frequencies of Light. Some astrologers say the Light that bathed the planet during that particular Lunar Eclipse occurs only once every *11,655 years*. For centuries, seers have observed this moment and proclaimed it to be the Age of the *"Return of the Goddess."* Our Mother God and all of the Feminine Aspects of Deity throughout Infinity are now poised and ready to reclaim this Earth to the path of Divine Love she was always supposed to experience.

For those who have trouble relating to the concept of *Mother* God, just realize that She is the Love of God made manifest, the Holy Comforter. She is the *Holy Spirit*. The fact that She is coming to the forefront in no way diminishes the all-encompassing Presence of our Father God. Our Father God is just as powerful and influential as He has always been.

The last 2,000 year-cycle prepared us for this miraculous moment. Through Jesus' various demonstrations during the pageantry of the Christian Dispensation, we witnessed the important part our Mother God will play in our return to Christ Consciousness.

When Jesus completed his eighteen years of training, which took place during the time referred to as the lost years, he was ready to demonstrate the return of The Christ to the world. The first thing he did was to be baptized by John the Baptist in the Jordan River.

The water element is associated with our emotional bodies and our feeling natures. Both of these vehicles are governed by the Divine Feminine within us. When Jesus entered the Jordan River to be baptized, he was demonstrating the need for our Mother God—The Holy Spirit—to wash away our "sins" of the past through the power of Divine Love.

We have all seen pictures of Jesus' baptism, and he is always shown with the descending Dove of the Holy Spirit above his head. The descending Dove reveals that the Holy Spirit—*the Love of our Mother God*—will cleanse our pasts and lift us into Christ Consciousness.

Another dramatic demonstration Jesus gave us to show how important our Mother God is in our return to Christ Consciousness is the Path of Divine Love. The Path of Divine Love is the full expression of our Mother God made manifest on Earth.

After Jesus' resurrection , he gave us another profound demonstration of the importance of our Mother God. The disciples were held in the embrace of the balanced Light of The Christ for 40 days after Jesus' resurrection. During that time, they were able to perform all of the miracles Jesus performed. When it was time for Jesus to Ascend into the realms of Light, however, everything changed.

When Jesus Ascended, his physical presence was withdrawn from the planet, and the disciples were left with only their own expressions of Light. Since they had not reached Christ Consciousness on their own, they began to falter. They became afraid, and they could no longer perform the miracles they had been able to accomplish when they were in the presence of Jesus.

It became very clear to Jesus and the Company of Heaven that without superhuman assistance, the disciples were not going to be able to fulfill their Divine Mission of bringing Jesus' teachings of the Path of Love and Christ Consciousness to the rest of world. Just ten days after Jesus' Ascension, the disciples were called into the *"Upper Room"* and bathed in the Love of our Mother God through a powerful baptism of the Holy Spirit. That event is celebrated every year as Pentecost.

Through the baptism of the Holy Spirit, the disciples' right-brain hemispheres and their spiritual brain centers were activated, and their Crown Chakras were opened. Those activities of Light lifted each of them into Christ Consciousness. We often see pictures and statues of the disciples after the baptism of the Holy Spirit with a Flame coming from the top of their heads to demonstrate the opening of their Crown Chakras.

The *"Gift of Tongues"* was also given to the disciples, but we have often misunderstood that gift. The Gift of Tongues does not mean speaking in unintelligible syllables and sounds as some claim. It simply means that the disciples were able to travel anywhere on the face of the Earth and teach the Path of Divine Love and the reality of Christ Consciousness to people in their own language.

The Dawning Age of Spiritual Freedom

On September 21-22, 1997, during the Autumn Equinox and the initial impulse of the Sun Cycle of Libra, the Goddess of Liberty rang the Liberty Bell and sounded the Cosmic Tone of Earth's Liberation throughout the Universe. With Humanity's Bands of Forget-fulness removed, the Age of Pisces was permanently sealed in a forcefield of Divine Love. The Legions of Light associated with the Seventh Solar Aspect of Deity—the Aquarian Age—moved to the forefront for the next phase of their Divine Service.

All of the Temples of Light in the Etheric Realms surrounding the planet were initiated into the Divine Plans they will fulfill during the next 2,000-year-cycle. The Sacred Flames blazing on the altar in each temple were empowered with the Immaculate Concept of the Solar Age of Spiritual Freedom, Eternal Peace and Limitless Abundance.

The complex of Etheric Temples above Arizona and the Middle East Ascended from the Sixth Solar Aspect of Deity—the Piscean Age—into the frequencies of the Seventh Solar Aspect of Deity. In addition to the enhancement of the existing Sacred Flames, new temples were created within the Holy Cities and above the Holy Land to expand the service of these Foci of Light:

St. Germain established magnificent *Temples of the Violet Flame* that expand, without limit, the new technology of the Violet Flame.

The Goddess of Liberty created *Temples of Liberation* and projected her luminous Presence to the cardinal point to the north of the Earth. She now bathes all life with the Violet Flame of Liberation.

The Goddess of Justice created *Temples of Justice* and projected her luminous Presence to the cardinal point to the east. She now bathes all life with the Violet Flame of Divine Justice.

The Goddess of Freedom created *Temples of Freedom* and projected her luminous Presence to the cardinal point to the south. She now bathes all life with the gifts of the Violet Flame of Freedom.

The Goddess of Victory created *Temples of Victory* and projected her luminous Presence to the cardinal point to the west. She now bathes all life in the Violet Flame of Victory.

The World Teacher, Kuthumi, also known as Saint Francis of

Assisi, created new temples within the Holy Cities and above the Holy Land, as well. He created the *Temples of Solar Enlightenment,* which have the new *Flames of Solar Enlightenment* blazing on their altars. This is a magnificent sunshine yellow Flame with a violet radiance.

On December 2, 1997, there was a rare alignment of planets that will not occur again for one hundred years. During that unique alignment, Mercury, Mars, Venus, Neptune, Uranus, Jupiter and Saturn assisted in ushering in the Light for the dawning Age of Spiritual Freedom, Eternal Peace and Limitless Abundance.

As that unprecedented Light of God poured into Earth, astronomers operating telescopes at Kitt Peak Observatory in Tucson, Arizona, photographed a colossal burst of energy at the far edge of the Cosmos. The scientists said the explosion of Light was the most powerful since the birth of the Universe. They reported that the 40-second flash spewed forth as much energy as ALL OF THE SUNS AND STARS IN THE UNIVERSE COMBINED! Astronomers said it was more energy than they thought possible in their wildest imaginations. The Light came from a source 12-billion light years away. Isn't that amazing?

The expanse of the Universe is mind-boggling, but we must remember that as insignificant as we feel when we ponder the Cosmos, the inward journey into quantum physics and subatomic particles makes us seem huge.

Every particle of life is intelligent and critical to the success of the Divine Plan. Minuscule, subatomic particles as small as the top quark play very important roles. The top quark is one of the necessary building blocks of matter. It is smaller than a *trillionth* of the thickness of a human hair, and it exists for only *a trillionth of a trillionth of a second.* Just imagine.

We have been preparing for this Cosmic Moment for hundreds of thousands of years. We must never underestimate our ability to make a positive difference. Opportunities are being presented to us every day. We must be alert, pay attention and respond. It is time for us to fulfill our purpose and reason for being. It is time for us to BE God in action on Earth. Our Light and love are needed more than we will ever know.

We are now bridging our inner and outer worlds. This life-affirming activity is enhancing our creative faculties and providing opportunities for personal, professional, emotional and spiritual expansion. Humanity's social structures are gradually being rebuilt with greater wisdom and balance between our heads and our hearts. We can now experience life more fully, feeling deeper compassion, tolerance, patience and greater self-expression.

The Golden Light of Eternal Peace and Limitless Abundance

In 1998, the Seventh Solar Aspect of Deity increased on Earth, and we experienced the initial embrace of Aquarius and the Violet Flame of Limitless Transmutation and Physical Perfection. That cleared the way for the next facet of the plan, which involved expanding the *complementary spectrum* of the Violet Flame: the Golden Flame of Eternal Peace and Limitless Abundance.

August 1998, was the twelfth Harmonic Convergence. Beginning with the first Harmonic Convergence in August 1987, and continuing on the anniversary of Harmonic Convergence every year, one of the Twelve Solar Aspects of Deity was expanded through Humanity's Twelve Solar Chakras and anchored into the Solar Chakras along the axis of Mother Earth.

1987 - 1st Solar Aspect - Blue - God's Will & Power
1988 - 2nd Solar Aspect - Yellow - Illumination & Enlightenment
1989 - 3rd Solar Aspect - Pink - Divine Love & Adoration
1990 - 4th Solar Aspect - White - Resurrection & Ascension
1991 - 5th Solar Aspect - Green - Truth & Healing
1992 - 6th Solar Aspect - Ruby - Grace & Devotional Worship
1993 - 7th Solar Aspect - Violet - Freedom & Forgiveness
1994 - 8th Solar Aspect - Aquamarine - Clarity & Discernment
1995 - 9th Solar Aspect - Magenta - Balance & Harmony
1996 - 10th Solar Aspect - Gold - Peace and Prosperity
1997 - 11th Solar Aspect - Peach - Divine Purpose & Joy
1998 - 12th Solar Aspect- Opal -Transformation & Transfiguration

In 1998, the Twelfth Solar Aspect was secured. That event completed the preparation for the activation of the Divine Matrix and Blueprint for the complementary spectrum of the Violet Flame.

In 1987, we were asked by the Spiritual Hierarchy to hold the First Annual World Congress On Illumination at Diamond Head in Hawaii. At that time, the First Solar Aspect of Deity was secured. In 1998, when it was time for the Twelfth Solar Aspect of Deity to be secured, we were asked by the Company of Heaven to return to Hawaii for the Twelfth Annual World Congress On Illumination. This time we were to be in Maui.

Pulsating in the Etheric Realms over Maui is the Temple of Eternal Peace and Limitless Abundance. This forcefield of Light creates a portal through which the Golden Flame from the Central Sun enters the Sun of Even Pressure in the center of the Earth. The original Divine Intent was for the Golden Flame to bless all life with Eternal Peace and Limitless Abundance as it poured into the physical plane through the portal in Maui. Unfortunately, after the fall everything changed. Humanity could no longer withstand the intensity of the Golden Light, and it had to be tempered and defused to a mere trickle of its original power. That tragic event compounded our belief in lack and limitation and perpetuated our ego's poverty consciousness.

In 1998, several activities of Light took place to help pave the way for the activation of the Divine Matrix and Blueprints for Eternal Peace and Limitless Abundance. On February 26, 1998, we experienced a powerful Solar Eclipse. On that same day, Venus was the brightest she had been in 100 years. As the Moon passed between the Earth and the Sun, Venus empowered the Solar Eclipse and blessed all life in our Solar System with intensified frequencies of the Love of God.

The path of the total Solar Eclipse passed directly over Venezuela. Pulsating in the Etheric Realms above Venezuela are resplendent Temples of Peace. During the moments of the total Eclipse, the Golden Light of Peace from the temples above Venezuela flooded the planet and prepared every particle of life to receive a merciful and compassionate purification by the Violet Flame of Limitless Transmutation.

After the Earth was bathed in the Golden Light of Peace, the total Solar Eclipse proceeded through the portal of the Violet Flame in the Caribbean Islands. When the total eclipse occurred over the erupting volcano in Montserrat, the Violet Fire blazed into the Sun of Even Pressure in the center of the Earth and expanded out through the Crystal Grid System. It blazed through every electron of energy, purifying ALL life. During that purification, our God Selves worked to release us from the bonds of poverty consciousness.

On March 21, 1998, there was a rare alignment of planets that the ancient Mayan civilizations said would be the Celestial sign that heralds the return of Enlightened Consciousness, Kundalini Wisdom, to Earth. That alignment consisted of Mercury, Saturn, Mars, the Sun, Jupiter, Venus, Uranus, Neptune, the Moon and Pluto. The alignment marked 1998 as the time of the *Awakening Power Within.*

As we pass into new dimensions of Solar existence, we are realigning with all of the Realms of Perfection in the Universe. These Divine Frequencies are infusing the planet with the energy we need to physically transform our reality into the perfection of Heaven on Earth. As the Light from the alignment of planets bathed the Earth, the Company of Heaven took full advantage of the opportunity.

On April 26, 1998, pictures were taken for the very first time of incredible solar storms on the Sun. Solar tornadoes with winds up to 310,000 miles per hour were captured on film. The tornadoes were 5,000 miles wide and as large as the continent of Africa. Never before has such activity been seen on the Sun.

On August 7, 1998, we experienced a Full Moon Lunar Eclipse. That Celestial event brought with it frequencies of Light that were specifically qualified to assist Humanity in releasing the old, obsolete patterns of abuse of power. These ego-based energies involve irresponsible, selfish, self-centered, uncooperative, immature, obsessive, fanatical patterns of response.

As the Light of God increased through the Lunar Eclipse, the negative patterns were pushed to the surface to be transmuted and healed. This had the unfortunate effect of amplifying the negative tendencies in rebelling human egos. To the horror of the world, we witnessed the heinous terrorist bombing of the United States' embassies in Nairobi, Kenya, and Dar es Salam, Tanzania, in Africa. In those senseless acts, 257 people lost their lives, and 5,500 were injured. That tragedy inspired a new level of commitment within the hearts and minds of the Lightworkers, and our efforts were redoubled as we intensified our calls for God's Light and Peace.

On August 15, 1998, the day celebrated in the outer world as *Mother Mary's Ascension Day,* a Global Prayer for Peace was organized around the world. It was promoted as the *"Silent Minute."* At 3:00 p.m. local time, millions of people all over the planet stopped what they were doing to pray for peace and planetary healing. That created a wonderful wave of Healing Light that encircled the globe.

That evening we began the Twelfth Annual World Congress On Illumination in Maui, Hawaii. The Opening Ceremonies of Light began at 7:30 p.m., and after a glorious day of preparation in both the inner and outer realms, all was in readiness. Beloved Mother

Mary, who had been enveloped in the love and devotion of millions of people throughout the day, was joined in the atmosphere of Earth by Feminine Aspects of Deity from throughout the Cosmos.

There were 400 people from 22 countries physically in attendance at the World Congress. Twenty-two is the master number that reflects power on all planes and the ability to change the course of history.

The countries represented were:

Aruba	Dominican Republic	Scotland
Argentina	England	South Africa
Australia	France	Suriname
Austria	Germany	Sweden
Bolivia	Ireland	Switzerland
Brazil	New Zealand	USA
Canada	Paraguay	Venezuela
	Puerto Rico	

On that day, Heaven and Earth blended together in a wondrous synchronicity. Six Heavenly bodies—Mercury, Saturn, Pluto, Uranus, Jupiter, Neptune and the Comet Chiron—were in retrograde positions. That event held all life on Earth in a breathless, multidimensional instant of suspended consciousness. During that timeless, spaceless moment, our Mother God and the unified Aspects of the Divine Feminine breathed the Breath of the Holy Spirit into ALL life and baptized every particle of life on Earth in the Divine Love of our Mother God. The unspeakable wonder of that baptism of the Holy Spirit lifted Mother Earth and all her life into higher frequencies of healing and purification.

On August 16, 1998, the Lightworkers, in unison with our Father-Mother God and the Builders of Form—the Elohim—worked to create a fluid field of unmanifest potential that could receive and hold the patterns of perfection that were originally expressed as the body of Mother Earth. This was the verdant paradise we called the Garden of Eden.

Humanity has mistakenly tried to interpret the allegory of Adam and Eve in the Garden of Eden literally when, in fact, the story is symbolic; it is a metaphor. The Garden of Eden is not a specific location on the planet. It represents the pristine beauty Mother Earth reflected when she was first created. Adam and Eve were not the first two Human Beings to embody on Earth. They represent the masculine and feminine polarities of our Father-Mother God, which must be present in order to birth the Children of God—The Christ.

The original Divine Intent of the Earth was to provide a school of learning within the constraints of a time and space continuum. In this school, the Sons and Daughters of God would learn to use their gift of free will and their creative faculties of thought and feeling to expand the Kingdom of Heaven on Earth. The plan was designed to teach Humanity to become cocreators with our Father-Mother God.

The body of Mother Earth was created to reflect the beauty of the Heavenly Realms, so that the Universal Law of *"As above, so below"* would be the order of the day in this Earthly experience. Everything Humanity needed to exist in the physical dimension was provided by the Elemental Kingdom. The Limitless Abundance of our Father-Mother God was our Divine Birthright, and God's supply of ALL good things was to be our everyday experience.

Our God Parents gave us *one* commandment in order to protect and sustain that Divine Plan. The commandment was that we *"must not partake of the Tree of Knowledge of good and evil."* As long as we had no knowledge of poverty, disease, war, hatred, death or any of the other mutated human miscreations, they could not be part of our consciousness. Therefore, it would be impossible for us to bring them into our daily life experiences through our creative thoughts, words, actions and feelings.

When Humanity began experimenting with our gift of life and began cocreating patterns of imperfection that were not present in the Causal Body of God, we experienced pain and suffering for the first time. That caused us to close our Heart Chakras, the portal of the Divine Feminine, forcing our Mother God to withdraw. That is why it is said that Eve, the Feminine nature within us, ate the apple from the Tree of Knowledge of good and evil. The distorted perception of Eve eating the apple has probably caused more pain and suffering for women than any other of Humanity's beliefs.

Adam and Eve were not literally two people. The reason it is said that Adam/masculine was created first is because in the creation of any physical manifestation, our Father God sounds the Keynote or Cosmic Tone, which forms the vibrational pattern for the matrix of that particular creation. *"In the beginning was the Word, and the Word was with God."* Our Father God reverberates through our Throat Chakras—the Power Center of the Spoken Word.

In the second phase of creation, our Mother God—Eve/feminine—projects a Sun of Divine Love into the heart of the matrix. The Sun of Divine Love has the cohesive power to magnetize the primal Light into the matrix, which will form the patterns for the person, place or thing being created. Our Mother God reverberates through our Heart Chakras—the Cohesive Center of Divine Love. Eve represents Adam's *heart* not his rib.

There is perfect balance in the creative process, and both the masculine and feminine polarities of God are necessary in order for any creation to manifest in physical form.

Reactivating the Garden of Eden

There is a very sacred valley on the Island of Maui that is dedicated to the Immaculate Concept of the original, pristine beauty of Mother Earth—the Garden of Eden. It is called the *Iao Valley*, and it has been a sacred place of pilgrimages since ancient times. *Iao* means Supreme Light. After the fall, when most of Lemuria sank beneath the healing waters of the Pacific Ocean, the Directors of the Elemental Kingdom and the Mighty Elohim agreed to encapsulate the Iao Valley within an invincible forcefield of protection. The Divine Intent of the plan was that one day Humanity's God Selves would reclaim responsibility as stewards of the Earth and reactivate the Divine Blueprints for the Garden of Eden.

On August 17, 1998, all of the Lightworkers attending the World Congress On Illumination went to the *Iao Valley*. We were joined by the God Presence of ALL Humanity and the Company of Heaven. As we traversed that hallowed ground, the Divine Matrix and Blueprints for the Garden of Eden were reactivated. Once those patterns of perfection were secure, our Father-Mother God breathed the Breath of Life into them, and the Immaculate Concept of the Garden of Eden swept around the globe in a wave of Light. In every location on the planet, the genetic codes for the Garden of Eden were imprinted on the Elemental Kingdom at a cellular level, and the pristine beauty of Mother Earth was God-Victoriously reclaimed.

Now it is our responsibility to daily and hourly energize the patterns of perfection for the Garden of Eden until they are tangibly manifest for all the world to experience.

On August 18, 1997, the Elohim worked through the God Presence of Humanity to reinforce all of the faults, cracks, fissures and tectonic plates in the body of Mother Earth. The reinforcement of all of the weak points in the body of Mother Earth assured that the incoming Twelfth Solar Aspect of Deity—the Light of Transformation and Transfiguration—would have only harmonious effects with no possibility of cataclysmic destruction.

On August 19, 1998, at 2:45 a.m., the buses arrived at the hotel to take us to the sacred mountain of *Haleakala* to witness the most mystical Sunrise any of us had ever seen. Haleakala is a volcano on Maui that is a natural conductor of Cosmic energy. Even the United States Air Force indicates that Haleakala is *the* strongest natural power point in America. Not only is there an energy configuration coming from within the Earth, but there is also a high focus of radiation coming from outside of the atmosphere. The name Haleakala means *House of the Sun.* Kahunas take their novitiates there to perform final rites of initiation. Students of higher consciousness from around the world are attracted to the natural Cosmic forcefield because of its rarefied energy.

We gathered at the summit of Haleakala to create a grounding transformer that would balance the incoming Light of the Twelfth Solar Aspect of Deity. We arrived at the crater in the pitch black darkness of predawn, and the crescent Moon was high in the sky. The stars sparkled with scintillating clarity, and the air was crisp and cold. The winds swept through the ethers, clearing away the last traces of effluvia that might attempt to impede the anchoring of the transforming, transfiguring Light of our Father-Mother God. The Lightworkers who were physically present had been prepared by their God Presence at a cellular level to be able to withstand the intensity of the Light that was to be anchored through their Heart Flames into the center of the Earth.

The summit of Haleakala is 10,023 feet, and as we looked out to the distant horizon, our vision flowed across the sea of billowing clouds below us. Ever so slowly, the pink radiance of our Mother God's Love began to appear on the eastern horizon. It bathed the clouds in a splash of color and created a sea of love that welcomed the first rays of the Sun. As the brilliant Light of the Sun burst into view, our Father-Mother God Breathed the Twelfth Solar Aspect of Deity from the core of Creation through our Heart Flames into the center of the Earth. As the Sacred Fire blended with the Divine Momentum in the heart of Mother Earth, it expanded out through the Crystal Grid System, and the Opal Ray of Transformation and Transfiguration was anchored in the Heart Flame of every man, woman and child.

The anchoring of the Twelfth Solar Aspect of Deity was the final step of preparation before the Golden Light of the Era of Eternal Peace and Limitless Abundance could be permanently established on Earth. On August 20, 1998, we consecrated our hearts, heads and hands to be the instruments of God in the world of form. Through a Divine Ceremony of Light, the portal of the Golden Light of Eternal Peace and Limitless Abundance was opened to full breadth.

A few days after the portal of the Golden Light of Eternal Peace and Limitless Abundance was opened, the Washington Associated Press reported that an immense wave of radiation from a bizarre star smashed into the upper atmosphere of the Earth with enough energy to power civilization for a *billion billion years*. Astronomers said at a news conference that the eruption was the most powerful burst of x-rays and gamma rays from beyond the Sun ever recorded. *"We've been monitoring things like this for 30 years, and we have never seen anything like this before,"* said Kevin Hurley, a research physicist at the University of California. *"The burst of gamma and x-ray radiation struck the Earth over the Pacific Ocean at 5:22 a.m., Eastern Daylight Time, on August 27, 1998. It was so powerful that it temporarily ionized the upper atmosphere just as the Sun does in the daytime,"* Hurley said.

Seven scientific satellites, five orbiting the Earth, one approaching an asteroid far beyond and one near the orbit of Jupiter all detected the massive eruption. Hurley said the burst was so intense that two of the satellites were forced to shut down to protect their electronics. The eruption came from a neutron star in the constellation on Aquila (Eagle) some 20,000 light years away. Astronomers said it is extremely rare for such a distant stellar explosion to have an effect on the Earth, attesting to the immensity of the release of energy.

The scientists estimated that the energy, if captured and put to use, could power all of the Earth's energy needs for a billion billion years. *"In that five-minute-long flash, we saw as much energy as there will be coming from the Sun in 300 years,"* Hurley said. *"If we could harness that energy, we would have enough power to power every city, every village and every light bulb until the end of the Universe and far beyond."*

We are finally realizing that we are truly multidimensional Beings, and we are beginning to get a glimpse of the other realities we abide in. No matter how awestruck we are, we are only perceiving an infinitesimal portion of the things taking place during this unprecedented experiment on Planet Earth.

Countdown to the Millennium

On November 17-18, 1998, the Earth's orbit around the Sun carried us through the Leonid meteor stream which originates from the Comet Temple-Tuttle. In most years, we encounter relatively sparse parts of the stream, but every 33 years (33 reflects Christ Consciousness), our planet passes through a thin, dense ribbon of cometary debris that accompanies the Comet Temple-Tuttle. During this time the atmosphere is bombarded with a Leonid meteor shower which creates a spectacle of thousands of shooting stars.

That influx of meteors is called a Leonid shower because the meteors appear to come from the direction of the constellation Leo, which represents the Lion Heart of God, the most powerful force of Divine Love in the Universe. As the Earth passed through the Leonid shower, our Father-Mother God charged the meteoroids with new frequencies of the Solar Cosmic Christ.

Equinoxes and Solstices form a cross in the sky as they orbit through the Precession of the Equinox, which takes 24,000 to 26,000 years. Every 6,000 to 6,500 years either the Equinoxes or the Solstices are brought into perfect alignment with the equator of our Galaxy. On December 21, 1998, the center of our Sun came into precise alignment with the center of the Galactic Equator creating an open portal through which major celestial energies from Galaxies and stars far beyond our System of Worlds poured into Earth. It was a time of great initiation for the Earth, a time of new beginnings. The precise alignment of the Sun with the center of the Galactic Equator lasts for about three years.

The Winter Solstice is known to mark the birth of the Solar Child as the Light of the Sun returns to Earth. It is the moment when we reaffirm the emergence of life on Earth and prepare for the Resurrection of Eternal Life that occurs in the spring.

Contrary to the prophecies of a few fear mongers, the concerns over Y2K (Year 2000) computer problems and the expectations of people who thrive on drama and trauma, 1999 provided an opportunity for Humanity to reach into untapped octaves of Divine Potential.

August 1999, was the thirteenth Harmonic Convergence. It was also thirteen years until the Cosmic Year of 2012.

Thirteen = Divine Alchemy

Jesus and his twelve disciples = 13, initiated the remembrance of Christ Consciousness during the Piscean Age.

The Twelve Solar Aspects of Deity plus the Solar Christ Presence of Humanity reflect the 13 facets of Solar Being for the Age of Aquarius. In ancient Aztec lore, the center of the human brain, the Alta Major Center, is known as 13 Cane. In the Mystery Schools, that center was thought to be the core of Divine Inspiration, Attainment and Completion.

There are 13 major joints in the Human Body. Our joints symbolize freedom, motion and pivots of change. Our joints are also known as *energy gates*.

Thirteen is a model of efficiency in physical, 3rd-Dimensional space. Twelve spheres fit exactly around a central 13th sphere in the most efficient arrangement.

Thirteen is a basic structural unit in nature. It is the *attracting center* around which elements focus and collect.

In Aztec cosmology, 13 refers to the sky—the Twelve Constellations and the Sun.

There are 13 Lunar Cycles in one Solar Year, and our Moon travels 13 degrees per day across the sky.

Thirteen is an octave of semitones on the musical scale. *It moves us into a new octave.*

The original intent of the founding of America was to form a new archetype for the family of Humanity. We were to model the I AM RACE, a race of God Conscious souls living together in harmony and mutual respect—one nation under God. Our Founding Fathers reached into the Divine Heart and Mind of God to transcribe the sacred documents for this country. They created the Great Seal of the United States of America and encoded it with mystical symbols that would hold the Immaculate Concept for this country in the face of all adversity.

The mystical number 13 was woven in many ways into the archetype for the New World. There were originally 13 colonies. The first flag contained 13 stars and 13 stripes and the Great Seal of the United States of America used the number 13 many times.

The Great Seal has:

13 Stars above the Eagle.
13 letters in "E Pluribus Unum."
13 leaves and 13 berries on the branch grasped
in the Eagle's right talon.
13 arrows clutched in the Eagle's left talon.
13 stripes on the emblem on his breast.
13 layers of stone to the capstone of the Great Pyramid.
13 letters in "Annuit Coeptis."

In February 1999, the International Gem & Mineral Show was held in Tucson, Arizona. This is the largest gem show in the world, and tens of thousands of people come from all over the planet bringing the most exquisite gems, crystals and minerals from the body of Mother Earth. This has been an annual event in Tucson for close to 50 years that rhythmically energizes and expands this portal of Light. In 1999, Lightworkers from Israel came to the gem show and, together, we utilized the Light of the sacred gems to intensify the forcefield of Light that connects Tucson to the Middle East.

In March 1999, I was asked to speak at the Universal Lightworkers Conference in Dallas, Texas. During that sacred conclave, a Chalice of Light was formed to cradle the unified Spirit of all world religions. That event was the initial impulse for healing the schism between world religions.

As Lightworkers at the ULC formed a Chalice of Light, another outer-world activity was taking place. The United Nations proclaimed the year 2000 the *International Year of Thanksgiving,* and one hundred and eighty-five countries participated in the event. A global gathering of religious and political leaders was meeting in Dallas at the Center for World Thanksgiving the same weekend as the Universal Lightworkers Conference.

Among the distinguished guests at that historic gathering were the Lord Archbishop of Canterbury, the Editor-in-Chief of the Encyclopedia of Hinduism, the President of the Vatican office of Interreligious Dialogue and a renowned Talmudist from Jerusalem. They were joined by religious and spiritual leaders from around the world. That auspicious group brought a powerful healing through gratitude and thanksgiving.

In 1999, we experienced the eleven-year-cycle of Solar Flares. The number 11 signifies the transformation from the physical into the Divine. Scientists reported solar storms more colossal and massive than they had ever seen before. They called them the *"storms of the century."*

On March 25, 1999, we held one of our Free Seminars in Albuquerque, New Mexico. The Spiritual Hierarchy revealed to us that a unique healing was taking place through the body of Mother Earth that day. New Mexico is a training center for the Deva Rajas in the Elemental Kingdom. These are powerful Beings in the Elemental Kingdom who have evolved to the point of being caretakers of large segments of the body of Mother Earth. The reason Los Alamos, New Mexico, was the focus for the original building of the atom bomb is because the Directors of the Elements hoped that the advanced Elemental Kingdom located in that area would be able to balance the incredible negative effects of that wayward human endeavor.

Interestingly, on the day of our seminar, the first of a very massive collection of toxic nuclear waste was placed in a cave in New Mexico. That event had been protested for a long time by environmental activists, but their efforts were in vain.

During our seminar, the *portal of the Sacred Earth,* which enters New Mexico and nourishes the body of Mother Earth with Light from the Central Sun, was expanded by the Deva Rajas. The Directors of the Elements then breathed Healing Light through the portal into all of the wounds in the body of Mother Earth that had been created by bombs, wars and human aggression. The Deva Rajas throughout the world absorbed the Light and healed the wounds in the body of Mother Earth in preparation for the next phase of the Divine Plan.

Humanity has been numbed by the paralyzing grip of pain and suffering for so long that the only thing we seem to respond to en masse is more pain and suffering. In order for the next phase of the Divine Plan to be fulfilled, it was necessary for the collective consciousness of the world to be actively involved. The general tendency for Humanity is that unless we are shocked and horrified by some outer-world calamity, we are too numb to respond with the necessary fervor and enthusiasm.

There is an ancient vortex of negativity in the Balkans, in Kosovo, that for aeons of time has energized the consciousness of hatred, aggression, prejudice, terrorism and war. This seething vortex of human miscreation has fed the entity of war on Earth since the "fall" of Humanity. It has perpetuated separation and fear, and those who live within the reach of this festering pocket of human depravity and violence have often been the instigators of global conflicts.

The vortex in Kosovo is called *"the Field of Blackbirds."* A conflict called the Battle of Kosovo took place in that location on June 28, 1389, between a Christian Coalition led by Tsar Lazar of Serbia and the Turkish Muslim forces led by King Murad. Both men were killed in the battle, and neither side could claim victory. For a span of 400 years, a rare legacy of diverse religious and ethnic cultures all lived together in peace and harmony. This was a model of hope for the area and for the future of the world. It was a stand against religious fundamentalism and fanaticism.

Unfortunately, the vortex of negativity kept spewing forth its accumulated effluvium and eventually overwhelmed the souls living in the area. On June 28, 1914, the anniversary of the Battle of Kosovo, a Serbian man named Gavrilo Princep assassinated Archduke Ferdinand in Sarajevo. That event triggered World War I, which in turn paved the way for the rise of Adolph Hitler and the Nazi party, the Holocaust and various other human atrocities in the area, which resulted in World War II.

On June 28, 1989, the 600th anniversary of the Battle of Kosovo, President Milosevich of Serbia gave a speech at the Field of Blackbirds. His intent was to rally the last vestiges of a greater Serbia. This act of betrayal to the other ethnic people of the region set into motion all of the terrible things that happened over the next ten years in Bosnia, Croatia, Slovenia and Kosovo.

Contrary to outer appearances, there is indeed a method to the madness. After the Chalice of Light was formed to cradle the unified Spirit of all world religions and the healing took place through the wounds in the body of Mother Earth, it was time once and for all to address the vortex of the Field of Blackbirds. To draw the attention of the numbed consciousness of the entire world, a human crisis of Biblical proportions was initiated in Kosovo when President Milosevich intensified his barbaric acts of ethnic cleansing. As the world watched in horror, it became clear that intervention needed to take place. There was much conflict on just what should be done, but the great majority of Humanity realized that Milosevich was not going to stop the carnage on his own.

The 19 countries associated with NATO decided that since President Milosevich was refusing to honor his previous peace agreement to stop the murderous attacks on the ethnic Albanians, the only recourse was to bomb his military installations. When the bombing began, it created the catalyst to shock Humanity out of our complacency and motivate us into the necessary prayers and invocations for Light and Peace.

On April 10th, 1999, the Peace Troubadour, James Twyman, traveled to Kosovo to give a Peace Concert at a refugee camp and to serve as a surrogate to anchor the unified prayers of millions of people into the vortex of the Field of Blackbirds.

Through a series of incredible acts of Divine Intervention by both Mother Mary and Mother Teresa, James was able to get past all of the obstacles and reach the refugee camp at Brazde on the border of Macedonia just in time for the scheduled Global Peace Meditation. As millions of Lightworkers joined in consciousness, James sang Saint. Francis' Prayer for Peace. During that moment, the Light of God blazed into the Field of Blackbirds in Kosovo and expanded out through all of the Balkan States. That influx of Light began a powerful process of both purging and healing.

The negative energy in that vortex was so dense that it was practically impossible to penetrate. It was like black, crystallized tar, and it took a very long time for even the powerful Violet Transmuting Flame to blaze through a single layer. To assist with the purification, Mother Mary and Mother Teresa projected their luminous Presence into the atmosphere over Kosovo. Mother Teresa was born in Albania, and an important part of her mission was dedicated to projecting Light into the Field of Blackbirds in preparation for the time when it could be purified.

The two exponents of our Mother God breathed Divine Love into the crystallized human effluvia. Their love penetrated deep into the negativity causing that unholy substance to soften and become fluidlike. Once that occurred, Legions of the Violet Flame projected bolts of Violet Lightning into the black tarlike substance. The Violet Lightning struck again and again until the mass of negativity began to shatter and break apart. The Violet Flame then blazed in, through and around the effluvia. Mother Mary and Mother Teresa sustained their efforts until the fragments of human miscreations were transmuted back into Light.

The Awesome Summer of 1999

After the purging in the Field of Blackbirds, Humanity was able to more effectively integrate the new frequencies of Solar Light . The veil between dimensions became gossamer, and Humanity became attuned to deeper levels of our own spirituality. Even the most sceptical people began to realize that things were changing and that something unusual was going on. People started seeking a spiritual connection in their lives, which opened them up to the possibility of cocreating Heaven on Earth.

The stage was set for one of the largest gatherings for Peace ever organized: *The Hague Appeal for Peace Conference.* Over 8,000 people from all over the world attended the gathering in the Netherlands.

That Global Conference for Peace began a long-term campaign to achieve the following basic conditions for human security:

*   A physical environment that can sustain human life.
*   Adequate food, clothing and shelter for all Humanity.
*   Respect and dignity for all Human Beings and for their different cultures.
*   Protection from avoidable harm.

During the conference, viable solutions and possible options for curing the problems of the world were discussed, as well as realistic alternatives for human security based on research, analysis and practical experience.

The Hague Appeal for Peace asks us to minimize the need for armed forces by challenging us to take seriously the many existing options for assuring security. The Peace Appeal invokes us to find the moral and political desire and the *will* to change our thinking about security. When conflicts arise, as they are bound to, it calls on each of us and our governments to resolve them without resorting to violence. Those gathered at The Hague expressed the belief that the term *"military security"* is an oxymoron.

The Birth of the NEW Renaissance

Florence, Italy, is where the Renaissance originated 500 years ago. That event was part of the master plan to accelerate the return of our Mother God by awaking Humanity's right-brain hemispheres and spiritual brain centers, so that the Earth and all her life could move up the Spiral of Evolution with the rest of our Solar System.

The Renaissance was a literary and artistic movement that was birthed in the 1400s. It stimulated the study of classical literature, art, dance and music and signaled the close of the dark ages and the beginning of modern history. It was the start of a new Era that differed sharply from the barbaric darkness which preceded it, and it inspired civil liberty and a new internal order of culture and political development. The reform of Christian society through classical education created a Golden Age of Creativity.

The Renaissance was a time of enlightenment and played a critical part in liberating the human mind from the superstition and error identified with the interpretation of Christianity at the time. Individualism and self-empowerment rose up in the hearts of Humanity, and people pulled away from the oppressive control of the church. The Renaissance person did not abandon Christianity, but rather adopted new attitudes about their spiritual beliefs. Rigidly dogmatic concepts were challenged and cast aside, which inspired vigorous religious impulses. This marked a momentous turning point in history.

In the midst of unrivaled, barbaric darkness, the Renaissance birthed a civilization of a higher order. It created a resurgence of the Human Spirit that made possible all of the great achievements of modern Humanity. It inspired the great discoveries beyond the seas, the new science, modern literature, art, dance and music.

People were converted from contemplative scholars into conscious and patriotic citizens with a new sense of responsibility for the future of the world and new feelings of historical destiny.

This was a striking, innovative moment on Earth that catapulted Humanity forward into new processes of formal thought, economic life, science and the discovery of the true man and woman.

The Renaissance initiated an atmosphere that was favorable to new ideas, innovative accomplishments and creative enterprises in every human endeavor. New concepts developed about global economy, and interdependent commerce and banking generated a new Era of great prosperity and cultural development.

Initially, there were dichotomies and confusion in the Renaissance, but eventually success was achieved. The archetypes for the "New World" were established, and Humanity was set on a path that would lead to this Cosmic Moment.

On June 6, 1999, my friend, Kay Meyer, and I traveled to Florence, Italy, to meet with several Lightworkers from various parts of the world. We were told by the Spiritual Hierarchy that the birthing of a *new* Renaissance was necessary in order for Humanity to be raised up further in consciousness and vibration into our Solar Reality. The Beings of Light said that the birth of the new Renaissance was an important part of the final preparation for the new millennium and would result in lifting Humanity's spiritual brain centers into Solar frequencies of Light. That activity would create a whole new paradigm of spiritual development for every person.

We were asked by the Spiritual Hierarchy if we would be willing to travel to various places in Italy to serve as surrogates on behalf of Humanity and to offer our vehicles as transforming instruments through which the Light of God could flow to complete the activation of the new Renaissance. In deep gratitude, we volunteered for that sacred pilgrimage.

On June 7, 1999, we began our mission at the Piazzale Michelangelo. This is a beautiful plaza at the top of a hill overlooking Florence. At the apex of the hill is a church called San Salvatore al Monte. On the floor in the center of the church there is a mosaic of the Zodiac that was placed there in the 1400s. The Twelve Solar Aspects of Deity are anchored at that point and radiate out over all of Florence like the beacon of a mighty lighthouse.

As we entered the church and stood on the Zodiac, it was revealed to us that the archetypes for the new Renaissance would expand from the microcosm of Florence, Italy, to the macrocosm of Planet Earth. At that moment, the Twelve Solar Aspects of Deity containing the archetypes for the new Renaissance blazed forth from the Central Sun into the Zodiac and expanded out to engulf the entire planet.

Next we were directed to go to Uffizi Plaza. Within the grounds and buildings of that plaza are many of the wonderful masterpieces of the first Renaissance. As we walked through those hallowed grounds, the archetypes for the new Renaissance were projected by our Father-Mother God into every statue and painting. As those patterns of perfection blazed through the priceless masterpieces, a new dimension and level of perception to awaken Humanity's spiritual brain centers was anchored in every painting and every statue. Our God Parents then expanded the new archetypes throughout the world and anchored them into every other expression of art on the planet.

The Spiritual Hierarchy said that with the birth of the new Renaissance the Divine Purpose of the arts, which include not only art but music, dance, literature and every other form of artistic expression, will be raised to a whole new level. No longer will the arts be appreciated for aesthetic beauty alone. They will now be elevated to new levels of expression that includes healing, transformation, awakening, enlightenment, purification, inspiration, adoration, harmony, peace, balance, abundance, love and every other Divine Quality of God.

On June 8, 1999, our pilgrimage took us to Fiesole and Siena. Fiesole is a charming little town about five miles north of Florence. It was founded by the Etruscans in the 7th century B.C. and colonized by the Romans three centuries later. The archaeological site of this mystical town contains an Etruscan altar and temple from the 4th century B.C. and a Roman temple, altar, baths, road and theater from the 1st century B.C.

As we walked along a very beautiful road on our way to Fiesole, we were met by a lovely Italian woman in her mid-seventies. She led us up a very steep hill to a little church called the *Church of San Domenico*. Saint Dominic (1170-1221) was a Spanish priest and the founder of the Roman Catholic order of friars known as the Dominicans.

According to legend, in 1212 Mother Mary appeared to Dominic and taught him to pray the Rosary. Dominic developed the system of counting the Rosary prayers on a string of beads. He taught the Rosary to all of his students and encouraged them to recite the prayers every day. By saying the Rosary daily, Dominic and his students opened the door for the eventual return of our Mother God .

The part of the Rosary given to St. Dominic by Mother Mary is:

> *Hail, Mary, full of Grace,*
> *the Lord is with thee.*
> *Blessed art thou amongst women, and*
> *blessed is the fruit of thy womb, Jesus.*

Mother Mary gave the affirmation in a way that could be easily comprehended by the devotees at that time. The mystical meaning of the Rosary is the revelation that through the womb of the Divine Mother, The Christ is born.

The additional portion of the Rosary was added later by the Catholic Church. That portion states:

> *Holy Mary, Mother of God, pray for us sinners now*
> *and at the hour of our death.   Amen.*

We entered the church of San Domenico and sat in front of a famous painting that was completed in 1430 by Fra Angelico. The painting is called *Madonna and Child with Saints and Angels.* As we absorbed the beauty of the painting in silence, Mother Mary revealed to us that preparation for the birth of the new Christ Child—the *Solar* Christ Presence—within the heart of every soul, was in the final stages. She asked us to be alert, pay attention, listen to our hearts and be in the eternal moment of now throughout the rest of our holy pilgrimage.

When we left the church, we went to the archaeological site in Fiesole. We walked up a very steep road to an ancient church that stands on the site of an Etruscan Temple. The church is called *Sant' Alessandro.* A little beyond it are the church and monastery of San Francisco. In that church, to the left of the high altar, is a painting of the *Madonna and Saints*; next to that painting is a picture of the *Immaculate Conception,* and above the high altar is a painting of the *Annunciation.*

Those three paintings depict the activities of Light that ushered in the birth of Jesus The Christ at the dawn of the Piscean Age 2,000 years ago. As we walked through the grounds, we were told by Mother Mary that it is now time for the activities of Light that will usher in the second coming of The Christ—birth of the *Solar* Christ Presence of the Aquarian Age.

We then went to the Roman and Etruscan temples. We were guided to an area where there are three arches. We sat and meditated for a while, and, as we did, we each had the very distinct feeling of "*coming home*." We experienced the multidimensionality of the location, and we witnessed the archetypes from all past Ages coming together to be lifted into the new Renaissance.

We watched the Transfiguration with our mind's eye, and when it was complete, the Languages of Light were spoken. As these ancient sounds reverberated through the Ethers, they shattered the obsolete patterns of hatred, prejudice, war and inhumanity which for aeons of time have plagued and sabotaged Humanity's hopes for peace. Through the Languages of Light, the Sound Ray pierced into the etheric stratum of Earth. A Divine Keynote rang though the Universe and formed the matrix for new patterns of Eternal Peace, Divine Love, Happiness, Abundance, Joy, Reverence for ALL Life and all of the other Divine Attributes of the New Heaven and the New Earth.

Next, we were directed by the Spiritual Hierarchy to travel to Siena, the home of Saint Catherine (1347-1380). Saint Catherine is the Patron Saint of Italy. She is known for her fervent faith and the ensuing mysticism that surrounded her. During her unusual child-hood, she experienced visions. At the age of 16, she donned her nun's habit of the Mantellate Order. Although Catherine was illiter-ate, she dictated many works. Nearly four hundred of her letters to potentates and prelates have survived. She holds a high place in Italian literature.

During her short, mystical life, Saint Catherine devoted her spiri-tual vocation to promoting peace in a divided Italy. She is the Heav-enly Presence who spoke to Saint Joan of Arc (1412-1431) and guided her on her mission to unite France. Joan began hearing the voice of Saint Catherine when she was only ten years old. She fol-lowed the directions that were given to her, and when she was 16, she began her mission, which eventually resulted in freeing France from British rule.

Saint Catherine and Saint Joan of Arc are models and expo-nents of the Divine Power of our Mother God. They are coming to the forefront at this time to assist Mother Mary, Mother Teresa and the other Aspects of our Mother God in transmuting the archetypes and patterns of war and human degradation once and for all.

In the wondrous Divine Plan, nothing is happening by accident. Everything is being orchestrated in perfect synchronicity to assist in the glorious events unfolding before our very eyes. In May 1999, a four-hour miniseries on the life of Joan of Arc was shown on na-tional television. At that time, the war in Kosovo was raging, and the message of Saint Joan of Arc was profound.

The legend of Joan of Arc reflects, symbolically, that unity and peace will be brought to Earth by the return of the Divine Feminine. As the legend goes, in the days of Camelot and King Arthur (400-500 A.D.), a prophecy was made by Merlin the Magician who was one of the embodiments of St. Germain. Merlin was a poet, a prophet of Celtic history, a mentor, a seer of the Arthurian circle and the protector and counselor of King Arthur. His prophecy stated that in the future a young maiden, guided by the Hand of God, would come from the province of Lorraine to unite France and free her from British rule. Merlin foretold that it would take seven years, but in the end, the Maid of Lorraine would be victorious.

For almost a thousand years, the people of France waited for the Maid of Lorraine to come and free them from their terrible plight. While they waited, their country was pillaged and plundered. Their homes were burned, and they fled into the wilderness to keep from being murdered.

It was surreal to watch this depiction of the legend of Joan of Arc on television one moment, and then watch the nightly news depicting the refugees fleeing Kosovo the next moment. The stories were identical even though they were taking place 600 years apart.

When Joan of Arc united the people of France under the guidance of Saint Catherine and the Hand of God, she helped pave the way for the return of the Divine Feminine. The fear-based church leaders called her a heretic and tried to suppress her message by burning her at the stake. The legend claims that Joan's heart did not burn in the fire but remained whole and continued beating. That phenomenon revealed that nothing can suppress the return of our Mother God's Love.

Joan of Arc became a martyr, and seven years after her death, just as Merlin had predicted, France was united and freed from British rule. The legend of Joan of Arc was brought to the forefront of Humanity's attention in May of 1999 to empower the archetype of the Divine Feminine in preparation for the next phase of the Divine Plan.

After the activities of Light in Fiesole, we traveled to Siena. As soon as we got off the bus, we were directed to Saint Dominic's Basilica. When we entered the church, we felt a sense of awe. The quiet grandeur of the church and the sacred paintings hanging on the walls are magnificent.

Within the church is a chapel dedicated to Saint Catherine. We quietly sat before the altar, and at 5:00 p.m., the bells rang and the priest began reciting the Rosary. As the traditional words of the Rosary echoed throughout the church, we were lifted into what seemed to be a parallel dimension. The church was the same, but it was more rarefied and more filled with Light. As the priest said the Rosary in the parallel dimension, he was joined by Choirs of Angels, and the words were changed into the Rosary of the New Age, which was given to the world by Mother Mary in 1983.

ROSARY OF THE NEW AGE

*Hail, Mother, full of Grace,
the Lord is with thee.*

*Blessed art thou amongst women, and
blessed is the fruit of thy womb, I AM.*

Hold for us now the Immaculate Concept of our

>   *true God Reality from this moment unto our*
>   *Eternal Ascension in the Light.*
>   *I Am that I Am.*

As these words were sung by Choirs of Angels, they rang through the Universe and invoked a new frequency of the our Mother God beyond anything the Earth had ever experienced.

After leaving the church, we went to the Piazza del Campo in Siena and absorbed the wonder of the moment. We spent the night in Siena while the new frequencies of the Mother God were assimilated and integrated into the core of purity in every electron of life on Earth.

The next morning we returned to Florence, and the Spiritual Hierarchy directed us to go to the *Accademia Gallery in San Marco Square.* This is the most famous art gallery in Italy. It contains the sculpture of David by Michelangelo and many other magnificent pieces of art from the first Renaissance. That day, the new frequencies of our Mother God flowed into the masterpieces and further shifted the Divine Purpose of the arts into the paradigms for the New Renaissance.

On June 10, 1999, we were guided to Boboli Gardens. This is a beautiful complex of labyrinths, fountains, wooded areas and gardens that was originally created in 1550. This garden is a glorious expression of the Elemental Kingdom, and it is holding the patterns for Heaven on Earth.

High on a hill, at the apex of the garden stands a colossal statue of the *Goddess of Abundance*. As we entered the aura of her august Presence, we were asked to sit and quiet ourselves. We were then told by the Mighty Elohim that the Elemental Kingdom is standing in readiness to assist Humanity in manifesting the Limitless Abundance and the Limitless Physical Perfection of the Permanent Golden Age. All Humanity has to do to receive that unprecedented assistance is to stay focused on the vision and commit our thoughts, words, actions and feelings to cocreating the New Heaven and the New Earth.

As we contemplated those words, the floodgates of Heaven opened and the Golden Light of Limitless Abundance and Eternal Peace poured through the statue of the Goddess of Abundance in Boboli Gardens and expanded out to flood the Earth.

After leaving Boboli Gardens, we were guided to go to a very special church in San Marco Square called *Church of the Santis-*

simo Annunziata. This church is dedicated to the Servants of Mary and was first built in 1250. To the left of the entrance is a small temple that contains a greatly venerated 14th century painting of the Annunciation. The legend indicates that part of the picture was actually painted by an Angel. It is referred to as the "miraculous painting."

We entered the church at 5:00 p.m. and sat before the painting of the Annunciation. Just as we quieted ourselves, the bells rang and the priest began saying the Rosary. Once again we were lifted into multidimensional reality and experienced a glorious activity of Transfiguration. The Archangel Gabriel was standing in the atmosphere of Earth sounding his mighty trumpet. The Angels were heralding the coming of the Immaculate Conception of the Solar Christ Presence within the heart of every Human Being.

On June 11, 1999, we traveled to Venice, the City of Divine Love. After we arrived by train, we went directly to Piazza San Marco. The original layout of this Italian, architectural jewel dates back to the 9th century A.D. The Piazza San Marco is dominated by a lofty bell tower about 100 meters high with a pyramidal steeple at the top. Standing at the apex on the capstone of the pyramid is a beautiful golden statue of Archangel Gabriel.

Within the piazza is the *Basilica of San Marco* (Saint Mark) which is a magnificent edifice that contains the remains of Saint Mark's Earthly vehicle. It is believed that Saint Mark wrote the first Gospel in 70 A.D. Mark wrote that the coming of Jesus The Christ fulfilled the prophecies of the Old Testament which proclaimed the coming of the Messiah.

He wrote that Jesus (modeling the Consciousness of The Christ) had power over sickness and the forces of evil in the world. Mark taught that Jesus The Christ had the authority to forgive sin and that he was inaugurating God's Kingdom on Earth in a new way among Humanity.

Humanity is now preparing for the second coming of The Christ, the birth of the *Solar* Christ Presence within every Heart Flame. Saint Mark is now fulfilling the second phase of his Divine Mission by proclaiming that Humanity's Solar Christ Presence has the authority to inaugurate God's Kingdom on Earth in a brand new way. This is the fulfillment of the New Testament.

As we sat in the beautiful Piazza San Marco, Archangel Gabriel once again sounded his mighty trumpet to announce the second coming of The Christ and the birth of the New Heaven and the New

Earth.

After that activity of Light, we then walked through the beautiful streets of Venice and took a boat trip down the Grand Canal. Later that evening we returned to Florence.

That same day, the United Nations Security Council approved the Kosovo Peace Settlement. Foreign ministers from the big power Group of Seven and Russia gathered in Cologne, Germany, to meet with Secretary of State Madeleine Albright. The group consisted of foreign ministers from the United States, Great Britain, France, Germany, Italy, Japan, Canada and Russia. As they met, final arrangements were made to end the war. The war in Kosovo lasted 11 weeks, and on the 11th of June, the Serb army was given 11 days to withdraw their troops. Eleven reflects the transformation of the physical into the Divine.

On June 12, 1999, we went to the *Piazza San Giovanni* in the heart of Florence. This is an awesome cathedral and baptistry that dates back to the 5th century A.D. It is dedicated to Saint John the Baptist—the Patron Saint of Florence.

Saint John the Baptist is considered the last of the prophets of the Old Testament and the first of the Apostles. Therefore, he is considered the link between the Old and the New Testaments. He baptized with water, symbolizing the washing away of sins by the Divine Love of our Mother God. He taught that the one who comes after him, however, will baptize with Fire—the Solar Fire of Divine Love of our Mother God—the Holy Spirit.

As we meditated in the cathedral, various Aspects of our Mother God joined John the Baptist in the atmosphere above the church. A Cosmic Tone sounded, and our Mother God breathed in the Solar Fire of Divine Love from the core of Creation. As She exhaled, She breathed the Sacred Fire into the Heart Flames of the representatives of the Divine Feminine who, in turn, breathed the Flame of Divine Love into the Heart Flames of every evolving soul on Earth. As the God Presence of each person absorbed that baptism of the Holy Spirit, the final preparation for awakening our spiritual brain centers was completed. For three days, that glorious Light bathed the physical brain structures of every person, which brought Humanity's right- and left-brain hemispheres into balance the maximum that Cosmic Law would allow.

On June 14, 1999, we traveled to Assisi, the home of Saint Francis (1182-1226). Assisi dates back to the 7th century B.C. The incredible beauty and splendor of the countryside around Assisi is awe inspiring. It has a mystical aura and a sacred feeling that is undeniable.

On June 15, 1999, we went to *Saint Francis Basilica.* A portion of the church was still under construction from the earthquake in 1996. As we sat in silence in the lower chapel that houses the body of Saint Francis, we experienced his Presence. We were told by Saint Francis (also known as the World Teacher, Ascended Master Kuthumi) that his service to Humanity was being expanded. He said that he is now bringing a new level of understanding and clarity to the world regarding the Laws of Abundance and God's limitless supply of all good things.

Saint Francis said that God's Abundance, used according to the highest good for ALL concerned, is a key factor in transforming this planet into Heaven on Earth. He affirmed that through the expanded consciousness of The Solar Christ, we will be able to use the Abundance of God and further our service to the Light by solving the maladies occurring on Earth.

Saint Francis said that this is a very different message than the one he exalted while in embodiment as Francis during the Piscean Age, but this is the need of the hour as the Seventh Angel begins to sound.

The rebuilding of Saint Francis Basilica is symbolic of what occurred during Francis's lifetime. One day, while Francis was praying, Jesus spoke to him from the crucifix in the old church of San Damiano. The church was falling into ruins, and Jesus said, *"Francis, repair my house which you can see is in ruins."* Saint Francis did not understand the deeper meaning of the message and set about repairing the physical structure of the church.

Saint Francis said that now our Father-Mother God is invoking us to repair the temple where God abides. This time we clearly understand it is not the physical structure of the church that must be repaired. It is the Temple of the Living God—our hearts and minds.

As Saint Francis breathed in the Holy Breath of God, his luminous Presence expanded to engulf the entire planet. Legions of Light throughout Infinity joined with him, and as he spoke the words of his famous prayer, he was lifted into his new octave of service. As he was lifted up, ALL Humanity was lifted up with him.

PRAYER OF SAINT FRANCIS

O Lord, make me an instrument of Thy Peace.
Where there is hatred, let me sow Love.
Where there is resentment, let me sow Forgiveness.
Where there is discord, let me sow Unity.
Where there is doubt, let me sow Faith.
Where there is despair, let me bring Happiness.
Where there is sadness, let me bring Joy.
Where there is darkness, let me bring Light.
O Divine Master, grant that I may desire, rather
To console than to be consoled,
To understand, rather than to be understood,
To love, rather than to be loved.
Because it is in giving that we receive,
In forgiving that we are forgiven,
In dying that we Ascend to Eternal Life.

After Saint Francis said his prayer, the sunshine-yellow Light of Divine Illumination flowed into his Crown Chakra and blazed into his spiritual brain centers. When the Light of God Illumination completed activating his spiritual brain centers into a new level of service, he breathed the Light forth to bless all Humanity.

The Flame of God Illumination expanded into the pituitary, pineal and hypothalamus glands and the ganglionic centers at the base of the brains of ALL Humanity and began reactivating the spiritual brain centers of every person on Earth.

After that activity of Light, we walked the hallowed streets of Assisi and traced the steps where Saint Francis had walked. The experience was transcendent and multidimensional. In the late afternoon we took the train to Rome.

On June 16, 1999, we took a bus tour that circled the city of Rome and gave us an overview of the mystery of that historical place. The wealth of culture and history is amazing. Rome represents both the depths and the heights that Humanity has experienced in our Earthly sojourn.

Rome has been a very significant factor in our evolution from the time of the vast Roman Empire to the time of the birth of the first Renaissance when it became the spiritual capital of the world.

One of Saint Catherine's most important accomplishments dramatically affected Rome and the spiritual direction of Humanity. Through the sheer power of her faith, her firmness of purpose and her commitment to God, Catherine convinced Pope Gregory IX to bring the Papal Seat from Avignon and restore it back to Rome. That event occurred in 1377, and it changed the spiritual course of history.

During the next few days, we traversed the city of Rome and took in the monumental grandeur of the architecture and fountains of Rome. As we walked the streets, we felt a deep sense of humility and gratitude for the sacred opportunity of being instruments of God during this wondrous moment on Earth. It was very clear to us that the God Presence of ALL Humanity were joined with us in one-pointed consciousness whether their physical presence were aware of it or not. Jesus spoke to the collective body of Humanity's God Presence and said, *"Humanity, has finally reached a point of awakening that will support the flowering seeds of physical transformation."*

On June 18, 1999, we left Rome and traveled to Pisa. Pisa is renowned for its history and artistic treasures. While we were in Pisa, the Elohim expanded the archetypes for the new Renaissance and accelerated the activation of Humanity's spiritual brain centers.

After visiting Pisa, we returned to Florence which completed our pilgrimage. The next day we left Italy to return to the United States.

The Immaculate Conception of Humanity's 5th-Dimensional *Solar* Christ Presence

The summer of 1999 was a wondrous time that brought to fruition some important prophecies by Michael de Nostradamas (1503-1566). In his mystical quatrains, Nostradamas foretold of the initial return—the second coming—of The Christ. This began with the Immaculate Conception of the 5th-Dimensional Solar Christ Presence in every Heart Flame. His terminology is different, of course, but now that the Spiritual Hierarchy has revealed to us what took place during the time Nostradamas refers to in his prophecies, it is easy to make the correlation.

Interestingly, the name Nostradamas means *Our Lady.* The prophecies he gave proclaiming the rebirth of the Era of Peace on Earth very much involve the return of our Mother God.

Nostradamas knew that Humanity would not fully understand the meaning of his prophecies until we awakened spiritually. He also knew that would not occur until the end of our 500-year period of

Grace. In Century III, Quatrain 94, he indicates that for five hundred years his predictions would be diligently studied but not comprehended. He said that at the end of the 500 years his prophecies would finally be interpreted accurately. It is 500 years from the time of Nostradamas birth in 1503 to 2003.

Nostradamas usually identified specific time frames by astrological configurations and rare celestial events. Rarely did he actually give a date. The exception to that rule was the prophecy he made for July 1999. In Century X, Quatrain 72, Nostradamas made a profound prediction. He said that in July 1999, a great King of terror will come from the sky to bring back life to the great King of the Angolmois. This refers to the East, the Far East and Middle East.

Another important reference that coincides with Nostradamas' predictions is in Chapter 16 of Saint John's Revelations. It states that *"the sixth Angel poured out his bowl upon the great river Euphrates, and its waters dried up, that the way of the King of the East might be prepared."* Nostradamas also refers to this area by stating *"From the Black Sea and the great Tartary, a great King will come..."* Both of these statements refer to modern Turkey within whose territory are the headwaters of the Euphrates River.

It is important for us to remember that the Divine Intent of the Nostradamas prophecies was to reveal to Humanity the negative things that would occur if our human egos continued on their wayward paths. The prophecies also revealed the transformational things that would occur if we changed our course of direction and reclaimed the Path of Light.

The reason the quatrains are so hard to interpret is because they have multiple meanings. Either the positive or negative interpretation could be correct depending on the actions Humanity has taken. The actions of awakened Lightworkers, specifically since the first Harmonic Convergence in August 1987, have been lifetransforming. Consequently, the prophecies for July 1999, resulted in the most positive scenario possible.

Let's compare the prophecies to the events that transpired in the summer of 1999.

"In July 1999, the great King of terror will come from the sky to bring back life to the great King of Angolmois."

Beginning on July 13, 1999, and continuing through August 17,

1999, we experienced a series of celestial events that were a once-in-a-lifetime occurrence. These events were instrumental in opening a portal of Light from the heart of the Great, Great Central Sun into the Heart Flames of every person evolving on Earth. That glorious activity of Light allowed the Immaculate Conception of the 5th-Dimensional Solar Christ Presence in every person's Heart Flame. That was the first step in the second coming of The Christ—bringing the great King back to life.

The reason this aspect of our own Divinity was referred to as *"the King of terror"* is because the Light of God amplifies everything in its path. If Humanity had not raised the energy, vibration and consciousness of all life evolving on Earth to the degree that we did after the first Harmonic Convergence, the Light from our 5th-Dimensional Solar Christ Presence would have amplified all of the negativity in our physical bodies, which would have been excruciating.

The first coming of The Christ took place in the Middle East. The second coming of the 5th-Dimensional Solar Christ Presence within every heart meant *"bringing back life to the great King of Angolmois."* The *East* also symbolizes the Dawn of a New Day.

Now, I will share with you a few of the events that transpired during the momentous summer of 1999. The spectacular celestial events began on July 13, 1999, with a Grand Cross Alignment. Another Grand Cross Alignment occurred on July 20, 1999. On July 28, 1999, there was a *Lunar Eclipse.* The configuration of the planets during that influx of Light facilitated the preparation for the thirteenth Harmonic Convergence and the Thirteenth Annual World Congress On Illumination.

On August 11, 1999, the Earth experienced a powerful *Solar Eclipse.* That eclipse was very unique and was heralded by some astrologers as the most significant event in the last 2,000 years. They said that it was visible to more people than any other eclipse in recorded history. Within moments of the total Solar Eclipse, the third *Astrological Grand Cross* of the summer was formed in the sky.

The planetary alignments were called Grand Crosses because almost all of the planets were in cross patterns while being held in the fixed signs of the Zodiac. On August 11, 1999, they were held in the *fixed signs of Leo, Taurus, Aquarius and Scorpio.* This began the opening of the portal of Light from the Great, Great Central Sun into each person's Heart Flame.

Those particular fixed signs are considered the "*Gates of Power,*" and they represent the symbols of the Four Sacred Beasts of the Apocalypse:

> The Bull - Taurus
> The Lion - Leo
> Man/Woman - Aquarius
> The Serpent/Eagle - Scorpio

In esoteric astrology, the Fixed Cross is described as a transition in consciousness and an initiation of the soul by the Fires of God.

A total Solar Eclipse combined with a fixed sign Grand Cross is very rare. But to have a total Solar Eclipse with a Fixed Grand Cross in the midst of three other Grand Crosses is a *once-in-a-lifetime occurrence.*

While we were in the embrace of the Light of the Grand Crosses and the eclipses, we experienced what the Mayan prophecies had predicted for centuries—*the Day of Destiny—August 13, 1999.*

On that day the door between Spirit and matter opened. With the assistance of our God Selves, we each had the opportunity to release and let go of the behavior patterns that no longer supported our highest good. Our Chakras and our spiritual brain centers were brought into alignment with higher frequencies of Solar Light. That was a moment of repositioning that paved the way for the Immaculate Conception of our 5th-Dimensional Solar Christ Presence. That event set the stage for massive and fundamental change and created a time of *self-transcendence.*

On August 14, 1999, at 5:45 p.m. in Tucson, Arizona, just prior to the Opening Ceremonies for the *13th Annual World Congress On Illumination,* there was a beautiful double rainbow in the eastern sky. That symbol of the Divine Covenant between God and Humanity was just the beginning of the miracles we would witness during that sacred conclave.

The participants came from all over the world to reignite ancient friendships and to offer themselves in service as a Holy Grail through which the Light of God would pour to fulfill the Divine Plan for that Cosmic Moment.

The God Presence of those physically present created a Chalice of Light that cradled the entire Earth and all her life in preparation for the Cosmic events that were going to take place during the week. The Elohim enveloped each person in an invincible armor of Divine Love and Protection.

On August 15, 1999, our Mother God came to the fore and performed a ceremony of Light to further awaken the Love Nature of the Divine Feminine within every human heart. That activity of Light brought the right-brain hemispheres of all Humanity further into balance. It also expanded our Heart Flames and created a *brazier or womb* within our hearts to cradle the embryo of our 5th-Dimensional Solar Christ Presence.

On August 16, 1999, the Divine Love of our Mother God was breathed into the Elemental Kingdom. That included the Elemental substance of Humanity's physical, etheric, mental and emotional bodies and the Elemental substance of the body of Mother Earth as well. That healing unguent bathed the battered body of Mother Earth and lifted all of the Elemental Kingdom into a new frequency of healing Light. That event further prepared the hearts of Humanity to receive our 5th-Dimensional Solar Christ Presence.

The final Grand Cross of the series occurred on the thirteenth Harmonic Convergence, August 17, 1999. The Grand Crosses on August 11th and 17th were comprised of almost entirely different planets; they had only the Moon in common. All but one of the planets were in the same Zodiacal signs as the Grand Crosses. The last time anything even remotely close to that took place was on January 11, 1910. For that unusual phenomenon to occur within a time frame of only six days was rare in the extreme. The importance of that celestial event cannot be overestimated.

During that Cosmic Moment, the *Immaculate Conception of Humanity's 5th-Dimensional Solar Christ Presence took place within the wombs of our Heart Flames.*

On that same day at 3:00 a.m., during the early predawn hours of the morning, *Turkey* experienced a devastating earthquake. Our Father-Mother God informed us that the earthquake was a critical facet of the Divine Plan as foretold in the prophecies and that it had to occur in order for the Immaculate Conception of our 5th-Dimensional Solar Christ Presence—the return of the King—to be fulfilled. Our God Parents said the plan had been a work in progress for many centuries, and contrary to outer appearances, it was merciful beyond the comprehension of our present level of understanding.

The Elohim shared with us that in the original plan, it was believed that *hundreds of thousands* of people would have to leave the Earth during that earthquake, but because of the incredible purification that had taken place with the assistance of Mother Mary and Mother Teresa in the Field of Blackbirds, the Divine Plan was able to be fulfilled by a few thousand people. The reason for the earthquake is complicated, but this is what the Elohim revealed to us.

The Earth is Ascending up the Spiral of Evolution into the 4th Dimension. Now, the goal is for ALL Humanity to be vibrating at a frequency of Light that is high enough to make the natural evolutionary shift onto the 5th-Dimensional Spiral of Evolution with the rest of our Solar System. This means that every person must lift up in energy, vibration and consciousness.

A few millennia ago the Company of Heaven realized that in order for the densest human miscreations to be transmuted in time for the Earth to Ascend, we were going to need Divine Intervention. To assist in this project, Turkey was made into a portal of the Divine Mother. This was done in order to try to balance the incredible negativity that was seething in the Field of Blackbirds nearby.

Ephesus was settled before *1000 B.C.* by Ionian Greeks from Athens. During the seventh century B.C. they erected the earliest-known temple of the Oriental Fertility Goddess later identified as the Greek Artemis. Ephesus became part of the Persian Empire in *546 B.C.*

In *356 B.C.* the Temple of Artemis was burned down by Herostratus, who was considered a fanatic, but its restoration was soon begun and was supported by Alexander the Great. The restored Artemisian Temple was celebrated as one of the Seven Wonders of the World during the Hellenistic Era. In Roman times, it became known as the Temple of Diana of the Ephesians. Each phase of this temple magnetized the Light of our Mother God into the world of form.

After Jesus' Ascension, the Christians were badly persecuted in Jerusalem, and Mother Mary, John the Beloved and Joseph of Arimathea fled to Ephesus. For many years, Mother Mary magnetized the Love of our Mother God into the physical plane from her home in Ephesus and permanently expanded the portal of the Divine Feminine to envelope the region that is now known as Turkey.

Ephesus became famous because of Saint Paul's visits and because it was a meeting place for many ecumenical councils during the fifth century of the Christian Era. The public attention amplified and sustained the portal of our Mother God.

In *532 A.D.* Emperor Justinian assisted in increasing the portal of the Divine Mother by erecting *Hagia Sophia, the Church of Holy Wisdom,* in what was then Constantinople. Sophia is an Aspect of the Divine Feminine that bathes the Earth with Divine Wisdom and the Breath of the Holy Spirit. As people from all over the world were drawn to that historical site, the breath of the Holy Spirit increased and flooded into the effluvia in the Field of Blackbirds.

Several decades ago, the Spiritual Hierarchy determined that the black crystallized pockets of hatred in the Field of Blackbirds were not responding to the efforts of the Lightworkers. It became obvious that those pockets could not be transmuted through normal means in time for the Earth to make the shift into the 5th Dimension with the rest of our Solar System.

With that realization, the Spiritual Hierarchy sent forth a clarion call and asked for assistance. This time hundreds of thousands of Lightworkers from the Inner Realms responded to the call. Those Lightworkers volunteered to embody in Turkey within the portal of the Divine Mother. They agreed to abide there and absorb the residue of hatred that could not be transmuted in the allotted time through normal means into the Divinity of their own Heart Flames. Those souls understood through their God Selves that when the time was right, they would leave the Earth together. They knew that the precise moment of their departure would be determined by the Godhead.

After the influx of Light that bathed the planet during the eclipses and the Grand Crosses in July and August 1999, all was in readiness for the next phase of the Divine Plan.

On August 17, 1999, at 3:00 o'clock in the morning, the Lightworkers who selflessly volunteered to assist Humanity by removing the densest frequencies of human hatreds from the Earth left the physical plane through the earthquake in Turkey.

In a single Cosmic Moment, they collectively formed one unified force and Ascended through the portal of the Divine Mother into the heart of the Great, Great Central Sun. As they left the Earth plane, they carried within their Heart Flames the black effluvia that the Lightworkers were having problems transmuting in time for our shift into the 5th Dimension. That mass of human miscreation was returned to the heart of our Father-Mother God to be transmuted and repolarized back into Light. In that sacred moment, the precious souls in Turkey God-Victoriously fulfilled their Divine Mission.

The Elohim said the souls left the physical plane instantaneously and painlessly while they were sleeping. The earthquake lasted for only 45 seconds. It measured 7.4 on the Richter Scale and was 400 times more powerful than the bomb that was dropped on Hiroshima.

In a Ceremony of Light, the Ascending souls were welcomed with great glory into the Heart of God. Through their sacrifice, the Earth and ALL Humanity were freed from the ancient hatreds of the world, and the way was cleared for the Immaculate Conception of our Solar Christ Presences.

The remainder of the souls affected by the earthquake in Turkey were cloaked in a forcefield of Divine Love and Comfort by our Father-Mother God. At inner levels, each one knew and understood the sacrifice they volunteered to participate in, and they knew of the mercy and Grace of God involved when hundreds of thousands of people did not have to leave the physical plane.

As the news of the earthquake spread through the media, people who thought the Solar Eclipse and the Grand Crosses would cause cataclysmic Earth changes were terrified that their fears were coming true. A sense of panic began to sweep through the hearts and minds of those expecting the worst, and their collective fears were building. Many people thought this was the beginning of the *"grand terror coming from the sky"* that Nostradamas had predicted.

The Elohim and the Company of Heaven asked the Lightworkers at the World Congress On Illumination to assist in calming the building chaos. We were asked to intensify the *Flame of Healing Through the Power of Limitless Transmutation* through all of the cracks, faults, fissures and tectonic plates on the planet. That sacred Fire was then projected through the Crystal Grid System, and the Mighty Elohim reinforced the weak points on the body of Mother Earth with additional Light so that Humanity's panic would not cause more earthquakes.

Later that same afternoon, the Cicini satellite was scheduled to pass within 750 miles of the Earth. It was carrying radioactive plutonium fuel. Many people were afraid that a mishap would occur and that the fuel would contaminate the Earth. Their fears had the potential of magnetizing the satellite into the atmosphere of Earth.

Archangel Michael and his Legions of Protection asked us to assist in creating a *Ring-Pass-Not of God's First Cause of Perfection* around the Earth.

Fortunately, the Light of God is *always* Victorious. The satellite passed without a problem and the earthquake that did occur in the San Francisco area at 6:05 p.m. that day was only 5.3 on the Richter Scale. There were a few other earthquakes that occurred in the next several days in Montana, Illinois and Costa Rica, but fortunately, they were minor with no loss of life.

On August 18, 1999, through Divine Ceremonies involving sacred movement and dance, the Light of God flowed through the hearts of the Lightworkers at the World Congress to soothe the grief stricken hearts of those remaining in Turkey. That Light then expanded to embrace all the people on Earth who were suffering from grief and the loss of a loved one.

On August 19, 1999, at 5:45 a.m. in Tucson, Arizona, another brilliant double rainbow appeared; this time it was in the western sky. We experienced that celestial gift just prior to the Closing Ceremonies of the World Congress On Illumination. It was confirmation from our Father-Mother God that the Divine Plan had been fulfilled. Humanity's 5th-Dimensional Solar Christ Presences were Immaculately Conceived in the wombs of our Heart Flames, and the nine-month gestation period had begun.

Many Sightings of Strange Lights After Turkey Quake

The earthquake in Turkey left several major mysteries in its wake. A spokesman for the Turkish UFO and Paranormal Organization shared the following information:

"Ever since the earthquake, some very strange lights are clearly seen all over western Turkey. They are incredibly clear, circular or triangular in shape, white, yellow, red and blue colored and remain visible in the sky for 50 to 60 minutes, following a materializing/dematerializing pattern. It has become a routine thing, as they have been showing up two or three times a week. They have become an inevitable component of the TV news and media.

"Furthermore, just before the quake, the bottom of the sea in Izmit went red, and the sea temperature went up to 104-113 degrees Fahrenheit—incredibly hot for seawater. Izmit, the epicenter of the 7.4 magnitude quake, is located on the easternmost edge of the Sea of Marmara. However, there are no underwater volcanos in the Sea of Marmara! Starting two days

before the quake, hundreds of fish, crabs and other sea life-forms died. Somehow they were burned. The fish nets of the fishermen were burned, and we have several rock and stone samples from the sea which turned black in color.

"That organization is cooperating with the Smithsonian Institute and a few universities in the U.S. They sent them some rock and burned fishnet samples upon their request. Some fishermen also said that they witnessed an explosion under the sea and, then, fireballs, strange lights and sightings in Turkey."

CNI News noted: *"So-called 'earthlights' are sometimes associated with strong seismic forces, and TUVPO investigators are taking that into account in the research, but the frequency, brilliance and duration of the sightings of anomalous Lights is highly unusual. Coupled with the heating of the Sea of Marmara, it would appear that a sustained source of very high energy is at work in the region of the earthquake."*

A few interesting footnotes:

Everything in the Universe is Connected

Our own scientists at the very cutting edge of Quantum Physics have discovered what is called the Quantum Hologram. They say this very complicated math confirms *"Everything in the Universe is connected to everything else, and it all knows what it is doing."* Our own scientists are now telling us, *"All is resonance."*

Edgar Mitchell, former astronaut and cofounder of the Institute of Noetic Sciences, is one of the scientists who are working with the Quantum Hologram theory. Through this discovery, the scientists believe there is a way to tap into the patterns of creation in order to create a better existence for us all.

The Year of the Light

According to Kabbalistic calculations, 1999 was the Jewish New Year 5760, which was *the year of the Light*. It is said that was the first time since the Jews were at Mt. Sinai receiving the Torah that this energy was *directly* available to Humanity. It was a powerful force of Light, designed to assist both our individual and collective efforts in reaching critical mass.

Earth's Inner Core is a Spinning Crystal Ball

Researchers are now probing what may turn out to be the most curious sphere in the Solar System. It is a globe the size of the Moon, and it appears to be a crystalline substance. This globe is in the center of the Earth. Two seismologists have demonstrated that this strange crystal sphere is turning slowly within the rock and liquid metal that keeps it all but hidden from scientific investigation.

Geophysicists realized decades ago that a solid inner core exists in the Earth, but they knew little about it. They believed the inner core and the liquid shell surrounding it were made largely of iron, yet other features in the core of the planet remained enigmatic.

Seismologists examining earthquake waves that pierce the inner core made a startling find. Rather than being "isotopic" (the same in all directions) in its physical properties, the inner core proved to be somewhat like a piece of wood with a definite grain running through it. Waves traveling along the planet's north-south axis go 3 to 4 percent faster through the inner core than those that follow paths close to the equatorial plane.

Geophysicists have struggled to explain why this grain should exist. The leading theory is that at the immense pressures of the inner core, iron takes on a hexagonal crystal form that has inherently directional, physical properties. Some force apparently keeps the hexagonal iron crystals all in close alignment.

Scientists at the Georgia Institute of Technology and the Carnegie Institution of Washington note that whatever texturing mechanism operates to form the anisotropic grain of the inner core, it must be almost 100 percent efficient. In an article published in *Science Magazine* the scientists stated, *"The very strong texturing indicated by the results of the study suggests the possibility that the inner core of the Earth is a very large single crystal."*

The Birth of Humanity's 5th-Dimensional Solar Christ Presence

After every person's 5th-Dimensional Solar Christ Presence was conceived in the womb of the Heart Flame, we experienced a nine-month gestation period. During that time, many incredible activities of Light paved the way for the miraculous birth, which was destined to take place during a rare alignment of planets on May 3, 2000.

On September 19, 1999, we held one of our Free Seminars in Los Angeles, California. Los Angeles is the portal through which the Divine Love of our Mother God entered the physical plane during the darkest hours on the continent of Lemuria. When Lemuria sank beneath the healing waters of the Pacific Ocean for purification, it broke apart, and a portion of it was pushed against what is now North America. The area west of the San Andreas fault was once part of Lemuria. The vortex of the Goddess or Divine Mother is located in Los Angeles and radiates through all of southern California.

During our seminar, our Mother God projected forth the most intensified frequencies of Divine Love Humanity was capable of enduring. As that crystalline pink essence flowed through the portal in Los Angeles, it bathed all life in the comfort and balance of the Holy Spirit. The Light reinforced the vulnerable areas in the body of Mother Earth and, once again, strengthened the cracks, faults, fissures and tectonic plates throughout the planet.

Then on October 17, 1999, we gave a Free Seminar in Pittsburgh, Pennsylvania. Pittsburgh is called the tri-river city because of the convergence of the Ohio, Allegheny and Monongahela Rivers. This city is very significant during this unique moment of renewal and rebirth for several reasons.

Because of its prolific steel industry, Pittsburgh became one of the most polluted cities in the world between the late 1800s and the 1940s. It epitomized the grime-incrusted filth of the contemporary cities of the Industrial Age. Then in the mid 1940s, the people of Pittsburgh joined together and undertook one of the most ambitious urban-renewal projects in history. The community-wide reconstruction program was termed the "Pittsburgh Renaissance," and it largely dispelled the blight and smog that plagued the city.

Pittsburgh was transformed into a bright and modern metropolis, modeling to the world what a unified Humanity, focused in one-pointed consciousness, can accomplish. The focal point of the transformation took place in an area that is referred to as the *"Golden Triangle."* This area is surrounded by rivers and hills forming an almost perfect triangle.

The *water element* is associated with the emotional stratum of Earth and our emotional bodies. At a point within the Golden Triangle where the three rivers converge, a portal into the Heart of God is formed. Through that portal, the emotional stratum is fed and nurtured with the harmony and balance of God.

During our seminar, we were joined by the Company of Heaven, the Solar Elohim and the Directors of the Water Element. These august Beings magnetized from the Heart of the Great, Great Central Sun frequencies of Healing Light specifically consecrated to heal Humanity's emotional bodies.

At 11:11 a.m. that day, a double helix of Light was projected from the Heart of the Great, Great Central Sun through the portal in Pittsburgh into the center of the Earth. One spiral of the double helix is emerald green Healing Light and the other is crystalline pink Divine Love. The Light was anchored in the center of the Earth and then expanded out to every particle of life through the Crystal Grid System. The Divine Intent of this Light is to prepare our hearts and our emotional bodies so that we will more effectively integrate and assimilate the Love of our Mother God.

Reactivating the Record-Keeper Crystals

Prior to the sinking of Lemuria, the Elohim gathered the Record-Keeper Crystals that contained the original archetypes and codings for the Divine Plan for the Earth and placed them in a large monolith for safekeeping. The codings in the crystals were rendered dormant until a future time when Humanity would awaken and reclaim our Divine Birthright as stewards of the Earth.

When the continent sank beneath the water and broke apart, the portion containing the monolith was pushed far into the southern hemisphere. Australia is that portion of Lemuria, and the monolith is called Uluru or Ayers Rock.

Since it was not part of the original Divine Plan for Humanity to create distorted patterns of pain and suffering, there were no archetypes or codings in the Record-Keeper Crystals to teach us how to stop our horrific descent into oblivion. Consequently, a contingency plan had to be created by our Father-Mother God and the Company of Heaven. The plan for Earth's salvation was programmed into new Record-Keeper Crystals that were placed in the Earth's Crystal Grid System. The contingency plan had viable solutions to Humanity's pain and suffering as well as information on how we could regain our direction and continue our Ascension up the Spiral of Evolution.

Alas, once again, our human egos perpetuated behavior patterns that resulted in further negativity, and the Earth gradually fell deeper into the frequencies of chaos and pain. Another Fiat was issued by our Father-Mother God, and Atlantis was submerged beneath the waters of the Atlantic Ocean for purification.

This time the Elohim collected the Record-Keeper Crystals with the contingency plan encoded in them and placed them in a huge monolith on what is now the North American Continent. This monolith is Stone Mountain in Atlanta, Georgia. Atlanta is named after the continent Atlantis.

After aeons of time and myriad activities of Light, Humanity has finally lifted our heads above the effluvia of human miscreation effectively enough for the Record-Keeper Crystals to be reactivated. Since the most powerful force on the planet is the unified focus of Humanity's attention, a Divine Plan was set into motion that would create the largest focus of Humanity's attention possible. In 1996 and 2000, the Olympic Games were held in Atlanta, Georgia, and Sydney, Australia. No other event holds the positive, focused attention of over four-billion people for more than two weeks.

The Olympics are a metaphor that represents the family of Humanity coming together to achieve our highest level of excellence. In 1996, as the world turned its attention to the activities taking place in Atlanta, the Company of Heaven used the collective cup of Humanity's consciousness to reactivate the crystals in Stone Mountain. These crystals contain the contingency plan that will assist the masses of Humanity to regain our direction and change the course of history.

In November 1999, Lightworkers were asked by the Company of Heaven if we would be willing to go on a sacred pilgrimage to Uluru/Ayers Rock and other sacred sites in the Australian Outback. Our mission would be to prepare for the activation of the Record-Keeper Crystals, which would take place during the 2000 Olympic Games. Of course, we joyously accepted the opportunity. Sixty people traveled from various parts of the world to Uluru, and we were joined in consciousness by Lightworkers from all over the world.

Several events took place in Australia that November in order to draw the focused attention of the rest of the world.

*   Every year since the end of World War I, people in Australia, England and various other countries of the world have stopped what they were doing on November 11th at 11:00 a.m. for a moment of silence. This is done to honor those who died in the war and those who have served the cause of Freedom. The full-gathered momentum of that reverent moment helped prepare the way for the activity of Light at Uluru.

*   For the first time, Australians voted on whether or not they wanted to carry on with the Queen of England as head of state. That controversy drew global attention.

*   Australia won the greatly prized World Cup in Rugby.

*   Hundreds of celebrities came to Sydney for a massive celebration and the kickoff of a major new branch of the film industry.

*   And plans for the Olympic Games in Sydney expanded and were publicized all over the world.

On November 7, 1999, the Lightworkers who had traveled to the Outback began our pilgrimage in Alice Springs. We met outdoors in the afternoon under a very nice ramada. As we began our sharing, an eagle circled above, and some black crows joined us and blessed us with their songs. One of the participants from Australia said that the Aboriginal people say when the crows come and sing during a Divine Ceremony, it means the Elders have joined in and are bringing their blessings.

After a little while, a "freak" rainstorm brought a beautiful rain and cleansed the air of dust and insects. We were then blessed with a beautiful rainbow. A few hours later after we were through with our meeting, we experienced another cleansing rain and the most brilliant double rainbow I have ever seen. The employees at our hotel said it never rains in Alice Springs in November.

The Elemental Kingdom blessed us with their obvious gifts throughout our entire trip. The Australian Outback is notorious for its fly and insect problems, and we were told to bring insect repellent and veils to protect our faces. Throughout our trip, however, we were blessed with a gentle breeze that followed us everywhere we went. It kept the insects in abeyance and cooled the air. Never once was it necessary to use insect repellent or veils.

After leaving Alice Springs, we traveled to an exquisite lake nestled in the hollow of a beautiful canyon. We gathered for a meditation at precisely the moment of the New Moon. As we meditated, an increased influx of Light bathed the Earth with powerful transformational energies, and the God Selves of Humanity projected Healing Light into the physical and etheric bodies of each soul. That energy caused strong biological and chemical reactions which triggered the necessary changes in Humanity's bodies in preparation for the birth of our 5th-Dimensional Solar Christ Presence. That New Moon was unique in that it was aligned with the same aspects as the August 11, 1999, Grand Cross and Solar Eclipse.

We were told by the Spiritual Hierarchy that the sixty Lightworkers on the pilgrimage had volunteered to serve as surrogates on behalf of Humanity. In deep humility and gratitude, we embraced that opportunity. We were told that the gifts and blessings being given to us were simultaneously being given to all Humanity.

We were then guided to enter the lake for a baptism of the Holy Spirit. As we entered the healing water, the Divine Love of the Holy Spirit flowed into our hearts, and our Mother God further balanced Humanity's right-brain hemispheres.

On November 9, 1999, we traveled to a huge 130-million-year-old, meteor crater that the Aborigines call the Mother's Womb. There, we invoked the Light of Healing and danced the sacred PanEuRhythmy. We danced to the Cosmic Tones of the heartbeat of Mother Earth as an eagle circled above us. As we danced, the full-gathered momentum of thousands of Lightworkers from all over the world who have held the Immaculate Concept and Divine Intent of the sacred PanEuRhythmy movements flowed into the Mother's Womb. These servants of Light have been energizing this sacred dance in the forcefield of the Rila Mountains of Bulgaria for over 75 years. As they merged their Light with ours, our humble efforts were expanded a thousand-times-a-thousandfold.

As we performed each movement, the Light of our Father-Mother God poured through our Heart Flames and blazed into the cause, core, effect, record and memory of all of the atrocities Humanity has inflicted on each other, the Elemental Kingdom and every other lifeform on Earth since the initial impulse of the "fall." The Violet Transmuting Flame of Limitless Mercy, Compassion and Forgiveness poured through our hearts and blazed in, through and around every particle of that misqualified energy, instantly transmuting it back into Light.

After our sacred time in the crater, we traveled to beautiful Palm Valley were we hiked in the glorious canyon and basked in the radiance of the swaying palms. There, we contemplated the wonder of the moment and assimilated the events of the day. Later that afternoon we traveled to Wallace Rockhole, which is an Aboriginal community.

On November 10, 1999, we were told by the Spiritual Hierarchy that some final preparation was necessary prior to the influx of Light that would take place the next day for the 11:11 Activation. We got up early in the morning and were taken by a guide to an Aboriginal watering hole. There were sacred symbols, paintings and writings on the rocks that are believed to be thousands of years old. As we walked that hallowed ground, we made a deep heart connection with the ancient Elders who hold the portal of Light open in that location.

We then traveled to the majestic Kings Canyon where we hiked along a beautiful creek into the arms of the magnificent canyon. Many of the Lightworkers brought Aboriginal music instruments. They brought didgeridoos, music sticks, drums, flutes and a guitar. In addition, we had a CD player and several CDs of traditional Aboriginal music. We all gathered together, sitting in a circle on the rocks above the creek. We were joined by the entire Company of Heaven, the God Selves of all Humanity and the ancient indigenous Elders from all time frames and dimensions. As we played our music and connected with the Cosmic Tones of Beloved Mother Earth, the Elohim and the Directors of the Elements joined us.

As the music built in power and momentum, the Elders projected bolts of Violet Lightning through the cup of our consciousness into the crystallized matrixes, archetypes, patterns and blueprints of Humanity's human miscreations. These old, obsolete forms were shattered into fragments and lovingly transmuted by the power of the Violet Flame.

The ancient indigenous Elders who joined with us from inner levels were Ascended Beings from the human evolutions who had been tenaciously holding onto the Immaculate Concept of the original Divine Blueprint of Heaven on Earth since Humanity first fell from Grace. For untold millennia, they had been waiting for the Cosmic Moment when the blueprints and archetypes for Heaven on Earth could once again be projected onto the fluid field of unmanifest Divine Potential for the Earth. They had been waiting for the moment when the Record-Keeper Crystals would finally be reactivated, and, at long last, *the moment had arrived.*

After the crystallized patterns of Humanity's miscreations were transmuted, the particles of the Comet Linear that were passing the Earth began to shake the ethers crumbling the polluted, stagnant atmosphere and clearing the way for the formation of a new fluid field of unmanifest Divine Potential.

The Comet Linear was discovered on May 12, 1999, and made its closest passage to the Sun in September 1999. It is believed to enter the inner Solar System only once every 63,000 years. On November 10-11, 1999, in Heavenly synchronicity, the Earth arrived at a point in space that brought us close to the path that the comet had passed 40 days earlier. This created a meteor shower that appeared to emanate from the bowl of the Big Dipper. This was the first known apparition of the "Linear particles." During the activities of Light on November 10, 1999, the patterns of perfection from the Divine Heart and Mind of God began gently reflecting onto the fluid field of unmanifest Divine Potential in preparation for the unprecedented activity of Light that was to occur the next day.

November 11, 1999, we broke camp early and left Kings Canyon for Uluru. As our caravan traveled toward that sacred site, the Light from the first time zone on the planet began pouring through the portal at Uluru. We could feel our hearts being prepared to withstand the building momentum of Light that was destined to blaze through the planet on that Holy Day.

From 11:11 a.m. to 12:12 p.m., in each consecutive time zone, the most intensified frequencies of Light that Humanity could endure poured from the heart of our Father-Mother God into the center of the Earth. The 24-hour wave of Light entered the Sun of Even Pressure and expanded out through the Crystal Grid System.

As 11:11 a.m. approached in our time zone, our caravan stopped a short distance away from Uluru. We wanted to conduct our Divine Ceremony in private so we would not draw attention to ourselves at Uluru/Ayers Rock. We found a huge pine tree that was awaiting us with open arms. It cast a blanket of cool shade on the ground, and we were all able to sit within its radiance. The pine tree is Archangel Michael's symbol, and we felt his protective Presence.

As our music began, the Solar Elohim from the Great, Great Central Sun entered the atmosphere of Earth. They took their strategic positions around the equator and projected mighty rays of the Twelve Solar Aspects of Deity into the center of the Earth.

The Directors of the Elements projected their luminous Presence and embraced the elements of air from the north, water from the east, earth from the south, fire from the west and the ether element from the center of the Earth.

Mother Earth braced herself in great anticipation and joy. Then Humanity's Solar Christ Presence joined together to form One unified Light Being with the Earth cradled in its Heart Flame. Ever so gently, the Light of God poured through the Heart Flame of Humanity's collective Solar Christ Presence into the Record-Keeper Crystals being held in the heart of Uluru. As the Light of God penetrated into the core of purity in each Record-Keeper Crystal, it began activating the original codings and archetypes of the Divine Potential for this sweet Earth.

After the initial Activation of the Record-Keeper Crystals, the Mighty Elohim summoned legions of Angels from their Regal Court in the Great, Great Central Sun. These magnificent Angels descended into the heart of Uluru and gathered up the Record-Keeper Crystals. As the Elohim sounded a Cosmic Tone, the Angels traversed the planet north, south, east and west. They carried the Record-Keeper Crystals to every Chakra and Power Point along the Crystal Grid System and securely reestablished the crystals in their rightful positions in the body of Mother Earth.

After the crystals were in place, we played our traditional Aboriginal music instruments. As the tones from the heartbeat of Mother Earth reverberated through the planet, the patterns of perfection for the New Earth were intensified and sealed in the newly-formed fluid field of unmanifest Divine Potential. Our Ceremony ended at 12:12 p.m., and we sealed the activity by listening to John Lennon's song *"Imagine."* We then continued to Uluru for the remainder of our activities of Light.

As we approached the rock, it was an awe-inspiring experience. The power and majesty of that monolith is overwhelming. We spent some time walking around Uluru. We embraced the sacred monolith and connected with its Devic Presence. As Sunset approached, bus loads of people began to arrive for the spectacular show. We all gathered a short distance away from Uluru so we could witness the rare beauty of the Sun setting on the rock. In a wondrous display, the setting Sun bathed Uluru in celestial colors and brilliant hues of Light.

Joy and elation poured forth from the Heavenly Realms, and the Legions of Light bathed the Earth in supreme gratitude and love for Humanity's participation in all of the activities of Light that day. That night we camped out at Uluru and witnessed some of the shooting stars from the Comet Linear.

When we awoke on November 12, 1999, it felt as if the Earth had been reborn. Everything seemed sweeter and gentler. There was a feeling of gratitude wafting through the air and a sense of reverence I had never experienced before. As we prepared to break camp, a special activity took place. A tremendous shaft of Light from the heart of our Father God was projected through the portal of the Divine Masculine in Tibet into the axis of the Earth. Then another tremendous shaft of Light from the heart of our Mother God was projected into the axis of the Earth through the portal of the Divine Feminine at Lake Titicaca in Bolivia.

As these mighty shafts of Light spiraled through the axis forming a double helix, the blue Masculine Ray of Divine Will, Authority and Power merged and became one with the pink Feminine Ray of Divine Love, Adoration and Reverence for All Life. That event transformed the axis of the Earth into a spiraling shaft of previously unknown frequencies of the Violet Transmuting Flame of Limitless Physical Perfection. This Light is now blazing through the Twelve Solar Chakras of the planet, which are aligned along the axis of Beloved Mother Earth. The new frequencies of the Violet Flame gently prepared Humanity for the *birth of our 5th-Dimensional Solar Christ Presence*.

After we broke camp, we traveled to the Olgas or Kata Tjuta. This is a grouping of tremendous monoliths, which form a portal of *birth* from the 5th-Dimensional Realms of Perfection into the physical plane. When we arrived, we hiked back into the resplendent *"birth canal"* and, once again, experienced the wonder and awe of the majestic moment taking place on Earth. We were joined by the Company of Heaven and the Feminine Aspects of Deity throughout the whole of Creation.

Those of us who were gathered together in the physical plane expressed our Oneness with all Humanity and our gratitude for the opportunity we had been given to serve the Light. As our hearts opened, the Elohim breathed the Breath of Life into the portal of birth and prepared the *planetary birth canal* for the unprecedented birth of Humanity's Solar Christ Presence, which would take place during the Grand Alignment in May 2000. Upon the completion of that activity of Light, our sacred pilgrimage was sealed and brought to fruition.

The next day we left Ayers Rock for our journey home. Kay and I went on to New Zealand for a few days as did several other people from our tour.

New Zealand is an Elemental Training Center. Within that forcefield of Light, the Elohim, the Deva Rajas and the Devas train the Elementals who are serving the Earth. The Elemental Beings include the Sylphs of the air, the Undines of the water, the Gnomes and

Nature Spirits of the earth, the Salamanders of the fire and the various Devas of the rarefied ether element. The Elementals are responsible for creating the substance that makes up all manifest form. This includes the elements that compose our physical bodies and the body of Mother Earth as well.

The first step in creating a manifest form is that our Father God sounds the Keynote which forms the matrix or pattern of the item being created. Then our Mother God projects a Ray of Divine Love into the center of the matrix that reverberates with the cohesive power to hold the unformed primal Light in the pattern of the matrix. After those two steps are successfully accomplished, the Elementals transform the unformed primal Light into the particular elemental substances that are necessary to sustain the creation in the physical plane.

The Elementals also have the job of sustaining the thoughtforms and feelings that Humanity expresses through our creative faculties. They observe what we send forth; then they are obligated to transform primal Light into the elemental substance that is necessary for our creations to manifest physically. This is true whether we are envisioning the perfection of Heaven on Earth or the depths of fear and despair.

On November 14, 1999, Kay and I rented a car and toured Christchurch in New Zealand. The new frequencies of the Violet Flame of Limitless Physical Perfection were blazing through the axis and Solar Chakras of the planet and penetrating deep into the entire land mass of the islands of New Zealand. A shift was taking place within the actual consciousness of the Elementals in the Elemental Training Center, and multidimensional levels of sacred knowledge were flowing into the hearts and minds of the Elementals from the Divine Mind of God. It was clear that their training was lifting into a higher octave of Divine Manifestation.

On November 15, 1999, we drove to Queenstown. The drive takes about seven hours, and it is the most beautiful, scenic drive you could ever imagine. We passed snow-capped mountains and aquamarine glacier lakes. There was a plethora of exquisite wild flowers along the road that exploded into a profusion of color against the backdrop of green hills and valleys that stretched as far as the eye could see.

As we approached Queenstown, it started to rain a little, and a gentle mist began to cloak the city, which gave everything a mystical, multidimensional appearance. We registered in a beautiful hotel that overlooks a lake and spent the evening admiring the beauty of the Elementals.

The next day we woke up early and prepared for sight-seeing. It was still gently raining and misty. The people at the hotel said it was not supposed to rain that day. The weather had been beautiful, and the rain came "out of the blue." We knew that something very special was taking place.

We took a gondola ride to the top of the mountain that overlooks all of Queenstown. As we ascended through the mist, it felt as though we were passing into a new dimension. The view was celestial. We felt the presence of the Elohim and the Beings from the Elemental Training Center, so we decided to sit and just *be* for a while.

The Record-Keeper Crystals that had recently been positioned along the meridians of the Crystal Grid System began to gently pulsate. Suddenly, the Elohim sounded a Cosmic Tone, and the original patterns for the Earth in all of her resplendent beauty began to flow onto the fluid field of unmanifest Divine Potential. The Elohim initiated the Elementals into a higher school of training, and the patterns of perfection for the New Earth were placed before their consciousness.

As that activity occurred, the intensity of the Light set off the fire alarm at the visitors' center, and we were all ushered outside while the fire department checked everything out. At the end of the experience, when everything calmed down, John Lennon's song *"Imagine"* was playing through the music system at the visitors' center.

Late that afternoon we left Queenstown by plane. We flew to Auckland and then left for America. We left at 9:00 p.m. Tuesday night on November 16th, traveled for twelve hours and arrived in Los Angeles at 11:00 a.m. Tuesday morning on November 16th. See, there really is no such thing as time or space.

This is just a fun observation: November 19, 1999 (11-19-1999), was the last totally odd-number day we will have until January 1, 3111 (1-1-3111). February 2, 2000 (2-2-2000) was a totally even-number day. The last time that occurred was on August 28, 888 (8-28-888).

On the Winter Solstice, December 21-22, 1999, the Full Moon reached Lunar perigee, or its closest point to the Earth. During that unique set of circumstances, the activation of Humanity's creative brain centers was intensified. That event catapulted us further into the *new Renaissance* and triggered new possibilities for technological discoveries.

Just to give you a glimpse of the things that are awaiting us, the last time the Full Moon, Lunar perigee and Winter Solstice all took place at the same time was in 1866. Thomas Edison's first invention was a voice recorder that was issued a patent on October 11, 1868. Shortly thereafter, Nikola Tesla discovered the alternate current power system (AC), which is the basis of our systems of electricity to this day.

Look at the amazing things we have accomplished in the way of technological advancements since 1866. The difference is, this time we are going to move forward into uncharted areas without polluting and destroying the body of Mother Earth in the process. Through our *awakened* consciousness, our newly-discovered technological expertise is going to allow us to heal the maladies on Earth. We are going to develop the viable solutions for poverty, hunger, homelessness, disease, health care, substance abuse, war, corruption, crime, pain and suffering, aging and death as we know it, pollution and every other distorted human miscreation.

January 1, 2000, was the midpoint of the gestation period of our 5th-Dimensional Solar Christ Presence. The new millennium ushered in the dawn of the *Permanent Golden Age of Spiritual Freedom, Eternal Peace and Limitless Abundance.*

Throughout history, Golden Ages have come and Golden Ages have gone, but for the very first time in the evolution of our planet, this Golden Age is being called *permanent*. The reason is that in past Golden Ages, illumined souls would come into physical embodiment, and through the radiance of their Light, they were able to lift up all of those who were within their spheres of influence. Unfortunately, when it was time for the illumined souls to leave the physical plane, their Light was withdrawn. Since the people they left behind could not sustain the higher consciousness without the support of the Light of the illumined soul, they faltered and fell to their previous states of awareness. That situation tragically resulted in the end of that Golden Age.

This Golden Age is going to be different. In this dawning Age, there is not going to be *one* illumined soul or Avatar who comes into the physical plane to bring the next level of Truth to Humanity. This time Humanity is awakening en masse, and we are remembering that we are Sons and Daughters of God. We are taking our power back and transforming our human egos into the Light. We are lifting up in consciousness and becoming One with our God Selves and the Divine Heart and Mind of God.

This is a Permanent Golden Age because one person will not leave the physical plane and withdraw his or her Light, thus causing those left behind to fall. This time, no matter who leaves the Earth, those remaining will have developed the ability to sustain Christ Consciousness on their own. This, in fact, is the true meaning of what Jesus was talking about when he referred to the second coming of The Christ.

On December 31, 1999, as each consecutive time zone struck the sacred moment of midnight, unprecedented Light from the heart of our Father-Mother God poured through the cup of Humanity's focused attention and bathed the Earth. During that Cosmic Moment, the Earth and ALL her life moved forward into the full embrace of the Age of Aquarius. Aquarius will now bathe the Earth in the Seventh Solar Aspect of Deity for the next 2,000-year cycle. This is the day of the Seventh Angel, and he is beginning to sound!

The Seventh Solar Aspect of Deity pulsates with the perfect balance of our Father-Mother God. The sapphire blue Ray of Divine Will, Power and Authority of our Father God and the crystalline pink Ray of Divine Love, Adoration and Reverence for Life of our Mother God created the perfect forcefield of Light for the birth of our 5th- Dimensional Solar Christ Presences.

In spite of all of the gloom and doom soothsayers and the fear about the Y2K (year 2000) computer problem, Humanity proved once again that when we join together in an attitude of cooperation and one-pointed consciousness, we can change the course of history. The potential for serious Y2K problems was real, but instead of succumbing to that potential, people all over the world joined together and developed viable solutions that averted a global catastrophe.

Instead of allowing our fear-based human egos to focus on the potential negative results of the Y2K bug, legions of Lightworkers around the planet joined forces to cocreate an alternative reality. Daily and hourly, Lightworkers invoked the God Presence of every person on the planet who could make a positive difference. We invoked the Light of God Illumination, Truth, Understanding, Wisdom and Enlightenment to flow into each person's conscious mind and feelings. That Light activated within them the knowledge necessary to solve the problems.

The result of Humanity's unified efforts confirmed beyond a shadow of a doubt that the Light of God is *always* victorious, and *we* are that Light!

It is imperative that we grasp the magnitude of that outer world demonstration. What it means is that when we are willing to pool our efforts and our resources for the highest good of all concerned, we can solve the maladies of the world. This is true, regardless of what we are talking about. At this very moment, we have all of the technology, resources, knowledge, skill, wisdom and ability we need to solve the problems of the world. This may sound like a monumental task, but it just takes a slight adjustment in our consciousness.

The moment we shift from a consciousness of separation to a consciousness of Oneness, we will know and understand that we have no choice but to live together in harmony if we want peace and abundance. The family of Humanity is totally and completely interdependent, interconnected and interrelated. What affects one person affects us all. We cannot harm another Human Being or another part of life without harming ourselves. When that Truth sinks into our awareness, then the concept of war, hatred, prejudice, crime, corruption, violence, selfishness, greed, poverty, dominance, aggression, abuse of power and every other destructive human behavior becomes ludicrous, self-destructive and obviously insane.

On February 5, 2000, during a powerful New Moon Solar Eclipse, the Chinese New Year of the Golden Dragon was born. The Year of the Golden Dragon has not fallen on a new millennium for 3,000 years. Amazingly, on that day tremendous Solar Flares that looked like a huge dragon were filmed expanding from the Sun. The pictures were posted on the Internet by astronomers and sent around the world.

The Year of the Golden Dragon represented a powerful, creative time. It enhanced clarity, purity, precision, structure and brought matters to the surface for healing. The Golden Dragon is a symbol of peace and prosperity.

With the assistance of the Solar Eclipse, new frequencies of Healing Light expanded through the Crystal Grid System, and a higher frequency of Solar Christ Light than Humanity had previously been able to withstand bathed the Earth.

Opening the Portal of Light in Thailand

Kay and I were asked to speak at the Silver Dove 2000 World Congress, February 14-19, 2000, in Chiang Mai, Thailand. On February 13th, we arrived in Bangkok. In spite of all of the difficult things that have occurred in that region, Thailand has very deep spiritual roots. The word Thailand actually means Freedom. Thailand is known as "The Jewel of the East," and Bangkok is called the "City of Angels."

For over 30 years, the actor Yul Brenner focused our attention on Thailand through his incredible performance in the movie and Broadway play "The King and I." Interestingly, in 1999 the movie was remade under the title "Anna and the King." That movie drew the attention of the world to Thailand once again for the activities of Light that were unfolding there. The movie is based on a true story and serves as a very important metaphor for Humanity.

The king represents the masculine side of our human nature that has abused its power by suppressing, dominating and controlling our feminine side which is represented by Anna. As the king opens his heart, he awakens and begins accepting and revering Anna. The evolving relationship between Anna and the king represents the balancing that is taking place between the masculine and feminine within each of us. Anna represents our feminine love nature who is gently teaching the masculine to accept and revere all aspects of life.

Upon arriving in Bangkok, we realized that multidimensional activities of Light were unfolding. Kay and I arranged for a tour of the temples, and when our tour guide arrived, there was only one other tourist with him. Our guide said he didn't know why, but for some reason there were only going to be three people on the tour. He said that was extremely unusual, but we were very lucky because we would be able to spend more quality time at each temple. We got into the van and introduced ourselves to the young man who was going to be with us. His name was Andrew, and he had just arrived from Australia. After touring the temples and spending a few days in Thailand, he was going to visit his mother in England.

The temples in Bangkok are exquisite, and the beauty, reverence and devotion to Gautama Buddha is awe-inspiring. The Thai people believe there is only one Buddha, and all of the statues in all of the temples in Thailand represent Gautama Buddha. Gautama serves in the Spiritual Hierarchy through the Second Solar Aspect of Deity. The Divine Qualities of this aspect are reflected through the yellow-gold Ray of Enlightenment, Wisdom, Understanding, Illumination and Reverence for Life.

At every temple, beautiful wreaths of golden flowers are placed at the feet of the enormous statues of the Buddha. Devotees buy incense, lotus blossom buds, candles and small squares of gold leaf to place before the statues in honor of the Buddha's service to life and the example of the Middle Way he modeled for Humanity.

As we toured each sacred temple, Light poured forth from the Heart of the Great, Great Central Sun into our Heart Flames. We went to the Temple of the Golden Buddha, the Temple of the Reclining Buddha and the Marble Temple. The Spiritual Hierarchy revealed to us that each temple represents an aspect of the Immortal, Victorious Threefold Flame—the Holy Trinity of Father-Power, Mother/Holy Spirit-Love and Christ-Wisdom.

When the three of us completed touring the temples, the Threefold Flames in our hearts expanded out in mighty plumes and formed a magnificent Threefold Flame that engulfed the entire country of Thailand. A Golden Lotus Throne formed in the atmosphere above Thailand, and Gautama Buddha projected his luminous Presence onto the Golden Lotus Throne.

As Gautama breathed in the Breath of Life, the Thousand-Petal, Golden Lotus Blossom of his Crown Chakra of Enlightenment began slowly spinning. As it gently turned, it radiated concentric circles of the Flame of Enlightenment and Reverence for All Life, which reverberated through all of Thailand. We were told by the Spiritual Hierarchy that the activity completed the final step of preparation for the events that would take place during the Silver Dove 2000 World Congress.

Later that afternoon, we traveled to Chiang Mai to join with Lightworkers from various parts of the world who had selflessly come to serve as instruments of God. The congress began on February 14, 2000, Valentine's Day, the day celebrated over much of the world as a day of love. The opening event of the congress was the Peace Pole Dedication Ceremony. The Peace Pole Project is a worldwide, grassroots effort to bring the powerful message of peace to the people of all lands. At that time, more than 100,000 Peace Poles had been dedicated in more than 160 countries.

As we were preparing to attend the Peace Pole Ceremony, the music playing through the sound system at the hotel was Whitney Houston's song *"The Greatest Love of All."* There could not have been a more appropriate song to celebrate Valentine's Day and the

Peace Ceremony.

The Peace Pole Dedication ceremony took place at the 700-Year Sports Stadium in Chiang Mai. When Peace Poles are anchored into the body of Mother Earth, they function as acupuncture needles and activate the acupuncture points along Earth's meridians. During that process, the frequencies of peace are magnetized through the poles into the Crystal Grid System. The Golden Light of Peace is then transmitted through the Earth to bless all life. Each Peace Pole has the words *"May Peace Prevail on Earth"* written on it in several languages

When the Peace Pole was anchored firmly into the Earth in Thailand, the acupuncture point at that location, which had been dormant for millennia, was activated. That began an incredible process of healing and awaking that continued throughout the entire week.

The attention of the world was turned to Thailand during that week because the United Nations was holding a special summit in Bangkok. According to newspaper reports, there were 198 world leaders gathered in Bangkok to discuss the problems and solutions for world trade on this increasingly, interdependent planet. The global focus of Humanity's attention created a Chalice of Light that enabled the God Selves of Humanity and the Company of Heaven to accomplish the next phase of the Divine Plan.

Once the Light of God began flowing through the meridians of the Crystal Grid System into the newly-activated acupuncture point in Thailand, the original Divine Intent of that land began to awaken within the very core of the Earth. The Spiritual Hierarchy revealed to us that Thailand was originally a powerful portal through which once flowed patterns of perfection from the Causal Body of God that were associated with reverence for the Elemental Kingdom.

Aeons ago, when Humanity fell into the throes of chaos and negativity, the portal in Thailand was closed and for all intents and purposes was rendered dormant. As the result of that tragic event, Humanity further separated ourselves from the Elemental Kingdom, and our knowledge about that lifeform was all but lost.

We forgot that everything existing on Earth is comprised of the substance created by the Elemental Kingdom. We forgot that the Elementals are intelligent lifeforms who are here to support and assist us in this school of learning. That lack of awareness caused us to perceive Mother Earth as a dead, inanimate object, and we actually came to believe that the Earth, the animals and the nature kingdom were here for us to use and abuse as we willed. This caused a great schism to form between Humanity and the Elemental Kingdom. The horrific effects of that breach resulted in the aging, degeneration, disease and death (as we know it) of our physical bodies. It resulted in plagues, famine, pestilence, destructive weather conditions, poverty, lack, limitation and all manner of physical imperfection.

Throughout the week of the Silver Dove 2000 Congress, the portal in Thailand was opened to full breadth and the Flame of Reverence for ALL Life flooded the Earth. The service that the Elemental Kingdom provides to Humanity will now filter into our conscious minds. People everywhere will begin to understand the necessity of working in harmony with the Elemental Kingdom in order to cocreate the perfection of Heaven on Earth.

One afternoon while Kay and I were shopping at the wonderful market in Chiang Mai, I was contemplating the significance of what was occurring in Thailand. All of a sudden, I became aware that another of Whitney Houston's songs was blasting out onto the streets from a little radio in the back of one of the stores. It was a song she sang for the opening ceremonies at one of the Olympic Games called *"One Moment in Time."* In every sense of the word, this is Humanity's one moment in time.

I am always astounded at how many signs are being given to each of us to encourage and support our humble efforts and our service to the Light. All we have to do is pay attention, and we will see God's support every single day.

On the final day of the congress, we went to a beautiful elephant reserve in the Chiang Mai mountains. There we experienced the beauty and regal presence of many magnificent elephants. Elephants are revered in Thailand and honored as sacred symbols of strength and wisdom. As we communed with the largest land mammals in the Elemental Kingdom, we experienced a new sense of trust, joy and healing.

Later that day we traveled to a retreat called Mount and Sky Resort. The retreat is glorious, and it is nestled in the last of the foothills of the Himalaya Mountains. If I had tried to envision a celestial-garden Shangri-La, I could not have come up with a more beautiful vision. We walked through the exquisite gardens amidst a plethora of flowers and stopped to refresh ourselves at a quaint tea house. As we basked in the beauty of the flowers, mountains, sky and fresh air, I had a profound inner knowing that the Company of Heaven was showing us what this planet will be like when Humanity and the Elemental Kingdom are working in harmony once again. I personally felt that our experience there was a gift from the Spiritual Hierarchy to let us know that the restoration of the planet is being accomplished God-Victoriously and to encourage us to "keep on keeping on."

That night we attended the final event for the congress, and we all gathered under the stars. We had a Full Moon meditation with a candlelighting ceremony, a Sacred Fire ceremony, prayers, heart sharings, laughter, love, joy, communion and friendship. It was the perfect way to expand the newly-opened portal of Reverence for ALL Life. The significance of the opening of that portal means that Humanity is finally ready to consciously work with the Elemental Kingdom. When our work together is complete, the planet will be restored to the limitless physical perfection of Heaven on Earth.

The next morning, Kay and I bid adieu to everyone and returned to Bangkok. We were not scheduled to leave for America until the following morning, so we decided to make our final hours in Thailand special. We went to the Grand Palace and visited the wondrous Temple of the Emerald Buddha. It is an understatement to say that it was an awesome experience. The grandeur of the palace is magnificent, and the feeling of reverence in the Temple of the Emerald Buddha is Heavenly.

After we left the Grand Palace, we walked across the street to the river and took a long-boat ride down to a beautiful hotel named Shangri-La. On Sunday afternoon, the Shangri-La serves High Tea, and we decided to attend. There were beautiful Thai girls carving magnificent sculptured arrangements out of fruit. There were ice sculptures, beautiful tables with an array of delicacies to eat, elegant floral arrangements and a wonderful orchestra. The orchestra played waltzes, mambos, tangos, cha-chas, fox trots and various other ballroom dances. We truly enjoyed watching the couples joyously glide across the dance floor on a Sunday afternoon. It was the perfect ending to a perfect trip.

The next morning Kay and I got up at 3:00 a.m. to begin our journey home to America. Our trip was long, but smooth. We were delighted to arrive home to the welcome embrace of our very special, loving husbands. Kay and I are both blessed beyond measure to have such wonderful, loving supportive husbands. What a gift!

Giant Rock Splits

The following event took place within days of the opening of the Elemental portal in Thailand.
(From the High Desert Star newspaper,
Wednesday, February 23, 2000.)

Landers, CA - Before Monday morning, Giant Rock in the Joshua Tree, California, area was considered by many the largest freestanding boulder in the world. It is now two boulders. A slice of the rock fell off from the boulder at 8:20 a.m. Monday, exposing a gleaming white granite interior.

A letter from James Twyman:

"In ancient times, Giant Rock was held sacred by the native peoples of the Joshua Tree area. So sacred, in fact, that only the chief was allowed to go near it. Everyone else had to wait nearly a mile away while the chief communed with the spirits of the "Rock" People who had prophesied the day when the Mother would split open and a New Era would be revealed. Most other traditions have pointed to this time in our history as the awakening of the Divine Feminine and the creation of a world based upon compassion and peace. Now that Giant Rock has split, many people believe that the prophecy has been fulfilled.

"In my latest book, *The Secret of the Beloved Disciple*, I wrote extensively about two important shamans in this area, Shri Naath Devi and Father John, a priest from Los Angeles. This letter is in regard to the important happenings that took place at an integration with Shri Naath Devi and Father John a mile away from Giant Rock during the two days prior to the boulder splitting. I believe that this story needs to be shared with as many people as possible, so we can focus our prayers and energy on the important Era we have so recently entered.

"On February 19 and 20, 2000, Shri Naath Devi was inspired to bring a number of powerful healers to the desert near Giant Rock to pray and meditate. She said that the native peoples were no longer doing ceremonies in this area and that the Earth itself was about to react with a violent upheaval. If the Mother accepted the prayers that were scheduled, then Giant Rock would crack at the side, relieving pressure on the Earth's tectonic plates. If the prayers were not accepted, then Giant Rock would split directly down the middle. The fact that Giant Rock has not moved for millions of years made remote the likelihood of such a change. And yet, the next morning, to everyone's amazement, the boulder had not cracked—rather one-third of the rock had split away and fallen to the desert floor. Shri Naath Devi interpreted this in the most positive Light. She said that the Mother had opened her arms to us, cracking open her heart for the whole world to see.

"Father John was there for part of the prayers. He, too, felt the incredible shift and joined two of my assistants who had participated in the prayers with Shri Naath Devi. As they stood in the kitchen discussing the events, lightning struck, sending a ball of Light through the center of the house in a north/south direction. Within moments, lightning struck again and shot through the house in an east/west direction. This was a very auspicious moment and was witnessed by all four people. Shri Naath Devi declared that the prayers were now complete and that the lightning was honoring the four directions as a sign from the Mother that supported this completion. The boulder split open only two hours prior to this gathering.

"What does all this mean?

"We stand at the threshold of an amazing opportunity. This is the time when we rediscover within ourselves the peace and compassion of the Divine, and the Earth itself will mirror this shift. There have been many signs over the last few years: the White Buffalo calf, comets that have come and comets that will come again over the next few months. All these lead us to believe that the time the ancients have called the 'Great Shift' is at hand."

Amazing Information from NASA

[Author's Note: On February 24, 2000, NASA reported the largest and most profound Solar Flares ever recorded. The increased influx of Solar Light pierced into our pituitary, pineal, hypothalamus glands and the ganglionic centers at the base of our brains. That Solar Light activation caused chemical changes within our brains, which opened us further to multidimensional experiences.

We were in the 11-year Solar Flare cycle, and our Twelve Solar Strands of DNA were gradually being recalibrated, preparing us to walk and talk with the Company of Heaven, Angels and Elementals. Some interesting reports from a NASA/GSFC press release confirmed the incredible Solar activation that had begun less than a year before.]

NASA Report

"On May 10-12, 1999, the solar winds that blow constantly from the Sun virtually disappeared—the most drastic and longest-lasting decrease ever observed.

"Starting late on May 10, 1999, and continuing through the early hours of May 12, 1999, NASA's AME and Wind spacecraft each observed that the density of the solar wind dropped by more than 98 percent. Because of the decrease, energetic electrons from the Sun were able to flow to Earth in narrow beams known as the strahl. Under normal conditions, electrons from the Sun are diluted, mixed, and redirected in interplanetary space and by Earth's magnetic field (the magnetosphere). But in May 1999, several satellites detected electrons arriving at Earth with properties similar to those of electrons in the Sun's corona, suggesting that they were a direct sample of particles from the Sun.

"Fourteen years ago, Dr. Jack Scudder, space physicist from the University of Iowa, and Don Fairfield of NASA's Goddard Space Flight Center predicted the details of an event such as occurred on May 11, 1999, saying that it would produce an intense 'polar rain' of electrons over one of the polar caps of Earth. The polar caps typically do not receive enough energetic electrons to produce a visible aurora. But in an intense polar rain event, Scudder and Fairfield theorized, the 'strahl' electrons would flow unimpeded along the Sun's magnetic field lines to Earth and precipitate directly into the polar caps, inside the normal auroral oval. Such a polar rain event was observed for the first time in May 1999, when the polar instrument detected a steady glow over the north pole in X-ray images.

"In parallel with the polar rain event, Earth's magnetosphere swelled to five to six times its normal size. NASA's Wind, IMP-8 and Lunar Prospector spacecraft, the Russian INTERBALL satellite and the Japanese Geotail satellite observed the most distant bow shock ever recorded by satellites. Earth's bow shock is the shock front where the solar winds slam into the Sunward edge of the magnetosphere.

"According to observations from the ACE spacecraft, the density of helium in the solar wind dropped to less than 0.1

percent of its normal value, and heavier ions, held back by the Sun's gravity, apparently could not escape from the Sun at all. Data from NASA's SAMPEX spacecraft reveals that in the wake of this event, Earth's outer electron radiation belts dissipated and were severely depleted for several months afterward."

On March 26, 2000, we held one of our Free Seminars in Atlanta, Georgia. We arrived on Saturday afternoon and joined some other Lightworkers at Stone Mountain. We took the sky lift to the top of the tremendous monolith and quietly walked around as we absorbed the incredible energy being transmitted by the Record-Keeper Crystals. After a while we sat and just listened to the silence as we watched a magnificent hawk circle below us. We became aware that off in the distance a carillon was playing, and the melody wafting through the ethers on the tones of the beautiful bells was Ave Maria.

The next day, approximately 250 people gathered at the hotel for the seminar. We were joined by the Company of Heaven, the God Selves of all Humanity and the focused attention of Lightworkers who were tuning in with us from around the world. The Spiritual Hierarchy asked us to assist with the preparation for the Grand Planetary Alignment that would take place in May.

Because of the rarity and strength of that upcoming planetary alignment, many people were responding to their fear-based human egos and predicting cataclysmic earth changes. The Spiritual Hierarchy asked us to reinforce the weak spots on the planet. Through music, meditations and visualizations, the Golden Light of Eternal Peace flowed through our Heart Flames into the vulnerable places in the body of Mother Earth and created an invincible forcefield of protection. It is very important for us to understand that Divine Intervention was necessary, not because of the potential danger of the Grand Planetary Alignment, but because of the thoughtforms of fear that were created and broadcast by people who were not perceiving the Truth of that glorious event.

The second thing we were asked to do in Atlanta was to assist in further activating the Record-Keeper Crystals that contain the contingency plan for raising the vibration of Humanity's physical, etheric, mental and emotional bodies. It was critical that our four lower bodies be lifted into a vibratory rate that would easily withstand the frequencies of our 5th-Dimensional Solar Christ Selves. During our seminar the expanded activation of those particular Record-Keeper Crystals was victoriously accomplished.

On May 3, 2000, the nine-month gestation period for Humanity's 5th-Dimensional Solar Christ Presence came to fruition. On that day, all seven visible planets: the Sun, Moon, Mercury, Venus, Mars, Jupiter and Saturn, aligned within a tight, geocentric sector of 27 degrees in the Sun Cycle of Taurus. The Grand Alignment of planets took place predominantly on the other side of the Sun, and we experienced very little physical stress on this side of the Sun. Astrologers say that the last time this particular alignment occurred was 2,000 years ago during the birth of Jesus. It is believed that the Light from that alignment was what the shepherds in the Holy Land and the three Wise Men referred to as the Star of Bethlehem.

The unique alignment of planets 2,000 years ago opened a portal of Light from the Heart of our Father-Mother God into the center of the Earth. The influx of Light that resulted from the opening of that portal ushered in the Age of Pisces and created the environment for the rebirth of Christ Consciousness on Earth.

Now, during the dawning of the Age of Aquarius, the same alignment was once again creating a portal of Light from the Heart of our Father-Mother God into the center of the Earth. This time, the opening of that portal was ushering in the Age of Aquarius and the initial impulse of the *second* coming of The Christ, *the Birth of Humanity's 5th-Dimensional Solar Christ Presence*.

The colossal portal of Light that was opened during the Grand Planetary Alignment on May 3, 2000, blazed forth from the heart of our omnipotent, omniscient, omnipresent Father-Mother God: the all-encompassing *Cosmic I AM—All That Is.* It then flowed into the hearts of the representatives of our Father-Mother God in the various dimensions of our Solar System: *Beloved El and Ela* from the *Great, Great Central Sun, Beloved Elohae and Eloha* from the *Great Central Sun, Beloved Alpha and Omega* from the *Central Sun* and *Beloved Helios and Vesta* from our *physical Sun.* The portal of Light was then projected through the birth canal for the Planet Earth in Australia and into the *Sun of Even Pressure* in the center of the Earth.

Once the portal was secure, the Light from our Christ Presence poured through the portal and expanded out through the Crystal Grid System. The Light blazed into the core of purity in every electron and prepared the Heart Flame of each person for the birth of the 5th-Dimensional Solar Christ Presence.

The birth took place within every Heart Flame during the apex of the Grand Planetary Alignment and the New Moon of Taurus. That Cosmic Hour occurred on May 3, 2000, between 8:41 p.m. and 9:41 p.m. Pacific Daylight Time. The New Moon occurred at 9:11 p.m. It is truly breathtaking to witness the synchronicity of the miraculous, unfolding Divine Plan.

The effect of the birth of our 5th-Dimensional Solar Christ Presence is going to be a very individual and unique experience for each of us. No two people will respond to this miracle in exactly the same way. What is actually occurring is that for the very first time in our Earthly sojourn, our 5th-Dimensional Solar Christ Presence have access to the physical plane through our physical bodies. In Ages past, this aspect of our own Divinity functioned in Realms of Light that were beyond the reach of our physical bodies. Now we have raised the energy, vibration and consciousness of our bodies effectively enough to withstand the 5th-Dimensional frequencies of Solar Light.

It is up to each of us to integrate our Solar Christ Presence into our physical, etheric, mental and emotional bodies. This will happen gradually according to our individual Divine Plans and our ability to sustain harmonious vibrations through our thoughts, words, actions and feelings. Our Solar Christ Presence will guide us and assist us in this process. We just need to pay attention and invoke their help.

The exciting news is that when this integration is complete we will reflect the Limitless Physical Perfection of our *Solar Light Bodies*. This means we will have bodies that are vibrantly healthy, eternally youthful and radiantly beautiful. The mutated manifestations of disease, aging, death, degeneration, decay and every other human miscreation cannot survive in the Solar Frequencies of the 5th Dimension.

Just imagine, this is the first step of our permanent Ascension into Limitless Physical Perfection. This is what we have been working and struggling toward for aeons of time.

After the Solar Christ Presence of each evolving soul was born in each heart, it was bathed in the Immortal, Victorious Threefold Flame. For *eleven* days, every Solar Christ Presence was nurtured and integrated into the physical plane through the Divine Balance of Love, Wisdom and Power. Then, on May 14, 2000, while people in the United States of America celebrated Mother's Day, the Feminine Aspects of our Mother God throughout the Universe descended into the atmosphere of Earth and blessed Humanity with an unprecedented gift of Light.

As hundreds of millions of people in this country focused on our Mother's love, Humanity's right- and left-brain hemispheres were brought into balance the maximum each soul could endure. After that balancing, Beloved Gautama in his full capacity as the Solar Cosmic Buddha and Beloved Jesus in his full capacity as the Solar Cosmic Christ breathed the Breath of Life into every souls' awakening Crown Chakra of Enlightenment. The Breath of Life blazed down into our Heart Chakras and opened the Stargate of our Mother God to full breadth. Our Mother God reclaimed full dominion of our Heart Chakras, and She will never be denied access to the physical plane of Earth again.

Opening the Portal for the Causal Body of God

When we were first breathed forth from the Heart of God, we were given a Causal Body as part of our Vehicles of Light. In the beginning, our Causal Body reflected all of the patterns of perfection contained in the Causal Body of God. The original plan was for our God Selves to observe the various patterns of perfection and through our creative faculties of thought and feeling, project those patterns onto the physical plane.

Once we fell into the paralyzing grip of our human egos who distorted our gift of life into horrendous mutations, a Divine Edict was issued to withhold the good of our Causal Bodies. In a merciful act of Divine Grace, God issued a Fiat to our God Selves to withhold the patterns of perfection in our Causal Bodies, so they would not be distorted into gross miscreations by our human egos.

A Cosmic Dispensation was issued at the same time declaring that every thought, word, action or feeling we expressed that was qualified with 51 percent or more Light would rise up into our Causal Bodies and be stored there until a future time when Humanity returned to Christ Consciousness. That Cosmic Dispensation was issued literally aeons ago, and the good of our Causal Bodies has been building in momentum for thousands of years.

We were told by the Spiritual Hierarchy that due to the incredible activities of Light that had taken place, the collective Solar Christ Presence of Humanity had finally reached a critical mass of vibration that would sustain Christ Consciousness on Earth. We were, at long last, in a position to have the good of our Causal Bodies released to us. That meant that the patterns of perfection from the Causal Body of God which had been withheld from Humanity for millennia could now return to Earth. To understand the full significance of that, we must realize that these are the patterns that contain all of the perfection of Heaven on Earth.

In order to fulfill that facet of the Divine Plan, we were asked by the Spiritual Hierarchy to gather Lightworkers within the portal of the Causal Body of God, which pulsates in the waters off the coast of Alaska for the fourteenth Harmonic Convergence. To comply with that request, we organized an Alaskan Cruise for the Fourteenth Annual World Congress On Illumination, August 14-21, 2000.

The Spiritual Hierarchy revealed to us that through the Heart Flames of the Lightworkers gathered on the Alaskan Cruise, the portal of the Causal Body of God would be opened to full breadth. The patterns of perfection from the Causal Body of God would then flood into Humanity's Causal Bodies and trigger the release of the good that has been accumulating there for thousands of years.

On August 12, 2000, my husband and I began our pilgrimage to the Fourteenth Annual World Congress On Illumination. First, we traveled to Vancouver, BC, and took a ferry to Vancouver Island for a couple of days. We stayed in the beautiful town of Victoria at the Ocean Point Resort.

When we arrived, there was a gentle mist rolling in off the water that engulfed Victoria in a rather mystical cloak of Light. Our coach driver, our taxi cab driver and the bell clerk at the hotel all told us that as long as they had lived in Victoria, they had never seen a mist like that before.

That evening my husband and I took a walk along the banks of the water and just absorbed the beauty and radiance of Victoria. We both felt the incredible power of the unfolding Divine Plan, and we felt like we were part of a glorious, multidimensional celebration that was taking place in the Inner Realms.

The next morning we arranged for a tour of Butchard Gardens, and we were to meet the tour guide in the lobby at 9:30 a.m. While we were waiting for the tour bus, the Canadian Olympic Basketball Team came into the lobby. They had played an exhibition game the night before, and they were preparing, at that moment, to leave for Australia.

The Divine Plan for the Summer Olympic Games in Australia was unfolding, and I knew it was not by chance that the Olympic basketball players were gathering in Victoria within the portal of the Causal Body of God. Nothing is happening by accident, and it is important that we all pay very close attention to the things occurring in our lives. We need to do this so that we will not miss an opportunity to be of service to God and the Light during this unparalleled moment on Earth.

As my husband and I waited for the tour bus, we realized that it was already ten o'clock. We inquired again at the front desk, and the woman said, "I don't know why they haven't picked you up. They are never late." She called the tour line, and they said they didn't understand why we weren't picked up, but they would send someone as soon as possible.

While we were waiting, I noticed that St. Germain's Keynote, the Blue Danube Waltz, was playing through the music system in the hotel. As I focused on the music, I observed that the basketball players were being enveloped in a tremendous forcefield of the Violet Flame. St. Germain revealed to me that the basketball players would carry the new Solar Frequencies of the Violet Flame from the portal of the Causal Body of God to the 2000 Olympic Games in Australia.

He said that as the basketball players traveled to Sydney, they would create a tremendous Rainbow of Light that would connect Australia directly to the portal of the Causal Body of God. Then, during the 2000 Summer Olympic Games, as approximately four-billion people turn their attention to Australia, the patterns of perfection pulsating within the Causal Body of God would flood through the collective Cup of Humanity's consciousness into Uluru—Ayers Rock.

St. Germain said that as those patterns of perfection blaze into Uluru, they would complete the activation of the Record-Keeper Crystals containing the original Divine Plan and the unmanifest Divine Potential for the Earth.

As the lilting strains of the Blue Danube Waltz wafted through the air, my husband and I went out on the balcony away from public view and waltzed to the beautiful music.

There is a very significant reason why St. Germain chose the Strauss Waltzes as his Keynote. The information on the Violet Flame began flowing into Humanity's consciousness toward the end of the 1800s, and, at that time, Humanity could not easily grasp the concept of the need to balance the masculine and feminine polarities of our Father-Mother God. Consequently, St. Germain and the Company of Heaven used the waltz as a way for Humanity to magnetize the frequencies of the Violet Flame into the Earth easily and effortlessly.

The masculine, sapphire blue Ray of Divine Will, Authority and Power activates our left-brain hemisphere and our Throat Chakras. Our *left* brain operates the *right* side of our physical bodies. The feminine, pink Ray of Divine Love activates our right-brain hemisphere and our Heart Chakras. Our *right* brain operates the *left* side of our physical bodies.

When a man and woman are in position to dance the waltz, she places her left hand (feminine) on the back of his neck (masculine Throat Chakra), and he places his right hand (masculine) on the middle of her back (feminine Heart Chakra). Then she places her right hand (masculine) in his left hand (feminine), and together they spin and twirl around the dance floor. As they do, the blue masculine polarity of our Father God and the pink feminine polarity of our Mother God are blended into the beautiful, balanced frequencies of the Violet Flame. For over a century now, men and women have joyously and effortlessly waltzed the Violet Flame into manifestation.

After my husband and I finished waltzing on the balcony, we returned to the lobby of the hotel. A short time later a young girl came in to get us for the tour. She said. "I am sorry, but the tour bus already left. If you don't mind, I am going to take you on a private tour of Butchard Gardens."

Butchard Gardens is an outer-world example of what the Garden of Eden must have looked like when the Earth was first created. It is truly a celestial array of the most beautiful flowers, plants, trees and water fountains. My husband and I wanted to go there before the World Congress because we wanted to connect with the spectacular beauty of this planet prior to offering ourselves as instruments for the opening of the portal of the Causal Body of God.

On August 14, 2000, we took the ferry back to Vancouver to board the cruise ship, which was called the "Dawn Princess." There were 130 people specifically attending the World Congress, and another 2,000 tourists enjoying the cruise with us. We left the dock at 5:30 p.m. to begin our wondrous adventure. That evening we relaxed, enjoyed a beautiful meal and a very special time of reuniting with our precious friends, both old and new, from around the world.

The next day was the Full Moon. It was also August 15th,

Mother Mary's Ascension Day. Each morning of the World Congress we met for two hours in the Princess Theater. During that sacred time, we were joined by the Company of Heaven and the God Selves of all Humanity as we learned the specific facet of the unfolding Divine Plan for the day and aligned with our holy mission.

When our morning activity of Light was complete, several people went out onto the deck of the ship and witnessed over one hundred dolphins joyfully leaping and swimming alongside the ship as they escorted us through the ocean waters.

On August 16, 2000, we were informed by the Spiritual Hierarchy that we had reached the time of the changing of the guard. At that moment, our Father-Mother God sounded a Cosmic Tone, and the Legions of Light who selflessly served Humanity and the Earth throughout the Piscean Age began coming from the far corners of the Earth into the heart of Shamballa. There are many 4th-Dimensional Temples of Light in the atmosphere surrounding the planet, but Shamballa is the Temple of Divine Government for the Spiritual Hierarchy.

Since ancient times, we have known of Shamballa as a Temple of Light pulsating above the Gobi Desert. With all of the shifts of consciousness and the exponential expansion of Light on the planet over the past few decades, that temple has greatly expanded its service. Shamballa now engulfs the entire planet, and the Earth is cradled within the Immortal, Victorious Threefold Flame that blazes on the altar of Shamballa.

As the Legions of Light who served the Piscean Age gathered before the altar at Shamballa, so did the Solar Christ Presence of every man, woman and child evolving on Earth. Humanity's Solar Christ Presence merged into one tremendous body of Light. Then, in a Divine Ceremony, the collective luminous Presence of the Spiritual Hierarchy from the Piscean Age passed their Staff of Power and Divine Service to the collective Solar Christ Presence of Humanity.

In order for us to grasp the magnitude of that honor, we must understand that after the fall, the Spark of Divinity within Humanity's hearts was not strong enough to claim our Divine Birthright as stewards of the Earth. During that very dark time, the Spiritual Hierarchy took over our responsibilities as Earth's caretakers. At the end of an Age, the Staff of Power and Divine Service was passed from the Spiritual Hierarchy representing the closing Age to members of the Spiritual Hierarchy for the dawning new Age. Until now, Humanity was never in a position to accept that role.

Now, for the very first time since the fall, Humanity collectively is resonating at a level of Christ Consciousness that enables us to reclaim our Divine Heritage as stewards of the Earth. During the Divine Ceremony on August 16, 2000, a new facet of the Divine Plan was set into motion, and the 5th-Dimensional Solar Christ Presence of all Humanity were empowered as the official stewards of the Earth.

After the collective body of the Solar Christ Presence of Humanity accepted the Staff of Power and Divine Service from the Spiritual Hierarchy of the Piscean Age, each Solar Christ Presence poured forth love and gratitude to those Beings of Light for the selfless service they have rendered to this sweet Earth for the past 2,000 years. Those precious Beings then gloriously Ascended into a higher octave of Divine Service.

When that phase of the Divine Ceremony was complete, the Seventh Angel, Archangel Zadkiel, sounded a Cosmic Tone. Instantaneously the Legions of Light associated with the Aquarian Age came into the Temple of Shamballa from the far reaches of the Universe.

This time the Spiritual Hierarchy is not coming to accept responsibility on behalf of Humanity as stewards of the Earth; they are coming for the exclusive purpose of working in unison with Humanity's Solar Christ Presence to cocreate the perfection of Heaven On Earth. These selfless servants of our Father-Mother God are bringing new levels of technology that are contained within the Solar frequencies of the Violet Flame.

After the Ceremony of Light, we disembarked and ventured into the little Alaskan town of Ketchikan. Approximately 20 percent of the population of Ketchikan are Alaska Natives. It is one of the wettest spots on the continent and averages over 13 feet of rainfall a year. The indigenous peoples of this region are the Tlingit Indians. The word Ketchikan is derived from a Tlingit phrase which translates into "Thundering Wings of an Eagle."

Our group chose various tours and traversed the little town north, south, east and west. Many of us were setting foot on Alaskan soil for the first time, and as we did, we connected with the Native People and the Elemental Kingdom at a deep, spiritual level. In the afternoon, we returned to the ship and continued our journey up the coast of Alaska.

August 17, 2000, was the fourteenth Harmonic Convergence.

On that day, the Beings of the Aquarian Age breathed in the new technologies associated with the 5th-Dimensional Solar frequencies of the Violet Flame and anchored them into the Sun of Even Pressure in the center of the Earth. Then, on the Holy Breath of God, they projected those technologies into the physical, etheric, mental and emotional strata of Earth.

The new technologies will allow us to download programs of perfection from the Causal Body of God in ways that were never before available to Humanity. Once we grasp these skills, we will be catapulted forward by leaps and bounds in our Ascension process.

On that same day, indigenous peoples from all over the world invoked the masses of Humanity to join them in celebrating the fulfillment of an ancient prophecy—the Native American Rainbow Dream Vision. That vision proclaimed that there would be a time when concerned people would come together to change the world. The indigenous peoples believe that time is now, and they sent forth a clarion all for "The World Gathering" to be held on August 17, 2000.

The prophecy states:

"When the Earth is sick and the animals are dying, there will come a tribe of people from all cultures who believe in words and actions, people who will restore this Earth to her former beauty. This tribe will be known as the Warriors of the Rainbow."

"The World Gathering" called for people all over the planet to gather at sacred sites and places of natural beauty to meditate, pray, chant, tone, sing, dance and commune in the silence. We were asked to participate in these activities for one hour beginning at 12:00 noon local time.

After our morning activity of Light, we disembarked in the town of Juneau. Juneau is the state capital, and it is the largest city in the United States. Juneau is 3,108 square miles, and it is the only state capital in the country that is not accessible by road. The only way to enter the town is by water or air. The population is 30,000.

Once again, our group chose various tours. People flew in float planes and helicopters over the awesome Mendenhall Glacier. They went on wildlife tours, white-water rafting, whale watches, tram rides up to the top of the mountain overlooking Juneau and various hiking trips. The pristine beauty of Alaska is awe inspiring, and it is clear to see why it is known as the last frontier. The rarefied clarity of the air and the pulsating lifeforce emanating from the plants and trees allowed us to commune with the Elemental Kingdom..

On August 18, 2000, the Solar Christ Presence of every person on Earth worked in unison with the Beings of the Aquarian Age and downloaded programs from the new technologies within the 5th-Dimensional Solar Violet Flame. These programs will now assist our Solar Christ Presences to reprogram our conscious minds into a higher perspective and to activate the dormant Divine Patterns within the deepest recesses of our memory banks. This new technology will reprogram the fragmented facets of our DNA and activate the genetic codings of our Divinity.

Our DNA is now a shimmering, waveform configuration that is being modified by Light, radiation, magnetic fields and sonic pulses. With the increase in Solar Flares and the new technology within the Solar Violet Flame, we are experiencing vast changes. The hands of time are shifting, and we are experiencing a rebirth and a new beginning. There is no turning back.

After our morning activities, we disembarked in the town of Skagway. This beautiful, tiny town has a population of 816, sometimes double that number in the summer. When the cruise ships dock, the population increases to approximately 7,000. Needless to say, the town is very focused on entertaining tourists, and it has beautiful shops, historical tours and nature experiences.

On August 19, 2000, the Directors of the Elements took their strategic positions. The Directors of the Air Element were at the cardinal point at the north; the Directors of the Water Element were at the cardinal point at the east; the Directors of the Earth Element were at the cardinal point at the south; the Directors of the Fire Element were at the cardinal point at the west, and the Directors of the Ether Element were in the Sun of Even Pressure in the center of the Earth. Once the Directors were in position, they sent forth a Cosmic Tone to alert the Elemental Kingdoms that an unprecedented moment of healing and transformation was at hand. The Elemental Beings stood in readiness.

Our Father-Mother God breathed in the Solar Violet Flame of Limitless Transmutation and Physical Perfection and projected it into every person's Heart Flame. Then our Father-Mother God sounded their Keynote, and this time the Mighty Solar Elohim responded. These powerful Builders of Form descended into the atmosphere of Earth from the Great, Great Central Sun. The Solar Elohim selflessly volunteered to remain in the atmosphere of Earth until this planet is wholly Ascended and free. They will now carry out their Cosmic Duties from this location in order to render Humanity and the Elemental Kingdom the maximum assistance during the remainder of our Ascension process into the 5th Dimension. This is an event unprecedented in the history of time.

As we basked in the radiance and splendor of the Solar Elohim, we opened our hearts on behalf of all Humanity and sent forth a heart of Divine Love to embrace them. From the deepest recesses of our hearts, we expressed our gratitude and appreciation for their commitment to life and the unfolding Divine Plan on Earth. We thanked them for the sacrifice they are making in order to assist Humanity and Mother Earth.

August 20, 2000, was the day the portal of the Causal Body of God was to be opened to full breadth. The patterns of perfection in the Causal Body of God contain the limitless Divine Potential pulsating in the Heart and Mind of God. They contain the viable solutions for the maladies of the world, and they contain the Divine Technology that will transform this planet into the perfection of Heaven on Earth.

The participants at the World Congress On Illumination gathered in the Princess Theater with a sense of abounding joy and great expectation. As the Divine Ceremony began, we each volunteered to be the Heart, Head and Hands of God in the world of form on behalf of ALL Humanity, and we gave full dominion of our four Earthly vehicles to our Solar Christ Presence.

Next, the Lords of Power and Protection from the Great, Great Central Sun descended into the atmosphere of Earth and stood shoulder to shoulder around the equator of the planet. These Beings of Light projected gigantic bolts of Violet Lightning into the weak spots in the body of Mother Earth. The Lightning shot back and forth through the weakened areas and wove powerful shafts of Light that strengthened and reinforced the vulnerable spots on the planet.

The Lords of Power and Protection then enveloped the Earth and all life evolving here in an invincible forcefield of Divine Comfort and Protection.

The majestic Solar Elohim then came to the fore and increased the Divine Love they had been blazing through the Elemental Kingdom, the Human Kingdom and the Angelic Kingdom. At that point, our Father-Mother God began projecting forth rhythmic pulsations of Light that were specifically designed to break down the crystallized patterns of the human miscreations.

Following that purification, the Solar Christ Presence of every evolving soul downloaded the new programs from the Solar Violet Flame that will result in each person fulfilling the Immaculate Concept of his or her Divine Plan. The new programs created a momentum within our Heart Flames that will help us to easily and effortlessly release the belief systems, behavior patterns and habits that no longer serve our highest good. Our Solar Christ Presence will now, more easily, burst the bonds of limitation and pierce through the walls and barriers that have prevented us from moving forward. As this occurs, we will each move to our next level of Divine Service, and we will step over the threshold of multidimensional awareness onto a glorious new path filled with Divine Purpose and Joy.

As the inner knowing of that Divine Truth awakened within the Lightworkers at the World Congress, we experienced an energy shift, and our Solar Christ Presence stretched us beyond what we previously perceived to be our comfort zones. We passed through the doorway into a new life experience. We moved into a totally different reality spectrum, and as we consciously chose to ignite our Light, we each experienced an *Epiphany!* The New Heaven and the New Earth became a tangible reality, and we perceived and understood with "*new eyes and new ears.*"

Under the guidance of our Solar Christ Presence, we then turned our attention to the Elemental Kingdom. In our new capacity as stewards of the Earth, we sent our love to the Elemental Beings and invoked them to prepare for the opening of the portal of the Causal Body of God. Each Elemental responded and stood in readiness. The Deva Rajas and Devas came from the four corners of the Earth and took their strategic positions within the forcefield of the portal of the Causal Body of God. They joined the collective body of the Solar Christ Presence of all Humanity and stood in readiness.

Then Legions of Light from Galaxies beyond Galaxies and Suns beyond Suns projected their luminous Presence into the forcefield of the portal of the Causal Body of God. Finally, the Angelic Kingdom and all of the various graded orders of Angels entered the forcefield. Once the Angels were in place, ALL was in readiness!

As one heartbeat, one breath, one voice, one energy, vibration and consciousness of pure Divine Love, those gathered in the portal of the Causal Body of God became One with the omniscient, omnipresent, omnipotent Cosmic I AM—All That Is. In perfect unison we inhaled the Breath of Life from the core of Creation and breathed it into the portal. In one glorious instant, the portal of the Causal Body of God opened to full breadth. The patterns of perfection from the Causal Body of God flooded into Humanity's Causal Bodies and triggered the release of the good that has been accumulating there for thousands of years. The patterns of perfection then flowed into the mental, emotional, etheric and physical strata of Earth. Now, the limitless Perfection of God is available to every facet of life on Earth, *"As it was in the beginning, is now and forever shall be. Amen!"*

The rest of our time on the cruise was spent absorbing the splendor of the glaciers, the wildlife and the beauty of Alaska. At various times during our sojourn, we saw orca whales, humpback whales and beluga whales. We also saw dolphins, sea lions, sea otters, salmon, sea gulls and jelly fish. On land we saw grizzly bears, moose, caribou, Dall sheep, eagles, hawks, marmots, Arctic ground squirrels, beavers and various other small birds and animals native to Alaska.

Our cruise ended at Seward where we disembarked and took land coaches to Anchorage. From there we all went in various directions. Some people returned home, and some took tours to other inland locations in Alaska. Several of us wanted to experience the spacious wilderness of Alaska, so after spending a night in Anchorage, we took an eight-hour, domed-train ride to Denali Park. Denali is a beautiful national park and wildlife preserve that covers six-million acres of land. It is home to 37 mammal species and 156 bird species.

Denali is also the home of Mt. McKinley *(The native people of Alaska refer to the mountain as Denali which means "the Great One.")* Mt. McKinley is the highest mountain peak on the North American continent. It is 20,320 feet above sea level. There are mountains in the world that are higher above sea level, for instance Mt. Everest is 24,000 feet above sea level, but the base of Mt. McKinley is only 3,000 feet above sea level, so from the base to the summit it rises an amazing 17,000 feet. No other mountain in the world ascends that quickly.

We took an eight-hour bus tour of Denali Park. It had snowed the night before our tour, and the clouds were still very thick as we began our adventure into the park at 5:30 a.m. Our guide said the weather had been very unusual during the summer and that no one had seen the mountain for months. He said due to the snow and rain, we wouldn't be able to see it that day either.

As we progressed on the tour, our guide, with great enthusiasm, said that the clouds had a slight break in them about halfway down the mountain, and we could see a bit of the snow on Mt. McKinley if we looked very quickly. The snow had a beautiful soft pink hue from the rays of the rising morning Sun, and the energy emanating from the mountain was incredibly powerful.

As we journeyed through the park, we saw grizzly bears, Dall sheep, bull moose, caribou and several different species of birds. The fresh layer of snow was absolutely beautiful. People kept apologizing to us about the rain and snow, but some of us were from Tucson, Arizona, where it had been between 106 and 110 degrees all summer, so we thought the weather was glorious.

After a while we turned a corner on the winding road through the park and, to the amazement of our tour guide, we beheld the awesome sight of a *cloudless* Mt. McKinley. Our guide took us to an outlook that was just 30 miles away, and by the time we got off of the bus, there was not a single cloud in the sky. The crescent Moon was radiating in the crystal blue sky, and the full view of the mountain glistened in a rare and beautiful brilliance.

Several other tour buses joined us, and one of the drivers said, "I have been driving this bus for seventeen years, and I have never seen the mountain this clear." All of us knew that we were being given a very special gift, and we expressed our gratitude to God and the Elemental Kingdom.

After spending time enjoying the view of Mt. McKinley, we boarded the buses and began our journey back to the resort. As soon as we were on the road, the clouds began to return, and by the time we got to the hotel, there was a thick cover of clouds in the sky again.

After spending a few more wonderful days in Alaska, we returned home.

The 2000 Summer Olympic Games

On November 11, 1999, the activation began for the Record-Keeper Crystals in Ayers Rock/Uluru and the activation of those crystals had been slowly building in momentum day by day.

The Olympic Flame

At midday on May 10th, 2000, the Olympic Flame was kindled from the Sun's rays in Olympia, Greece. The torch was carried for 10 days around Greece, then taken by plane to Guam. It spent the next 17 days traveling the tropical roads and waters of 112 Pacific islands that make up the Oceania Ring of Olympic nations. A replica of the torch was even sent into space for 10 days aboard the Space Shuttle *Atlantis*.

The Olympic Flame traveled in 14 canoes on its way through the Oceania Ring. In New Zealand, it rode on a gondola, a mountain bike and skied down Coronet Peak. On June 8th, it finally arrived by plane at Uluru, the ancient heart of Australia. *When the Flame was lit at Uluru, the full activation of the Record-Keeper Crystals began.* For the next 100 days, the Olympic Flame traveled in many different ways around the country.

The torch was carried on a surf boat at Bondi Beach, on the Indian Pacific train across the Nullabor Plain, on a Flying Doctor Service aircraft across the outback, by camel on Cable Beach at Broome and underwater by a scuba diver in the Great Barrier Reef.

In a spectacular, emotion-charged moment, a torchbearer entered the Sydney Olympic Stadium and a succession of athletes completed the longest torch relay in Olympic history. In Australia, 11,000 torchbearers carried the Flame 27,000 kilometers to its final destination.

Opening Ceremonies of the Olympic Games

On September 15, 2000, as an estimated four-billion people focused on the Opening Ceremonies, a tremendous Chalice of Light was formed, and the symbology and spiritual influence of the ceremonies opened the hearts of Humanity.

The 27th Olympiad of the Modern Era

199 Nations participated.
A *33*-year old *woman* read the Olympic Oath.

Various segments demonstrated the life and beauty of Australia. They were titled: *Awakening, Arrival, Eternity, Unity and Reconciliation.* A tapestry of the Wagina—Creation Spirit—was present to unite the group, and an enormous Dove of Peace blessed the ceremonies. Fire breathers, Aboriginal dancers, singers, children and people from all walks of life participated in the unfolding story. When the Olympic Flag was raised, Vanessa Amorosi sang a beautiful song. The music and lyrics are by John Gillard.

Heroes Live Forever

You are the Light that shines in everyone
The Truth that's there for all to see
You are the voice that speaks to everyone
You're the heroes we'd all like to be
You live the dreams that lie within us all
With a passion that cannot be denied
You bring the whole world together as One
And we'll always be by your side
And all the world will join in celebration
And all the world will share the joy you bring
And all the power, the hope, the inspiration
In all their glory, the nations will sing
Heroes live forever
Always we'll remember
Heroes live forever
Since the dawn of history
In searching for our destiny
To be the best that we can be
We've found our immortality

To honor the 100 years of women's participation in the Olympic Games, several women athletes who competed in previous Olympics took turns carrying the Olympic Flame into the stadium. As they did, a beautiful song was sung by Tina Arena. The words and music are by John Foreman.

The Flame

Is this the hope of the world in my hands?
I'll take this moment to be all that I can
I look to you; I see the future
Stronger and free

Today we will show who we are
We are the Earth and we're together again
My friends, will you show us the way?
We travel on, guided by the Flame
The fire within makes you reach out to the goal
You redefine 'the best' by stretching the soul
A world in need of inspiration
Looks to you and me

Since ancient times we've come together
In the Light of the Flame
And stand for all the world to see
People reaching out to greatness
And all we can be

Today you will show who you are
The best on the Earth
And you bring the world together again
My friends, you have shown us the way
Look to your hearts,
You will find the Flame

The final torch bearer was Kathy Freeman, an Aboriginal woman and participant in the 2000 Olympic Games. In a spectacular moment, she ascended the steps while carrying the torch and walked into the center of the water-filled cauldron. She touched the torch to the water and ignited a ring of fire that encircled her in Flame. The cauldron then ascended around her and continued ascending up to the position the Flame held throughout the Olympic Games. After the Flag was raised and the Flame was lit, John Farnham and Olivia Newton-John sang this beautiful song.

Dare to Dream

I Am my own believer
In my heart the reason
I will follow the Light from within
I'm not afraid of weakness
I'm gonna taste the sweetness
Of the power not to give in
I will see it through. I believe

In my moment of Truth
I believe, I believe, I believe
Dare to dream
Dare to fly
Dare to be the ever chosen
One to touch the sky
Dare to reach
Dare to rise
Find the strength to set
my Spirit free
Dare to dream
I will go the distance
Embrace resistance
I will lay my soul on the line
When the wait is over
And the hunger has spoken
If I give my all I will shine
I will see it through I believe
And the heart will shine like the Sun
A million voices together as One
I believe, I believe, I believe
Find the strength to do what I believe
Dare to dream

The moment the Olympic Flame was lit, the Record-Keeper Crystals containing the original Divine Plan and all of the unmanifest Divine Potential for the Earth were activated to their full original potential. That information is now available to each and every one of us at a genetic, cellular level. The original patterns for Heaven on Earth have now been activated within the DNA codes of Mother Earth and all life evolving upon her.

If each of us will ask our God Selves, our Father-Mother God and the Company of Heaven to charge our precious gift of life with the patterns of perfection from the Causal Body of God and the newly-activated Record-Keeper Crystals, we will begin to reclaim Earth's course of direction as we cocreate Heaven on Earth.

Divine Intervention
The Flame of Transfiguring Divine Love

In January 2001, in spite of the incredible activities of Light that had taken place on the planet, the Spiritual Hierarchy said that there were still millions of souls who were trapped in the paralyzing, mind-numbing grip of their human egos. Those souls who abided in every country in the world were resisting the influence of their 5th-Dimensional Solar Christ Presence and refusing to voluntarily move into the Light. They were functioning out of fear and anger and responding to their life situations with violence, greed and corruption. The Spiritual Hierarchy said that without superhuman, Divine Intervention, those souls were in danger of not awakening in time to make the shift onto the spiral of the 5th Dimension with the rest of Humanity.

Even though there was a tremendous awakening taking place on Earth at the time, and millions of Lightworkers were diligently working to heal Humanity's blatant transgressions of the Laws of Love and Harmony, there were still millions of souls who were not ready to make the quantum shift into the 5th Dimension.

With that understanding, Alpha and Omega set a plan into motion that would be, as they stated, *"Humanity's last, best hope to choose to move into the Light before the Cosmic Inbreath."*

Alpha and Omega sent forth a clarion call and invoked the assistance of all of the Solar Logos in the Universe. The Solar Logos, in turn, invoked the assistance of all of the Beings of Light in their particular Solar Systems. The response was tremendous. According to Alpha and Omega, never in the history of the Universe had that much Light and Love been offered to save one small planet.

The Beings of Light joined together and beseeched the Cosmic I AM for assistance. Whenever tremendous outpourings of Divine Love are offered to assist any facet of Creation, special dispensations are granted, and extraordinary assistance can be given. In this case, the assistance was unprecedented.

The Cosmic I AM sounded a Celestial Keynote and *activated* the most powerful frequency of Divine Love ever made manifest in the history of time—the *Flame of Transfiguring Divine Love.*

This Sacred Fire has been resting in dormancy in the Causal Body of God, awaiting the Cosmic Moment when a collective body of Divine Beings representing the entire Cosmos, would send forth the invocation to activate it. *This was that moment.*

The reason Alpha and Omega stated that the Flame of Transfiguring Divine Love is the last, best hope for the recalcitrant souls to choose to move into the Light is because this Flame contains a very unique *Divine Intelligence*.

Once the Flame of Transfiguring Divine Love is anchored in the Immaculate Heart of each person's 5th-Dimensional Solar Christ Presence, the Divine Intelligence within the Flame will expose the distorted beliefs and manipulations of the human ego. Every person will then have the opportunity to make the conscious choice to correct his or her negative behavior patterns.

The Flame of Transfiguring Divine Love will expose any belief that reflects a lack of reverence for life or justifies harming any other part of life for our own personal gain. Then the illusions of separation will be no more.

When we grasp the magnitude of that concept, it is clear that the Flame of Transfiguring Divine Love is a gift of Divine Grace beyond our knowing. But before the Flame could be anchored in every heart, Humanity had to be raised into a higher vibratory rate, and our wounded hearts had to be healed.

All of us have been through many difficult experiences. We use those experiences to form our attitudes, beliefs and behavior patterns. Our beliefs are usually based in illusions and limited and erroneous perceptions. The way we think and feel about things is often in conflict with the Truth and the reality of what is actually happening.

In January 2001, the Spiritual Hierarchy indicated to us that there would be several activities of Light that would need to take place in order to heal our hearts and prepare the Earth and Humanity to withstand the power of the Flame of Transfiguring Divine Love. We were told that if all was in readiness, the Flame would be anchored on Earth during the fifteenth Harmonic Convergence.

On February 12, 2001, NASA reported that astronomers witnessed an astounding, large scale Solar event as *the Sun's north and south poles changed places*. This amazing phenomenon occurs every 11 years during the maximum cycle of Solar activity.

The Sun's magnetic poles will remain as they are now, with the north magnetic pole pointing through the Sun's southern hemisphere, until the year *2012* when they will reverse again.

NASA reported that Earth's magnetic field also flips but with less regularity. Consecutive reversals are spaced five thousand years to 50 million years apart. The last reversal happened 740,000 years ago. Some researchers think our planet is overdue for another one, but nobody knows exactly when the next reversal might occur.

On March 3, 2001, Kay and I traveled to Kona, Hawaii, to participate in an eight-day *Awakening in Paradise* retreat. The retreat was co-presented by Sheoli Makara and myself. It was the eleventh retreat Sheoli had sponsored and even though men were invited to participate, it was the first retreat she had ever organized that was attended by only women. A total of twenty two women participated in that activity of Light.

We stayed in two beautiful beach houses on Kealakekua Bay in Kona on the Big Island. This is a magical bay that draws hundreds of dolphins year round, and it is a sacred portal of *Healing for the Wounded Heart*. We had wonderful gourmet vegetarian meals served to us every day, and we were pampered by practitioners of various healing modalities. Daily we swam out into the ocean to play with the dolphins and the ancient sea turtles who are known as the Angels of the Sea. We traveled to several sacred sites and performed Divine Ceremonies to assist in the preparation and the healing process that was taking place for Humanity and the Earth. Every evening we watched the Sunset together, and on many occasions, several whales came into the bay to bless us with their presence as the Sun sank beneath the horizon.

Each morning we gathered at Sunrise for meditations and various activities of Light that included the God Selves of all Humanity and the Company of Heaven. Day by day the Spiritual Hierarchy guided us through the events that were unfolding at both inner and outer levels. These events were specifically designed to accelerate Humanity's healing and to further prepare each soul and the body of Mother Earth to withstand the influx of the *Flame of Transfiguring Divine Love*.

After our morning meditation, we put on our snorkeling gear and swam about three-fourths of a mile out into the ocean to play with the dolphins for several hours. We could always tell when we were getting close to the dolphins. We swam through the rays of the Sun that were piercing into the ocean, and when the dolphins were near, the rays changed from white Light to brilliant colors of emerald, sapphire, amethyst and gold.

Dolphins are truly mystical Beings, and they seemed to clearly understand the magnitude of our Divine Mission. They encircled us and swam below us and next to us. As they bathed each woman in their sonic tones, the rhythmic pulsations blended into a symphony of sound, and the music of the dolphins penetrated through every fiber of our Beings. We each felt as though we were being lifted into previously unknown octaves of vibration by an atomic accelerator. The Solar Strands of our DNA were activated and encoded with new patterns of Divine Love and Healing from the Causal Body of God. Each woman received what she specifically needed to enhance her ability to be the Heart, Head and Hands of God in the physical plane.

On March 9, 2001, we experienced the Full Moon of Pisces. We went down to the bay, but due to the Full Moon, the tides were quite high and the water was rather turbulent. A few people decided to brave the rough waters, and the rest of us decided to take in the beauty of the dolphins from the shore. It seemed as though the dolphins wanted to express their joy for the miracles taking place. They were clearly aware that they had an audience, and they put on a spectacular show for us.

The dolphins in Kealakekua Bay are called Spinner Dolphins because they love to jump out of the water and spin and flip. That day they put on a display unlike anything we had seen before. Their antics were like a well-choreographed production. One dolphin jumped out of the water thirteen consecutive times and did a flip each time. Others leapt in the air and whipped their tail back and forth on top of the water very quickly, which propelled them forward as if they were walking on the water. Some of the dolphins turned upside down and slapped the water with their tails making splashes. Many of the other dolphins jumped, spun and flipped in unison with each other, creating a synchronistic ballet.

The buoyant, joyous dance of the dolphins went on for over an hour, and even the local people who gathered with us to watch the show said they had never seen anything like it.

On Sunday, March 11, 2001, each of us bid adieu to our sister coservers and began the journey home.

On April 1, 2001, NASA reported that the most powerful Solar Flares ever recorded erupted on the Sun. The Solar Flares were measured at Class X-20, and the electromagnetic fields of Earth were so profoundly affected that an Aurora of the Northern Lights was seen in Tucson, Arizona, that night. The phenomenon in the sky was reported on the evening news. No one remembered ever seeing such an aurora in Tucson.

Another thing that occurred on April 1, 2001, was the incident with the American spy plane and the jet fighter in China. From outer appearances, that event seemed to be a typically political situation, but in reality something far greater was taking place during the *eleven* days that the American soldiers were held in China.

Despite the consciousness of Communism that exists in China today, that country has very deep spiritual roots. One of the Beings of Light in the Realms of Illumined Truth who is playing a monumental role in the present healing and transformation taking place on Earth is Kuan Yin. She is known throughout the world as the Goddess of Divine Family Life, and her Temple of Mercy, Compassion and Forgiveness pulsates in the Etheric Realms above China. Kuan Yin's temple is associated with the Seventh Solar Aspect of Deity and for millennia has flooded the planet with the Violet Flame.

Since the dawn of the new millennium and the birth of the Aquarian Age, Kuan Yin's temple has come to the forefront. She magnetizes people into her temple in their finer bodies as they sleep at night and assists them to remember the Oneness of all life. She works perpetually to shift the consciousness of men, women and children toward the harmony and balance of Divine Family Life as she bathes each one in the mercy, compassion and forgiveness of the Violet Flame.

When pilot Lt. Shane Osborn, his copilot and their *twenty-two* member crew were forced to land on Hainan Island, the attention of the entire world was drawn to China. What we heard through the media reflected the typical political chatter of the human ego, but when we step back and focus on the greater message, we clearly see the various facets of that amazing Divine Plan.

In spite of the political jargon, the most profound message was from the families of the crew and the Chinese pilot. For *eleven days* they expressed, from the deepest recesses of their hearts, concern for their loved ones and an intense desire to bring the members of their families HOME. As billions of people around the world watched this pageant unfold, they opened their hearts and joined in invoking mercy, compassion and forgiveness into the situation. The focus of Humanity's attention created a vehicle for the Violet Flame.

Through the cup of Humanity's collective consciousness, Kuan Yin, the Company of Heaven and the God Selves of all Humanity were able to blaze the Violet Fire of Mercy, Compassion and Forgiveness through the etheric records associated with all forms and expressions of the lack of reverence for life. There were many requests by both China and the USA for apologies, forgiveness and expressions of regret and sorrow for the loss of life. Humanity's focus of attention on these things created further opportunities for purification, transmutation and healing by the Violet Flame.

On April 11, 2001, the eleven-day healing process was brought to fruition. China released the crew and gave them permission to return home. The crew carried the Violet Flame in their Heart Flames as they flew to Honolulu, Hawaii, and landed within the *forcefield of the ancient continent of Lemuria.*

Kuan Yin expanded the Violet Flame through the Heart Flames of the crew members. The Solar Christ Presences of all Humanity breathed the Violet Flame into the Etheric records of our fall from Grace, which began on Lemuria. Kuan Yin then bathed every electron of life with her gift of mercy, compassion and forgiveness.

After completing that facet of the Divine Plan, the crew flew to Whidbey Island Naval Air Station in the state of Washington. Throughout the entire ordeal in China, various politicians expressed it was America's intent to get the crew home to their families in time for Easter. The American soldiers arrived at Whidbey Island on April 14, 2001, which was Holy Saturday, the day before Easter.

Within the forcefield of Whidbey Island, there is a powerful portal of Resurrection that has for centuries been bathing the Earth with the Mother of Pearl Resurrection Flame . As the crew landed and billions of people around the world focused on Whidbey Island, Jesus The Christ, Mother Mary and Archangel Gabriel bathed all life on Earth with the Resurrection Flame.

Due to the various activities of Light and the God-Victorious purification and transmutation that had taken place over the past 11 days, the Earth and all her life were able to absorb higher frequencies of the Resurrection Flame than ever before.

May 2001, I was blessed to facilitate a group of *33* people on a pilgrimage to England. England is a portal of Light through which a frequency of God's Light flows to sustain the activation of Humanity's pineal glands. Our pineal glands are the spiritual brain centers that keep us connected to all of the various aspects of our own Divinity. When our pineal glands are working effectively in unison with our pituitary glands, the result is, literally, the bridging of Heaven and Earth.

In the beginning, many portals of Light around the world were opened, and Humanity was continually bathed in various frequencies of Divine Light to help us remain connected to our God Selves.

When Humanity made the free-will choice to use our creative faculties of thought and feeling to create mutated patterns that conflicted with the perfection in the Causal Body of God, the portals of Light were closed and the Light of God was withdrawn. When that happened, we lost contact with our God Selves.

Through Ages of time, one plan after another was set into motion so that the portals of Light could be reopened, and the Light of God would once again flow freely into the Earth and awaken Humanity. For thousands of years, very few souls were able to raise their heads above the sea of human miscreation effectively enough to remember their Divine Birthright as Sons and Daughters of God. The few souls who did managed to magnetize into the mental stratum of Earth the Divine Truth that would form the sacred doctrines that eventually became the world religions.

During the inception of the Piscean Age, a Divine Plan was set into motion to open the portal of Light in England that energizes Humanity's pineal gland. The Spiritual Hierarchy knew that portal would be a vital part of facilitating the second coming of the Christ— the birth of Humanity's Solar Christ Presence.

After Jesus' Ascension, some of the Disciples and many others who served with him were imprisoned for promoting his teachings. Jesus' uncle, Joseph of Arimathea, was one of the imprisoned teachers. While Joseph was in prison, he was visited by the Archangel Raphael. Raphael asked him to take the Chalice, the Holy Grail that Jesus used at the Last Supper, and the vials of the blood and water that were gathered from Jesus' wounds when he was on the cross to Ynis Witrin, the Sacred Land of Glass. This is the area in England now known as Glastonbury. It is the location of the mystical tales of Avalon, King Arthur, Guinevere, Merlin, the Knights of the Round Table, the Lady of the Lake, the magic sword Excalibur and Parsifal's search for the Holy Grail.

Joseph agreed to accept the mission and asked Mother Mary, John the Beloved, Mary Magdalene and nine other people to join him on his pilgrimage. On their way to Glastonbury, the little band traveled to several places in England. As they walked that hallowed land, they began reestablishing the ley lines and reconnecting the short circuits in the Crystal Grid System that occurred aeons ago when the portal of Light in England was closed. Each person clearly understood that Archangel Raphael had sent them on a mission to prepare the way for a future time when the portal of Light associated with Humanity's pineal glands and our return to Christ Consciousness would be reopened.

Jesus successfully anchored the matrix and the archetypes for Humanity's return to Christ Consciousness while he was on Earth, but he realized that it would be centuries before Humanity, en masse, would awaken enough to allow our Holy Christ Selves to have full dominion of our lives. In Revelations he told Saint John, *"In the day of the Seventh Angel, when he begins to sound, the mystery of God will be fulfilled, and time will be no more,"* during the time of the *"second coming of The Christ."*

Joseph of Arimathea and his entourage completed their Divine Mission by traveling to Glastonbury and established the Divine Blueprint that would one day open the portal of Light in England. They left the Chalice and the vials of blood and water from Jesus' wounds there. Joseph thrust into the ground the hawthorn staff that he brought from the Holy Land , and it took root and began to bloom. To this day, the miracle of the Holy Thorn bush on Wearyall Hill is seen in its flowering, which always occurs on December 25, Christmas Day, in memory of the birth of The Christ.

The very first Christian church was founded by Joseph of Arimathea in Glastonbury, England. That is why Glastonbury is considered the New Jerusalem. The traditional Christian song titled *Jerusalem* tells of England and its mystical green hills. The Abbey in Glastonbury, the Isle of Avalon, is known as *"a Christian sanctuary so ancient that only legend can record its origin."*

Our Modern-Day Pilgrimage

In May 2001, Humanity was finally ready for the opening of the portal of Light in England associated with the pineal gland and the maintenance of Christ Consciousness on Earth. Several Lightworkers were asked by the Company of Heaven whether we would be willing to complete the activity of Light that was started 2,000 years ago by Joseph of Arimathea, Mother Mary, John the Beloved, Mary Magdalene and the others from the Holy Land. We affirmed from the deepest recesses of our hearts that we would be honored to serve as instruments of God for that Holy Mission.

Several months before our trip was to begin, England began having problems with foot and mouth disease. Many people in England felt it was a politically contrived catastrophe but, nevertheless, three million cows were slaughtered in the process as well as hundreds of thousands of sheep. All of the sacred sites were closed to tourists, and even the elections were delayed to prevent people from traveling around England and possibly spreading the disease.

The Company of Heaven told us to be at peace, that all was in Divine Order, and our pilgrimage should continue as planned. The week before we were to leave for England, our travel agent called and said that all of a sudden the authorities had reopened all of the sacred sites in England to tourists, and none of our tour plans needed to be altered.

May is known as the mystical month because of the many spiritual events that take place during that time. We left for England on May 1, 2001, which is the day celebrated as St. Germain's Ascension Day, and it is the sacred Druid Celebration of Spring. It is also the day that Mother Mary's Temple of the Immaculate Heart is opened in the Celestial Realms. Her temple is open for the entire month of May every year, and every person on Earth is drawn into her Presence sometime during that month, as we sleep in our finer bodies at night.

When we arrived in London on May 2nd, we were told by the Spiritual Hierarchy to focus and pay close attention to everything that was happening. They said that every step of our pilgrimage was significant and represented facets of the fallen consciousness of Humanity that were being lifted up and healed in preparation for the reactivation of Humanity's pineal glands.

It was raining and cold when we arrived in London, and everyone who spoke to us mentioned that it had been raining in England for two solid months. They said it had been unusually cold, and the Sun rarely peeked out from behind the thick cloud cover.

After registering at the famous Strand Hotel where we were staying, the first trip the group took was to Saint Paul's Cathedral, which is considered the spiritual center of London. That magnificent cathedral rose out of the devastation of the Great Fire of London of 1666. The fire razed two-thirds of London to ashes in just four days.

Prior to his conversion, Saul, who became Saint Paul, was a man of the world. He was consumed with outer-world business affairs and making money. He refused to listen to Jesus' message of Oneness and Divine Love, and instead he committed his life to fulfilling the demands of his human ego. His stubborn resistance was not unlike what many recalcitrant souls are expressing today.

Then, one day after Jesus' Resurrection and Ascension, Saul was traveling on the road to Damascus, and Jesus appeared to him in his Solar Light Body. He revealed the Light of The Christ to Saul and asked him to change his name to Paul. Jesus revealed to Paul the path of Divine Love that he must travel in order to fulfill his purpose and reason for Being. In that instant, Paul awakened to the Truth of his own Divinity and became an avid crusader for the message of Jesus and the cause of The Christ.

The Spiritual Hierarchy said that the full reactivation of Humanity's pineal glands will have a similar effect on the awakening of those souls who are still resisting moving forward in the Light.

After the visit to Saint Paul's Cathedral, our group visited the Tower of London. The Tower has a brutal and bloody history, but within its walls lies the oldest church in London, the Chapel of Saint John, as well as the Chapel of Saint Peter ad Vincula and Saint Thomas's Tower. That one area represents the best and worst of human consciousness and the extremes into which Humanity has ventured.

After the visit to Saint Paul's Cathedral and the Tower of London, we gathered for dinner at the hotel. After dinner we had a guided meditation and created our unified Heart Chalice.

May 3, 2001, numerically was an eleven day. It was a beautiful day; the Sun was shining through the clouds, and it was warm. The Elementals blessed us with beautiful warm, sunny weather for our entire pilgrimage. We began by visiting Westminster Abbey which was founded in the 11th century. For 900 years, nearly every king or queen of England has been crowned in Westminster Abbey, and many English monarchs are buried there.

After connecting with that forcefield, we boarded our coach and passed by the financial area, Royal Courts of Justice, Mansion House (home of the Lord Mayor), Hyde Park Corner, Piccadilly Circus, Knightsbridge (Harrods), Trafalgar Square, Covent Gardens, Buckingham Palace, Downing Street, Big Ben, the River Thames and various other historical sites in London. When we arrived at *Kensington Palace*, which continued to be Princess Diana's home after her divorce from Prince Charles, we stopped for a meditation.

The scare of foot and mouth disease had prevented tourists from coming to England, so everywhere we went the crowds were minimal, and we were able to have our gatherings without making spectacles of ourselves.

Princess Diana was one member of the monarchy and aristocracy of England who was dedicated to healing the schism and separation imposed on people by the social class structure in that country. She reached across invisible boundaries through her love and devotion and united people from all classes and walks of life.

When we gathered within the forcefield of Princess Diana's Earthly home, the sky was perfectly cloudless. The warmth of the Sun enveloped us, and the Music of the Spheres wafted through the air. As we went within to the Divinity in our hearts, the august Presence of the Galactic, Solar Angel of Restoration descended from the heart of the Great, Great Central Sun and entered the atmosphere of Earth. Beloved Jesus expanded his luminous Presence, and within the embrace of his Heart Flame, the Earth and all her life were lifted up in energy, vibration and consciousness.

The Angel of Restoration breathed in the crystalline-white Flame of Restoration from the core of Creation and projected it forth into every particle of life on Earth. As that Divine Essence blazed through every facet of life, the old, obsolete archetypes and matrixes that have perpetuated the consciousness of separation in Humanity were transmuted into Light.

After our day tour, we returned to the hotel for a little rest and relaxation. We had a free evening, and people chose various things to do. Just for fun, some of us went to High Tea at the famous Savoy Hotel, which was just across the street from our hotel. It was wonderful!

There are 92 theaters in London, and that night several of us wanted to see the live performance of the Lion King. The reviews said the musical was spectacular, and the costumes were said to be incredible. Many of us also knew that, in many ways, the story of the Lion King is a wonderful metaphor for what Humanity is experiencing now. We felt it would be a perfect addition to our mission.

The concierge at the ticket desk at our hotel said that the Lion King was sold out, and it would be impossible for us to get tickets for that night. We did not let his words discourage us, and we went to the theater to see if, by chance, there were any tickets held back that were being released for that night. There were nine of us in our group, and the woman at the ticket counter said, *"Well, amazingly enough, I have nine seats together on the mezzanine that are available for tonight."* Isn't God fun!

The live production of the Lion King was everything everyone had said it was and more. I highly recommend seeing it if you have the opportunity.

On May 4, 2001, we checked out of our hotel and boarded

our coach in preparation for the next phase of our adventure. We drove a few miles out of London to Runnymeade and stopped at a beautiful park along the River Thames for our meditation. As we gathered along the riverbank, the Sun was shining. The grass, flowers, trees, water and the soft breeze all seemed to be singing.

We entered the Divinity of our hearts and joined the activity of Light that was unfolding in the Realms of Cause. Beloved Alpha and Omega sounded a Cosmic Tone, and the Universe stood in readiness. The Directors of the Elements sent forth their unified Keynote and invoked the indigenous Elders from all time frames and dimensions who have served and protected the Beings of the Elemental Kingdom since the inception of the Earth. For aeons of time, the Elders have embodied on every continent and in every culture on the planet. They have tenaciously held the vision for the limitless perfection of Heaven on Earth since Humanity's fall from Grace. When the Elders heard the call, they came from the far corners of the Universe.

The Directors of the Elements explained to us that the events that were taking place in England involving the cows and sheep were reflecting Humanity's abuse of the Elemental Kingdom. They said that the Lightworkers had been invoking assistance from On High to heal the Elemental Kingdom, and the call had been heard.

The Directors of the Elements then signaled the Elders to traverse the planet north, south, east and west. They took their positions above every city, town, village and hamlet on the Earth. When they were all in their places, they sang their song of healing and collectively invoked the most intensified Violet Transmuting Flame Humanity could endure.

The Elders projected the Violet Transmuting Flame into the psychic-astral plane and the physical plane. The Violet Flame penetrated the air, water, earth, fire and ether elements and transmuted the mutated patterns of pollution at causal levels.

Then the Elders called forth the Elemental Beings from the 3rd- and 4th-Dimensions who have served the Earth since the beginning of time. The Gnomes (earth), Salamanders (fire), Undines (water), Sylphs (air), the Mountain Gods, the Devas and Deva Rajas who have served the Earth since her inception came from the far reaches of the planet and entered the Golden Throne Room of Shamballa.

As these Beings stood before the altar, they were told by the Directors of the Elements that it was time for the changing of the guard. The Directors commended every Elemental Being and assured each one that they had served the Earth courageously in the face of horrendous adversity. The Directors then informed the Elemental Beings that they had earned the well-deserved right to return to the heart of the Central Sun.

With that announcement, the Angel of Restoration entered Shamballa and magnetized the Elemental Beings into the embrace of his Heart Flame. Then, in a flash of Light, the Angel of Restoration escorted the Elementals who have served the Earth since her inception back Home to the heart of Alpha and Omega.

The Spiritual Hierarchy said that those selfless Beings of Light will have a period of healing, rest and relaxation. Then they will progress to the higher schools of learning in preparation for their next level of service.

After that activity of Light, the Mighty Elohim sounded a Cosmic Tone, and the Elemental Beings from the 5th-Dimensional Realms of Limitless Physical Perfection descended into the atmosphere of Earth from the Great, Great Silence. These magnificent Elemental Presences entered Shamballa and were consecrated by the Elohim for their mission as coservers with Humanity in the creation of Heaven on Earth.

It is hard for us to fully comprehend what this changing of the guard will mean in our Ascension process, but the assistance of the 5th-Dimensional Elemental Beings will be wondrous. These Elementals vibrate at a frequency of energy, vibration and consciousness that transcends the distorted mutations of Humanity's miscreations. They are exclusively trained to manifest the perfection of the Heavenly Realms and the Causal Body of God in physical form. They are not committed to manifesting every thought, word, action or feeling that our human egos choose to express as the 3rd- and 4th-Dimensional Elementals were. They have taken vows to solely serve the God Selves of Humanity. Therefore, they will only expend their energy to cocreate the thoughts, words, actions and feelings of Humanity that are qualified with the frequencies of perfection from the 5th Dimension and above.

This means that without the support of the Elemental Kingdom, the distorted attempts of the human egos who are still operating out of greed, selfishness, dog-eat-dog consciousness and lack of reverence for life are destined to fail.

Since the physical plane is the very last dimension to reflect change, Humanity's human egos can use the residue of the previously manifested patterns of pollution and make it appear, for a short while, that they are succeeding in continuing the destruction of the Earth, but that will be a very short-lived illusion.

Once the 5th-Dimensional Elementals were consecrated into their new Divine Mission by the Elohim, they traversed the planet and descended into their rightful places within the air, water, earth, fire and ether strata in and around the body of Mother Earth. They then breathed in the patterns of perfection from the Causal Body of God and projected the matrixes and archetypes for the New Earth onto the fluid field of unmanifest Divine Potential.

Now, daily and hourly, as the Lightworkers around the world envision and energize the Immaculate Concept of Heaven on Earth, the Elemental Kingdom will assist us in manifesting this Divine Truth, right here and right now.

After that activity of Light was sealed in our Heart Flames and the Heart Flames of all Humanity, we boarded the coach and proceeded to Windsor Castle, the favorite home of Her Majesty Queen Elizabeth II. When we arrived, the Sun was shining, and the large clock on the wall said it was 11:11 a.m.

We toured through the regal splendor of the castle, and as we did, the healing of separation, class structures, prejudice and abuse of power was greatly amplified through all life on Earth.

After our tour of Windsor, we proceeded to Oxford. When we arrived, we were met by two wonderful tour guides. We split into two groups, so that we could clearly hear what our guides were saying.

As we walked down the historic streets, we noticed that there were beautiful baskets of flowers hanging on every lamppost. Our tour guide said that, *coincidentally*, the baskets had just been hung that very day. We felt it was a special gift from the newly-initiated Elemental Kingdom.

John Keats said, *"This Oxford, I have no doubt, it is the finest city in the world."*

Oxford is truly amazing. Squeezed into a tiny space less than a mile square is one of the greatest collections of buildings. These buildings have been home to an extraordinary number of statesmen, kings and saints. For over eight centuries, Oxford University has educated philosophers, poets and scientists who revolutionized the way we see the world.

On High Street there is a very famous clock, and at 3:00 p.m., we stopped and watched it perform its unique talents. The flag flying above the clock was the European Union Flag, which consists of twelve gold stars on a blue field. Our tour guide said it is the symbol of unity for people everywhere.

We then proceeded to Christ Church and various other wonderful buildings associated with Oxford University. As we walked through those hallowed halls, patterns of perfection from the Halls of Wisdom and the Temples of Knowledge in the Realms of Illumined Truth were projected by the Company of Heaven onto the fluid field of unmanifest Divine Potential. These patterns will assist in shifting the consciousness of Humanity. They will also accelerate the process of lifting us out of the distorted misinformation and disinformation being used to entrap and manipulate us by our human egos.

The Spiritual Hierarchy said the Divine Intent of the influx of Light from the Halls of Wisdom and the Temples of Knowledge is to inspire our teachers, professors, scientists, scholars, students and people in general to reach up in consciousness and to go within to get their answers from the Realms of Truth.

After we left Oxford, we traveled through England's beautiful countryside to the sacred site of the Rollright Stones. This stone circle measures 30 meters in diameter, and it is the easternmost circle in Britain. Very little is known about its true significance or the spiritual ceremonies that may have been performed there. The stone circle is aligned along the Crystal Grid System, and it is in a beautiful area that has a wonderful vista of the surrounding landscape.

We had a very special meditation within the circle. The Dove of the Holy Spirit amplified the Violet Flame through the Maltese Crosses that were placed within the Heart Flames of every man, woman and child. Although we didn't see it, as that influx of Light was taking place, we all heard a dove clearly cooing in the background. That activity of Light sealed the events of the day, and we all stood in wonder watching the Sunset as we experienced incredible feelings of love and gratitude.

After our meditation, we traveled to Stratford-upon-Avon and the beautiful Stratford Victoria Hotel where we were scheduled to stay for two nights. Stratford-upon-Avon is famous for being the birthplace of William Shakespeare. It is the home of the Royal Shakespeare Theatre, and it is just a few miles from Warwick Castle.

In the literary field, there has always been a debate as to whether or not there really was a man named William Shakespeare and whether he or Francis Bacon wrote the Shakespearean plays. In Stratford-upon-Avon, they insist that Shakespeare was born and died there, but, of course, that is their main claim to fame.

Francis Bacon was one of the embodiments of St. Germain, and he has indicated that William Shakespeare was a pen name he used to write the plays. St. Germain said that the name William Shakespeare was a code name that affirmed ... it is the ... WILL ... of the ... I AM ... to ... SHAKE ... a ... SPEAR ... at the sinister force. The spear, of course, is Archangel Michael's Sword of Blue Flame.

On May 5, 2001, our group participated in various events, as we opened our hearts to the facet of our sacred pilgrimage that was unfolding in that famous town. We were told by the Spiritual Hierarchy that there is a building momentum of the Violet Flame that St. Germain established in that area during his embodiment as Francis Bacon, and because of the worldwide attention Humanity has placed on the code name William Shakespeare, Stratford-upon-Avon is the portal for a very unique frequency of the Violet Flame.

The frequency of the Violet Flame that pours through that particular portal is specifically designed to cleanse the psychic-astral plane and to cut Humanity free from the interference of the forces of imbalance that abide in that realm of human miscreation.

In cooperation with the Company of Heaven, everyone on the pilgrimage volunteered to be an instrument of God, and we all agreed to allow the unique frequency of the Violet Flame to pour through the Maltese Crosses in our Heart Flames. We collectively offered ourselves as the Holy Grail through which the Light of God would pour to assist in awakening the discarnate souls who were trapped in the psychic-astral plane. We asked that those lost souls be lifted up, so that they could once again reach into the Realms of Illumined Truth and remember their own Divinity. As that process unfolded moment by moment, our group walked the streets of Stratford-upon-Avon and visited the various sites.

Later we went to see the magnificent Warwick Castle and experienced the exciting Renaissance performances. The elaborate production consisted of knights and their ladies, beautiful horses arrayed in their medieval garb, jousting and archery demonstrations, exhibitions of birds of prey with American bald eagles, golden eagles, falcons, owls and vultures and many other activities. We were told by our tour guide that the Renaissance performances take place only two or three weekends during the year and that we were very lucky to have happened to be there on that specific weekend.

That evening we all went to see a Shakespearean play at the famous Royal Shakespeare Theater. We saw the comedy *Twelfth*

Night, and it was wonderful.

An amazingly synchronistic facet of the Divine Plan was also taking place while the psychic-astral plane was being cleansed. Pope John Paul II was traveling in Greece and the Middle East to promote Peace and Interfaith Unity. He was the very first Pope to do so, and he was making history with his momentous journey. Pope John Paul II met with the leaders of the Greek Orthodox Church in Athens, Greece, and prayed to heal the schism between the Greek Orthodox and Roman Catholic churches. He then traveled to the Middle East.

For the first time in Islam's 1,400-year history, a Pope entered a Muslim mosque. Within the mosque, Pope John Paul II met with a Muslim cleric, and together they invoked Peace for the Middle East. They prayed at the tomb of Saint John the Baptist, which is inside the mosque and invoked Interfaith Unity.

On May 6, 2001, Pope John Paul II became the first Pope ever to travel to Syria. He went to Damascus, the capital of Syria, and traced the steps of Saint Paul the Apostle.

As the Pope walked the famous road to Damascus, Jesus projected forth the luminous Presence of his Solar Light Body and revealed the Truth of The Christ to the souls trapped in the psychic-astral plane just as he did to Paul 2,000 years ago. In the vulnerability of their astonishment, Jesus offered them the opportunity to go with him into the Temple of Divine Grace in the Holy Cities of John the Beloved in the Heavenly Realms.

Because of the incredible purification of the Violet Flame that had been blazing through the psychic-astral plane for the past two days, the lost souls were able to glimpse a flicker of Light in their Heart Flames, and they collectively accepted Jesus' merciful offer.

Archangel Gabriel sounded his mighty trumpet, and in a miraculous instant, every soul trapped in the psychic- astral plane was transferred to the Temple of Divine Grace. Saint John the Beloved beckoned each soul into the sacred Flame of Divine Grace blazing on the altar, and each one was lifted into a higher level of consciousness.

Alpha and Omega issued a Cosmic Fiat and decreed that the gift of free will for each of those souls be set aside for a moment in time. In that Cosmic Moment, each soul was required to peer into the Mirror of Life and perceive his or her own Divinity. For some of those souls, it had been hundreds of thousands of years since they remembered that they were Beloved Children of God.

Once that realization registered in their conscious minds, their free will was restored, and they were given the opportunity to choose to move forward into the next level of their learning experience. Each soul was shown what he or she would have to do to transmute the transgressions of the Laws of Love and Harmony that they had participated in. As a source of encouragement, each one was also shown the assistance and support he or she would receive from On High in their healing process.

To the great joy and relief of the Company of Heaven and the God Selves of embodied Humanity, every soul from the psychic-astral plane willingly chose to move forward into the next school of learning.

Once again, Archangel Gabriel sounded his mighty trumpet, and the souls were instantly transferred to the heart of Alpha and Omega. In a Divine Ceremony, the souls reaffirmed the vows they had taken in the heart of God to fulfill their Divine Birthright as Sons and Daughters of God.

Once their vows were reaffirmed, Alpha and Omega placed a laurel wreath upon their heads and a Violet Cloak of Forgiveness about their shoulders. An amethyst Maltese Cross medallion was placed over their hearts, and Alpha and Omega gave them a special blessing.

The souls consecrated their lives to serving God and agreed to embody on Earth in the very near future. They vowed to quickly assist in transmuting their transgressions of the Laws of Love and Harmony, and they promised to fulfill their Divine Potential in co-creating the Limitless Physical Perfection of Heaven on Earth. After that activity of Light was complete, the souls were taken to their schools of learning to prepare to reincarnate on Earth.

Archangel Michael then invoked the Lords of Power from the Great, Great Central Sun and directed them into psychic-astral-plane to shatter and transmute the residue of the empty shells, archetypes, matrixes and thoughtforms left behind by the previously trapped souls. That event cleared the veil of maya and illusion and completed the purification and transmutation of the psychic-astral plane of human miscreation.

After the God-Victorious accomplishment of the purging of the psychic-astral plane, we boarded our coach and began our scenic journey to Bath. We drove through the charming Cotswold villages of Shipston-on-Stour, Moreton-in-Marsh, Stow-on-the-Wold and Burton-on-the-Water. After lunch we took a tour of Sudeley Castle at Winchcombe, which was the home of Queen Katherine Parr, the sixth wife of King Henry the VIII. We then traveled through the Roman town of Cirenchester and arrived at Bath in the late afternoon.

Bath is famous for the healing properties of its magical hot springs. The Roman spa has drawn people from all over the world for nearly 2,000 years. Bath has a long and rich history and has been home to Stone Age hunters, Bronze Age craftsmen, Celts, Romans, Saxons and Georgian Era architects. It has also been the healing vacation spot of kings and queens for centuries.

May 7, 2001, was the Full Moon of Taurus and the celebration of Wesak. With the transmutation of the psychic-astral plane, the Earth was in a position to Ascend higher up the Spiral of Evolution. Taking full advantage of the millions of people around the world who were focusing on the Buddha's Love through the celebration of Wesak, Alpha and Omega seized the opportunity to make an adjustment in the Earth's axis.

Millions of years ago, the weight of Humanity's human effluvia actually bent the axis of the Earth and caused our planet to fall off of the Spiral of Evolution and onto the Wheel of Karma. Finally, after aeons of time and myriad activities of Light, on January 11, 1992, the Earth Ascended off of the Wheel of Karma and established her rightful place back on the Spiral of Evolution. Ever since that Cosmic Moment, Humanity has been awakening at an accelerated pace.

The Earth is now in a fluid state of flux. That is why we feel ourselves vacillating back and forth between the various dimensions. Sometimes we feel the bliss and wonder of the 5th Dimension. Other times we feel the peace and harmony of the 4th Dimension. And many times, we feel like we are smack-dab in the middle of the densest frequencies of the 3rd Dimension.

Since 1992, the axis of the Earth had been gradually adjusted by the Elohim and the Directors of the Elements. These adjustments were made in gentle a way that would prevent any cataclysmic backlash or loss of life. Now, for the very first time since the fall of Humanity, the psychic-astral plane of human miscreation was transmuted into Light, which created a unique window of opportunity.

On May 7, 2001, as our group welcomed the radiance of the Sun, we went into the Divinity of our hearts and joined the Ceremonies of Light taking place in the Celestial Realms. Archangel Chamuel and his Divine Complement, Archaii Charity, took their strategic positions at the north and south poles. These resplendent Solar

Archangels are the exponents of the Third Solar Aspect of Deity, the Ray of Divine Love, Comfort and Adoration.

In one synchronized breath, the Archangels absorbed into their hearts an intensified frequency of Divine Love and Comfort from the heart of God. Then they breathed that Divine Light through the axis of the Earth and expanded it out through the Crystal Grid System.

Chamuel and Charity then directed the 5th-Dimensional Elementals to blaze that Light through all of the cracks, faults, fissures, wounds and tectonic plates in the body of Mother Earth. The Light of Divine Love and Comfort reinforced every weak spot on the planet and secured the land masses, oceans, seas, mountains, winds and fire elements in an invincible forcefield of protection.

After the Earth was secured, Archangel Michael and his Divine Complement, Archaii Faith, joined Chamuel and Charity at the north and south poles. They invoked the Ring-Pass-Not of God's First Cause of Perfection from the core of Creation and projected it around the Earth. That forcefield of Light infused every particle of life with the Will of God in preparation for the straightening of the axis.

Next, St. Germain and his Divine Complement, Lady Portia, the Goddess of Divine Justice, took their positions at the north and south poles. These exponents of the Seventh Solar Aspect of Deity blazed the new Solar frequencies of the Violet Flame through the axis of the Earth. As that Light expanded through the Crystal Grid System, all life was bathed in the Divine Light of Mercy, Compassion, Forgiveness, Transmutation, Freedom, Justice, Liberty, Victory and Limitless Physical Perfection.

The Twelve Solar Elohim then magnetized the Twelve Solar Aspects of Deity into their Heart Flames and descended into the center of the Earth. Each Elohim anchored the Solar Aspect of Deity into the corresponding Solar Chakra along the axis of Mother Earth. Then, with all of the safeguards in place, the Mighty Elohim, ever so gently, adjusted the axis of the Earth.

That adjustment brought the magnetic poles of the Earth into alignment with the axis of the physical Sun of Helios and Vesta, the Central Sun of Alpha and Omega, the Great Central Sun of Elohae and Eloha and the Great, Great Central Sun of El and Ela.

May 8th is Gautama Buddha's Day of Enlightenment. It is rare for Wesak and Gautama's Day of Enlightenment to fall so close together, but during that Cosmic Moment, the synchronicity was obviously in perfect Divine Order.

With the axis of the Earth in alignment with the Solar axis of the Suns in this System of Worlds, Humanity could, once again, receive the Light from the various dimensions and aspects of our own God Selves. On that holy day, Gautama Buddha breathed the Flame of Enlightenment into Humanity's Crown Chakras and accelerated our awakening process.

Later that morning, after assimilating the Flame of Enlightenment, our group left Bath and traveled to Wells, a charming old cathedral town at the foot of the Mendip Hills. We took a tour of Wells Cathedral and absorbed the splendor of that magnificent edifice. After spending some time enjoying the shops and having lunch, we continued on to Street.

Street is a little village just outside of Glastonbury where we were scheduled to stay for six days. We arrived in the late afternoon and checked into our hotel. That night we had a meditation and integrated the building momentum of Light that was expanding on the planet through the celebrations of Wesak and Gautama Buddha's Day of Enlightenment.

May 9, 2001, we began our activities of Light in the mystical village of Glastonbury. Amazingly, within a ten-mile circle, the landscape of Glastonbury reflects the twelve astrological signs of the Zodiac.

A sculptor named Katherine Maltwood discovered the patterns in the landscape in 1925. It is believed that the Sumerian metal-traders, who were known to be astrologically aware, are the people who recognized the signs and developed them in about 2700 BC. Some believe that the ten-mile circle containing the twelve astrological signs was the model for the original Round Table of Avalon.

Within the circle, the astrological signs are in the correct order and proportion. The heads are toward the center facing west. The summer signs are in the sunny south and the winter signs are in the north.

Glastonbury is where the seed atom of the portal of Light associated with the pineal gland is located. Throughout the week as we traversed that sacred land, the Mighty Elohim expanded the Twelve Solar Aspects of Deity through the twelve signs of the Zodiac that are naturally carved into the landscape. That activity of Light further prepared the vortex for the opening of the portal.

We were told by the Spiritual Hierarchy that as we followed in the footsteps of Joseph of Arimathea, Mother Mary, John the Beloved, Mary Magdalene and the others, we would reconnect the circuitry of the Crystal Grid System in that area. The seed atom in Glastonbury will then be able to permanently hold open the portal of Light in England.

The Sun was shining as we began our pilgrimage. We walked from our hotel in Street to Wearyall Hill where the Holy Thorn bush still grows after 2,000 years. From the top of the hill, we were able to see the panorama of Glastonbury and connect with the beauty and expanse of that charming village.

We then walked to Chalice Well, which is a beautiful and mystical place. The well is surrounded by exquisite gardens, and the peace there is truly sublime. The water that flows through Chalice Well from deep within the heart of the Earth has been revered for millennia for its healing properties.

Water is truly a gift of the Earth, and it is the essence of life. It is pulsating with a lifeforce, and it sustains all lifeforms. The spring at Chalice Well is thought of as a symbol of the continuous and unbounded nature of that lifeforce.

Throughout time, people have perceived Chalice Well as a gateway to the spirit world where the veils between the Earth and the Celestial Realms are gossamer and where communication with the Beings of Light in the Realms of Truth can easily occur. Each of us spent some quiet time there in the silence meditating and assimilating the wonder of the moment.

After our meditation, we walked into the village of Glastonbury where we had lunch and spent some time in the metaphysical bookstores and shops. Later that afternoon we climbed the Tor.

The Glastonbury Tor is extraordinary. It is a 500-foot, conical hill surrounded by an ancient labyrinth. At the top of the Tor is a tall tower dedicated to Saint Michael. The Tor is the most striking landmark in Glastonbury, and it is considered by many to be a bridge between Heaven and Earth.

The climb to the top of the Tor is rather formidable, but it is well worth the effort. In our group, four women had problems with their legs, and interestingly, all of them limped on their left side. They each shared their feelings about their afflictions, and every one of them had the inner knowing that they were surrogates working toward healing the blocked feminine side within Humanity. All four of these courageous women succeeded in climbing to the top of the Tor.

As we started our climb up the Tor, a gentle mist began to

form, and the sky became cloudy. It felt as though we were entering another dimension. We truly experienced what is known as the mists of Avalon.

The vistas from the top of the Tor are magical, and the energy there is incredible. We were joined by choirs of Angels as the Light of God poured through our Heart Flames to bless all life on Earth.

When we were through with our meditation, we made our way down the opposite side of the Tor. By the time we reached the bottom of the hill, the mist had stopped falling and the clouds were clearing. We walked to a quaint little cafe to relish the moment and have our afternoon tea.

On May 10, 2001, we began our sacred pilgrimage to various enchanted sacred sites that were built by the Neolithic people in the ancient kingdom of Wessex. Those people lived in close harmony with the Elemental Kingdom and revered the earth beneath their feet as well as the Moon and Sun above. They had a loving kinship with their families and a very powerful relationship with their own Divinity and our Father-Mother God. They built a large number of mounds and stone rings to honor the Heavens, their ancestors and the seasons.

The ritual landscapes of the Neolithic peoples are always connected with water. The Avebury Complex stands near the confluence of two important rivers, the Winterbourne and the Kennet.

Avebury is the largest henge in Britain, and it was raised between 3710 BC and 2000 BC. That is approximately the same time the pyramids were being built in Egypt. Thirteen of the great pyramids could fit inside the Avebury circle. Some scholars have commented on the similarity between the design of the Avebury ritual landscape and Egyptian Sun and snake motifs.

There are actually three stone circles in Avebury which are all made of Sarsen stone. The outer circle consists of 98 stones, and there are two smaller inner circles. One of the inner circles is aligned to the north and includes the Cove, three huge flat stones making a square enclosure with an open side. The other inner circle is aligned to the south and includes a 21-foot tall stone obelisk, which itself is surrounded by 29 smaller stones that are set at intervals of 36 feet. All of the stones at Avebury are set at 36 foot intervals. The complete henge at Avebury consists of 247 stones. All of Stonehenge could easily fit into either of the smaller inner circles.

Our group formed a circle within one of the inner circles and connected with the heart of Mother Earth. The Mighty Elohim amplified the alignment of our spinal columns with the axis of the Earth and the axis of the Suns in this Solar System. Then our Solar God Parents sent forth the radiance of their Light and further prepared Humanity's right- and left-brain hemispheres for the activation of the pineal gland.

From our perspective at Avebury, we were able to see Silbury Hill. Silbury Hill is the largest man-made hill in all of prehistoric Europe. It is considered to be the most labor-intensive piece of construction in Neolithic Britain. It is estimated that it would have taken 800 men ten years to build it, if they worked year round. The hill was built about 2700 BC.

Silbury Hill is 5 ½ acres at the base and rises 130 feet. It contains 12 ½ million cubic feet of chalk and soil. The ditch around the hill was originally 16 feet deep and 70 feet wide. It is believed that Silbury Hill may have been a massive fertility figure, the pregnant womb of the Mother-Goddess, which was universally recognized by primitive farming societies at that time. During the mid-to-late Neolithic era, the earth had been depleted through over use, and the population had increased dramatically. It is assumed that the people had close association with the Female Deity and built a giant monument to invoke her assistance. The belief is that the construction of Silbury Hill, surrounded by her holy waters, was a desperate plea to bring fertility to the land.

One of the mysteries of Silbury is a very unusual tree that grows from the bank of the stream. It bears two different sets of leaves and flowers. A fully-grown sycamore tree springs from a fork in the trunk of an alder. Locals interpret the tree to be the vitality of life proclaiming itself.

After our trip to Avebury, we returned to Chalice Well to complete that phase of reconnecting the circuitry in the Crystal Grid System. We had a brief meditation and absorbed the peace pulsating there.

On May 11, 2001, we made our pilgrimage to Stonehenge. Stonehenge, like Avebury, is steeped in mysticism and folk lore. It stands on the Salisbury plain and is one of the most famous sites in the world. There is nothing else like it anywhere.

Stonehenge was constructed in three stages, the first beginning approximately 5,000 years ago, the second 4,900 to 4,600 years ago and the final stage about 3,600 years ago. The final phase involved the erection of Bluestones from the Preseli Mountains in Wales, which was followed by the building of the stone circle with

Sarsen stones from Marlborough Downs.

The most common theory is that Stonehenge was a very complicated observatory used in ancient times to count the cycles of the Moon and to predict eclipses. That would mean that the architects of Stonehenge were profound astrologers with very advanced knowledge of the lunar orbit. Since the Moon has a complex cycle that lasts nearly nineteen years, the builders of Stonehenge must have observed the skies for a very long time.

As our group walked the path encircling Stonehenge, the circuitry for that facet of the portal of Light in England was spliced into the Crystal Grid System.

We went directly from Stonehenge to the cathedral at Old Sarum which was built between 1077 and 1092. The ruins of Old Sarum stand on a windswept hill one mile away from Salisbury. The ancient cathedral was built on what is known as the Goddess ley line, which played a critical part in preparing the circuitry between Humanity's right- and left-brain hemispheres.

Our group gathered in a secluded place along the Goddess ley line at Old Sarum and joined with the Company of Heaven and the God Selves of all Humanity for an important activation. We were guided through a visualization in which the Light of God flowed back and forth between the right- and left-hemispheres of our brains. As the Light flowed back and forth, it formed an infinity symbol, which is a reclining figure 8. The Light expanded through the brains of all Humanity and prepared our physical brain structures at a cellular level for the activation of our pineal glands.

After that activity of Light, we went to Salisbury Cathedral, which was built without a break between 1220 and 1266. The cathedral houses the world's oldest clock and an important Recordkeeper Crystal that was buried in the foundation before the Abbey was built. When that leg of the circuitry was victoriously reconnected in the Crystal Grid System, we returned to our hotel in Street.

On May 12, 2001, numerically an 11 day, we participated in the final phase of reconnecting the circuitry of the Crystal Grid System.

On that day, the most prestigious soccer tournament in the world, the FA Cup Final, was schedule to take place at the Millennium Football Stadium in Cardiff, Wales. Two English teams were playing in the championship game, Liverpool and Arsenall. It was estimated that 450 million people around the world would be focusing on England during the game. That focus of attention created a Chalice of Light through which the Light of God poured to assist in bringing our Divine Pilgrimage to fruition God Victoriously.

In the morning, our group gathered for a meditation. We entered the Divinity of our hearts and joined the Divine Ceremony taking place in the Celestial Realms. The Feminine Aspects of our Mother God from Suns beyond Suns and Galaxies beyond Galaxies projected their luminous Presences into the atmosphere of Earth and stood shoulder to shoulder forming a circle around the Earth from the north to the south poles. Then, those exquisite expressions of our Mother God bathed the Earth in the healing unguent of a Mother's Love. Humanity's wounded hearts were lifted into a new level of healing and comfort.

After that blessing from our Mother God, we walked from our hotel to the Glastonbury Abbey. The Abbey was the first Christian church, and it was founded by Joseph of Arimathea. When our group entered the gates of the Abbey, the church bells tolled 11 o'clock.

We walked to the tombs of King Arthur and Queen Guinevere, which are located on the grounds of the Abbey. When our group stood at the grave sites, two beautiful white doves circled above us. We had not seen any white doves during our entire sojourn in England.

As we walked the hallowed grounds of the Abbey, the twelve-pointed Crown of the Solar Elohim that rests on the brow of every Human Being was activated with higher frequencies of the Twelve Solar Aspects of Deity than we had ever experienced before. That activation poured through our Heart Flames and permanently sealed the splicing that had taken place in the circuitry of the Crystal Grid System and physical brain structures of Humanity, thus completing the preparation for the opening of the portal of Light in England.

At the conclusion of our tour of the Abbey, we entered the building that was once the kitchen for the Abbot's house. The room has a high, domed ceiling, and when we entered the building, some of our group began toning a gentle Om. The celestial sounds reverberated through our Beings, and choirs of Angels joined in with us. When the toning stopped, we sat in awe in the breathless silence.

May 13, 2001, was Mother's Day in the United States of America, Canada and Australia. With hundreds of millions of people focusing on love for their mothers, the atmosphere was set for the opening of the portal of Light that will assist in returning Christ Consciousness to Earth.

We invited Lightworkers in England to join us for our activity of Light on May 13th. Fifty five people joined the thirty three people who had come with me on our sacred pilgrimage. Eight is the number that symbolizes the Universal Law *"As above, so below."* There were eighty-eight people physically participating in our activity of Light in Glastonbury and hundreds of thousands joining us consciously from all over the world.

During a three-hour activity of Light orchestrated by the Company of Heaven and God Selves of all Humanity, the portal of Light in England was successfully opened to full breadth. The pineal glands within the physical brain structures of every person on Earth were activated, and the *second* impulse of the second coming of the Christ was God-Victoriously accomplished.

May 14, 2001, we returned to London. To complete the final facet of our pilgrimage, we all went for a ride on the famous London Eye. In order to ride on that popular tourist attraction, we had to make our reservations a year in advance. When we picked up our tickets it was 11:11 a.m.

As we were lifted high above the London skyline on the Eye, the Light of God flooded through our Heart Flames and blazed forth from the newly-opened portal of Light in England to bless all life on Earth.

[This is just an interesting note. The Holy Cities of John the Beloved pulsate in the Etheric Realms above Arizona in the United States of America. Many years ago, a man in Arizona bought the London Bridge. He had the bridge transferred to the Arizona desert where it was reconstructed, brick by brick, in Lake Havasu City, along the Colorado River. That event actually formed a highway of Light between England and Arizona that has been building in momentum since that time.]

Healing the Wounded Heart

Eighty percent of Humanity's energy is released through our emotional bodies, and eighty percent of the lifeforce of Mother Earth is released through the emotional stratum of the planet as well. The emotional substance of our bodies and the Earth is reflected through the water element. That is why eighty percent of our bodies and the Earth are comprised of water.

Since the "fall" aeons ago, Humanity's emotional bodies have experienced levels of pain and suffering that have boggled our minds and overwhelmed our senses. Emotionally we have each faced extreme adversity and walked through trials and tribulations that would have shaken even the strongest Beings of Light to the very core. We experienced the *"dark night of the soul"* and struggled to persevere as we wept and wailed through our valley of tears.

Our pain and grief distorted our perception and caused us to close our hearts. That catastrophic event prevented the love of our Mother God from entering the physical plane. Without the love of our Mother God, our hearts became fragile and easily wounded. We became domineering, aggressive, controlling, violent and manipulative. Those destructive behavior patterns exacerbated the wounds in our hearts and catapulted us further into the throes of chaos and confusion.

In order for Humanity to withstand the 5th-Dimensional frequencies of the Flame of Transfiguring Divine Love, our wounded hearts had to be healed. Our abuse of power also had to be healed, and the Divine Authority, Will and Power of our Father God had to be restored.

After the Flame of Transfiguring Divine Love was activated by the Cosmic I AM in January 2001, myriad activities of Light took place to heal our wounded hearts. Our Solar Christ Presence were alerted to the need of the hour, and Lightworkers around the world responded to the call. People from every walk of life actively participated in improving the quality of life for themselves, their families and communities.

We were asked by Beloved Alpha and Omega to hold the Fifteenth Annual World Congress On Illumination within the *portal of the Flame of Healing Through the Power of Limitless Transmutation* in Tucson, Arizona, during the fifteenth Harmonic Convergence. People from all over the world came to Tucson to create the Heart Chalice that would secure the Flame of Transfiguring Divine Love in the physical plane. The first phase of that Divine Plan involved completing the healing of our wounded hearts.

The World Congress On Illumination began on August 11, 2001, which numerically equaled 11:11. As Lightworkers entered the beautiful forcefield of Loews Ventana Canyon Resort in Tucson, they were greeted by the Company of Heaven.

Every attendee experienced the loving embrace of our Father-Mother God and was lifted into the Great Solar Quiet. There each one was bathed in love, gratitude and deep appreciation for the sacrifices they had made in the expenditure of energy, time and money to come to that sacred conclave. They had come to selflessly serve as surrogates on behalf of ALL Humanity and to be the Heart, Head and Hands of God in the world of form. They had come to participate in an activity of Light that was unprecedented in the whole of Creation, and Heaven rejoiced.

In the late afternoon, a gentle rain baptized the Earth, and a double rainbow appeared in the sky. Over 500 people attended the Opening Ceremonies of Light that evening. Through beautiful music, sacred sounds, guided visualizations and the sharing of sacred knowledge, the final healing of Humanity's wounded hearts began. Our unified hearts created a tremendous Chalice of Light that cradled the entire Earth. The Solar Christ Presence of every person on Earth, whether they were in or out of embodiment, joined us in preparation for the week's activities.

On August 12, 2001, our Father-Mother God assisted Humanity to lift our Heart Chakras into a higher frequency of Divine Love. During the predawn hours of that morning, the *Perseid* meteor shower blazed through the atmosphere of Earth, and hundreds of meteors shot across the sky. The meteors shook the ethers and shattered the crystallized thoughtforms and archetypes of Humanity's lack of trust.

Every evolving soul knows at some level that if we had only trusted enough to hold open our Heart Chakras during the horrendous adversity we were faced with, the fall of Humanity would never have occurred. The Divine Love of our Mother God is omniscient, omnipresent and omnipotent. There is no destructive, outer-world event or human miscreation that can be sustained in the presence of that blazing force. It is the cohesive power of the Universe and the illusion of separation is dissolved in the Light of our Mother God's Love.

After the archetypes of Humanity's lack of trust were shattered, the Legions of Light flooded the Earth with the gift of Divine Trust which allowed our Solar Christ Presence to lift up our Heart Chakras.

After our Heart Chakras were raised in vibration, Saint Germain invoked the Lords of Power from the Great, Great Central Sun to descend into the atmosphere of Earth. Saint Germain then directed Violet Fire Angels from his Regal Court into the aura of every person on the planet. Once the Angels were in position, the Lords of Power breathed the most powerful activity of the Flame of

Healing Through the Power of Limitless Transmutation the Earth had ever experienced into the Heart Flame of every Human Being.

As the Healing Flame blazed through Humanity's Heart Chakras, it penetrated into the physical, etheric, mental and emotional bodies of each person and transmuted the crystallized patterns of fear, pain and suffering that were recorded there. The ancient wounds in Humanity's hearts were healed, and our Mother God was able to expand through every Heart Chakra.

On August 13, 2001, Beloved Serapis Bey and his Court of Mighty Seraphim descended into the atmosphere of Earth. Serapis Bey is an exponent of the Ascension Flame and the Fourth Solar Aspect of Deity. He has selflessly served this Earth since prior to our fall from Grace.

Serapis Bey revealed to us that he had come with his Legions of Seraphim to guide us through a quantum leap in the Earth's Ascension process. Now that Humanity's wounded hearts were healed, we were ready to Ascend further up the Spiral of Evolution than we had ever experienced. Serapis Bey directed a Seraphim of the Ascension Flame into the aura of every person on the planet, and the Company of Heaven stood in readiness.

Serapis Bey expanded his luminous Presence until our unified Heart Chalice cradling the Earth was held in his Heart Flame. On the Holy Breath, he breathed the Ascension Flame into the core of purity in every electron of precious life energy. For twenty-four hours the Ascension Flame gently raised the energy, vibration and consciousness of every atomic and subatomic particle and wave associated with the physical substance of the Human, Elemental and Angelic Kingdoms.

On August 14, 2001, everything was in place for the next step of the Divine Plan. Humanity had finally reached the evolutionary moment that required the archetypes and destructive patterns of Humanity's masculine abuse of power to be lifted into the Light. That was a necessary facet of the plan that had to be accomplished in order for the Earth to Ascend further up the Spiral of Evolution.

First, our Mother God invoked the Cosmic Dove of the Holy Spirit to breathe a miniature Dove into the Heart Flame of every person who has ever been part of the Earth's evolutions. This powerful gift from the Cosmic Holy Spirit will assist each of us to trust enough to hold our hearts open, regardless of the adversity we may face in our lives.

Next, Alpha and Omega revealed that it was time for the patterns and archetypes associated with our abuse of power to be lifted into the Light. We joined with those who had dedicated their lives to this service, and as one unified force, the collective Solar Christ Presence of Humanity Ascended into the heart of Alpha and Omega. As this occurred, an upward rushing flow of energy, vibration and consciousness was created. That allowed the thoughts, words, actions and feelings associated with our masculine abuse of power to be lifted into the Light.

After that miraculous healing, a mighty pillar of Light that extends from the heart of Alpha and Omega into the center of the Earth was permanently secured. Alpha and Omega then blazed the Solar Frequencies of the 5th Dimension through the pillar of Light and transformed the Sun of Even Pressure into a 5th-Dimensional Sun.

Alpha and Omega then expanded the Divine Authority, Will and Power of our Father God through their Throat Chakras. Those qualities of our Father God were then projected through the pillar of Light into the 5th-Dimensional Sun. They flowed into the spaces that previously contained the patterns and archetypes of Humanity's masculine abuse of power, and every empty void was filled with the perfection of our Father God. With the completion of that Cosmic event, *the Divine Authority, Will and Power of our Father God were restored on Earth.*

August 15th is celebrated as Mother Mary's Ascension Day. On that sacred and holy day, the Light of our Mother God poured through every person's healed heart and bathed the Earth in frequencies of Divine Love, Adoration and Reverence for Life. Simultaneously, the newly-anchored qualities of our Father God integrated further into every particle of life, and the Earth was bathed in the frequencies of Divine Authority, Will and Power. That long-awaited union of our Father-Mother God in the physical plane of Earth completed the final step of preparation for Earth's Ascension onto the initial rung of the 5th-Dimensional Spiral of Evolution.

For several years, Humanity has been existing in a fluid field of unmanifest potential. We have been fluctuating up and down the Spiral of Evolution, flowing back and forth through the 3rd-, 4th- and 5th-Dimensional frequencies. That is why things have seemed so confusing and so chaotic in our personal lives. Now it is time for us to stop vacillating up and down the Spiral of Evolution. It is time for us to begin our permanent ascent up the 5th-Dimensional Spiral of Limitless Physical Perfection.

On August 15, 2001, Beloved Jesus The Christ, expanded his luminous Presence to envelop the 12 Suns and the 144 planets in the System of Alpha and Omega, and all of Heaven stood in silence.

The Mighty Elohim and the Directors of the Elements reinforced the body of Mother Earth, and the Lords of Power strengthened the axis and Crystal Grid System. The Directors of the Elements flooded every Elemental Being with the Light of Divine Comfort and Peace. The Solar Christ Presence enveloped every soul in Divine Trust. All of the graded orders of Angels amplified the qualities of God they administer to Humanity during our Earthly sojourn. Finally, the 12 Suns and remaining 143 planets belonging to the System of Alpha and Omega joined in to assist the Earth in her final steps of preparation.

Each of the 12 Suns and 143 planets projected mighty shafts of Light into the 5th-Dimensional Sun of Even Pressure in the center of the Earth. Those shafts of Light held the Earth in her rightful position for her Ascent up the Spiral of Evolution.

When all of the safeguards were in place, Alpha and Omega sounded their Celestial Keynote signaling to the Cosmic I AM that their Solar System was ready to be breathed further up the Spiral of Evolution. On a mighty Inbreath of the Cosmic I AM, the entire Solar System of Alpha and Omega instantaneously Ascended onto the first rung of the spiral of the 5th Dimension.

That activity of Light placed the Solar System of Alpha and Omega in proper alignment for the next *Cosmic Inbreath,* which will lift the Earth into a new octave of learning in the 5th-Dimensional Realms of Limitless Physical Perfection. No one knows exactly when the Cosmic I AM will take that Inbreath, but according to the Spiritual Hierarchy, that Cosmic Inbreath is destined to take place in the very near future, and it will involve *every* Solar System in the Universe.

It is important for each of us to grasp the magnitude of this moment. The Solar System of Alpha and Omega has God-Victoriously Ascended onto the initial rung of the Spiral of the 5th Dimension. This means that Humanity can now begin to integrate the energy, vibration and consciousness of the 5th Dimension into our bodies and into the physical, etheric, mental and emotional strata of the planet. We now *truly* have the ability to manifest Heaven on Earth.

We still have free will, of course, and our thoughts and feelings are creative, so if we choose to descend down into the vibrations of the 3rd and 4th Dimensions, we have the ability to do so. But, if we consciously choose to hold our vision on the Limitless Physical Perfection of the 5th Dimension, *we have the absolute ability to remain in the harmonious frequencies of the 5th Dimension.*

We must be ever vigilant! We are creatures of habit, and it is very easy for us to let the old, familiar patterns surface. If we don't closely monitor our thoughts, words, actions and feelings, we will perpetuate patterns of pain, suffering, lack and limitation.

After the healing of our wounded hearts, the lifting of our Heart Chakras, the restoration of the Divine Authority, Will and Power of our Father God and our Ascension onto the spiral of the 5th Dimension, we were finally in a position to withstand the Cosmic Light of the Flame of Transfiguring Divine Love.

On August 16, 2001, the Solar Logos from Suns beyond Suns descended into the atmosphere of Earth in a regal procession. Each one assumed a strategic position around the planet in preparation for their awesome service to life.

As one breath, one voice, one heartbeat, those aspects of our Father-Mother God sent forth a Divine Edict, and for one timeless instant, Humanity's gift of free will was, once again, set aside. The Solar Logos commanded that every single lost, recalcitrant soul on Earth come forth in their finer bodies and stand before them. Even the most resistant souls who were buried in the densest frequencies of human miscreation were commanded to come forth in their finer bodies and stand before the Solar Logos. As each of these souls stood before the august Presence of the Solar Logos, they were *compelled* to remember their rightful positions in the family of Humanity.

Their Solar Christ Presence lovingly embraced them and spoke to them through their newly-healed hearts. As the souls listened, they were held in the gentle arms of our Mother God, and they began to awaken. After that activity of Light, the souls were drawn into the luminous Presence of Archangel Gabriel.

Archangel Gabriel held the Immaculate Concept for the Christ Presence of Jesus during the Piscean Age, and he is doing the same for all Humanity during the Age of Aquarius. On August 16, 2001, Archangel Gabriel intensified the Immaculate Concept of Humanity's Solar Christ Presence through the Stargates of our newly-healed hearts. He then sounded his mighty trumpet and burst asunder the remaining vestiges of the veils of illusion. The separation was no more, and the Solar Christ Presence of Humanity stood forth in readiness as One unified expression of God, prepared to fulfill the greatest mission we had ever been called to do on behalf of the Earth and all her life.

The Cosmic I AM—All That Is—sounded a Cosmic Tone, and the most powerful frequency of Light ever manifested in the history of time, the *Flame of Transfiguring Divine Love*, poured forth from the core of Creation. The Flame of Transfiguring Divine Love is a beautiful, deep rose-colored Flame with an aquamarine aura of Clarity. Radiating out from the heart of the Flame is an opalescent Sun of Transfiguration. This beautiful Flame was breathed into the Immaculate Hearts of the Legions of Solar Logos standing in the atmosphere of Earth and assimilated into their Heart Chakras.

These Light Beings then breathed the Flame of Transfiguring Divine Love into the Heart Chalice that had been created by the Lightworkers at the World Congress On Illumination. The Lightworkers, serving as surrogates on behalf of all Humanity, joined together and breathed into the 5th-Dimensional Sun of Even Pressure the Heart Chalice containing the Flame of Transfiguring Divine Love. Mother Earth joyously assimilated the Flame of Transfiguring Divine Love into her Heart Flame in preparation for the activity of Light that would take place the next day through the unified efforts of millions of Lightworkers around the world.

Interestingly, NASA reported that on August 15, 2001, a massive Solar Flare erupted on the back side of the Sun. Normally Solar Flares on the back side of the Sun do not affect the Earth because they radiate out in the opposite direction. According to scientists who monitor Solar activity, *"For some obscure reason which NASA cannot explain, on August 16, 2001, the flux of high-energy protons around the Earth soared to 1000 times the normal range hitting the Earth with a tremendous shock wave."*

That phenomenon caused an aurora borealis to be seen in many places throughout the globe. After that, the solar winds were above average, and sunspot activity was far above the peak scientists had predicted.

A high of 200 sunspots per day has been reached during the summer only a few times in the last 300 years. In the summer of 2001, however, we experienced a period of peaks up to 300 sunspots a day. That was a unique phenomenon that *had never before occurred in recorded history.*

The Lightworkers attending the Fifteenth Annual World Congress On Illumination came from all over the world. There were Lightworkers from England, Scotland, Switzerland, Germany, Canada, Argentina, Australia, Bolivia, Korea, Israel, Paraguay, Aruba, Equador, France and throughout the United States of America. On August 16th, when the World Congress was over, they each traveled to wherever their hearts directed them to go.

Some Lightworkers returned to their homes; some traveled to other locations on the planet, and some stayed in Tucson. Wherever they went, they created highways of Light from the Heart Chalice of the Flame of Transfiguring Divine Love to their points of destination. This formed a grid of Light that prepared the Earth for what would take place the next day.

August 17, 2001, was the fifteenth Harmonic Convergence. On that day, the Flame of Transfiguring Divine Love pulsated out from the Heart Chalice in the center of the Earth and blazed into the Crystal Grid System.

Millions of Lightworkers around the world joined together to assimilate and integrate that gift of Divine Love into the physical plane of Earth for the benefit of all life. Throughout the entire 24-hour period, the Flame of Transfiguring Divine Love blazed through the Crystal Grid System into the body of Mother Earth and bathed the planet in its healing Light. During that time, Humanity's Solar Christ Presences anchored the Flame of Transfiguring Divine Love in the permanent seed atom of each soul's heart.

Throughout that sacred and holy day, Lightworkers around the world focused their attention on the vision of Heaven on Earth. They empowered the thoughtforms of every single person on the planet awakening to the realization of his or her own Divinity and Oneness with all life. As those visions were empowered, the patterns of perfection from the 5th Dimension were imprinted into Humanity's RNA and DNA genetic codes.

Now, the Flame of Transfiguring Divine Love is gently building in momentum in every Heart Flame. Day by day, the Divine Intelligence is being released into the conscious mind of each soul.

During the Full Moon on September 2, 2001, the Divine Intelligence in the Flame of Transfiguring Divine Love shed new Light on our conscious fears and our erroneous belief systems. That helped to create the environment in which Humanity will experience a deeper sense of inner knowing and Divine Insight.

On September 4 and 5, 2001, six planets formed a Star of David around the Earth. A fire triangle was formed by the Moon trine Venus trine Pluto, and an air triangle was formed by Mercury trine Neptune trine Saturn. The ascending and descending triangles in the Star of David symbolize Humanity reaching up to God and God reaching down to Humanity. This forcefield of Light helped brace the Earth for what was to come.

September 11, 2001 — *911* — *an emergency call.* The seers of old said that during these end times we would experience "*screaming and the gnashing of teeth.*" They also predicted *Armageddon*—the ultimate battle between good and evil.

The reason for their dire predictions is that the seers witnessed what naturally occurs when the Light of God increases on Earth. They saw that when the Light of God penetrates into the physical plane and pierces into the core of purity in every electron, all of the humanly-created patterns of imperfection that conflict with that Divine Light are pushed to the surface to be healed and transmuted into Light.

For example, when Divine Love flows into the Earth, everything that conflicts with that love is pushed to the surface to be healed. That includes hatred, fear, intolerance, prejudice, abuse, anger, violence, war and every other expression of life that is void of love.

If people are not aware of what is happening, it appears as though things are getting worse in their lives. That causes them to become frightened, and when people move into fear, it is easy to latch onto the negative patterns that are coming up. When that happens, they often act out destructive behavior patterns which, of course, just exacerbates the situation. Tragically, that is what occurred on September 11, 2001.

Just for a moment, reflect on what happened in August 2001. O*ur Heart Chakras were lifted into higher frequencies of Light increasing the flow of Divine Love from our Mother God, and the Divine Authority, Will and Power of our Father God was returned to Earth.* The Light of both our Mother God and our Father God are now pouring into Earth and entering the core of purity in every electron of life. That Light is pushing to the surface of each person's life everything that conflicts with *Divine Love, Authority, Will and Power*. This is happening individually for each of us and collectively for the entire family of Humanity. Consequently, our individual abuses of love and power are coming up and so are

Humanity's collective abuses of love and power.

Now, with an open heart and mind, let's look at the bigger picture. Let's step back and observe the *SYMBOLOGY* of the horrendous things that happened on September 11, 2001.

Osama bin Laden and his al-Qaida organization are the number one suspects in this terrorist attack. These men model the *epitome* of abuse of power and the lack of love and reverence for life. They act out their lower human egos' manipulative, fear-based concepts of God, which are the antithesis of Divine Love, Authority, Will and Power. In their warped minds, they honestly believe that they are doing God's Will. They feel they are participating in a "holy war" (talk about an oxymoron).

Bin Laden and al-Qaida were harbored by Afghanistan, which is a country that severely abused women through the misuse of the masculine power of the Taliban, all in the name of God. The terrorists have total disregard for human life, and their participation in those horrific events SYMBOLICALLY represented *the very basest aspect of the human ego attacking the facilities that represent the masculine abuse of power and lack of reverence for life* in the most powerful country in the world.

The World Trade Towers represented the heart of the global economy and commerce. They were the financial center of the world in the most powerful country on the planet. Within those two towers were housed the movers and the shakers representing myriad corporations, investment firms, banks, businesses, traders and insurance companies. When the towers crumbled to the ground, they SYMBOLICALLY represented the demise of the old corporate structure and the consciousness of greed, selfishness and abuse of power. That is the "dog-eat-dog" consciousness that has resulted in the pollution of the Earth, governmental and corporate corruption, crime, war, famine, poverty, distortion of the medical system, imbalance in the economic system and every other abuse of power in the economic world.

The Pentagon is the nerve center of military power in the most powerful country in the world. The attack on the Pentagon SYMBOLICALLY represented the lack of reverence for life and the abuse of power that has been inflicted on Humanity through the death, pain and suffering of war.

The fourth plane's destructive mission was foiled, but according to reports, it was headed for the White House or the Capitol Building in Washington DC. Those buildings represent the seat of government in the most powerful country in the world. The negativity surfacing through an attack on the White House or the Capitol would have SYMBOLICALLY represented the abuse of power and lack of reverence for life associated with governments around the world.

The horrific attack on these symbols clearly reflects the distorted patterns being pushed to the surface to be healed and transformed by the influx of Divine Love from our Mother God and the influx of Divine Authority, Will and Power from our Father God.

We must remember that the Light of God is ALWAYS Victorious. I assure you that the increased Light from our Father-Mother God is not going to cause more harm than good. It only looks like things are getting worse through our limited perception. Any loss of life is devastating, but the potential was that tens of thousands of people could have died in those attacks. It was truly a miracle that fewer than 3,000 people sacrificed their lives in that tragedy.

When the news of the attack on America started spreading around the world, the open-hearted response was awe-inspiring. The leaders of the free world responded, expressing their solidarity with the United States. Within two hours after the attack, I had over 200 E-mails from Lightworkers all over the world invoking calm and imploring people to hold the Light, meditate and pray for Peace. The United States Congress and Senate members stood together on the steps of the Capitol and sang "God Bless America" with one unified voice. Communities throughout America banded together to offer assistance and give blood. All of these acts of compassion, love and genuine caring assisted in healing and transmuting the negativity being pushed to the surface.

The love and compassion that poured forth from people around the world in response to that tragedy caused Humanity to hold open the Stargates of our hearts in spite of the terrible adversity. Even though our reflex response reflected the old-paradigm of war, the things we learned from those tragic events will greatly assist in lifting the consciousness of Humanity into a new understanding of Divine Love and Divine Authority, Will and Power. Positive growth will result in the transformation of the way we do business on this planet, the way we manage the global economy, the way we govern ourselves, the way we interact with each other and the way Humanity respects and honors all life.

September 17, 2001, was a unique moment in the evolution of the Earth. During that New Moon, exactly one month after the Flame of Transfiguring Divine Love was assimilated and integrated into the Heart Flames of every man, woman and child, the 5th-Dimensional Sun in the center of the Earth expanded its Light a thousandfold to envelop the entire planet.

That expansion of Light birthed Beloved Mother Earth into her initial existence as a SUN.

Here is some very interesting information that was reported regarding September 17, 2001.

Day of Truth
by Kiara Windrider
(This was shared over the Internet)

"There is a 6,000-year calendar encoded in stone within the Great Pyramid of Giza, which has accurately predicted significant historical events including the birth of Jesus Christ and the global wars of this century.

"The calendar began in *3999 BC* and ends, amazingly, on September 17, 2001.

"According to this calendar, there are three things we might expect at this time of ending. It is a time for *a shift in Earth's relationship with the Sun*. It is time to complete the balance of planetary karmic cycles. And it is time for a global spiritual initiation.

"What are the implications of this? Earth's relationship to the Sun is shifting. We have been experiencing more Solar Flares this year than ever before in recorded history. The magnetic polarities of the Sun have gone through a significant shift, and scientists are indicating this could soon happen on Earth as well. The Earth's magnetic fields hold our collective thoughts, feelings and consciousness. Could the shifting of the magnetic fields perhaps be mirroring the evolution of human consciousness that we are currently experiencing? Could it also have to do with our entry into a region of space known as the 'photon band,' which has, in previous cycles, indicated quantum shifts in planetary evolution?

"As we prepare for such a quantum shift, we will simultaneously be experiencing the completion and balancing of long-range karmic cycles. On a 3rd-Dimensional level, what we do to the Earth, we do to ourselves, and we are beginning to see the repercussions of this. On a higher level, we may evoke a Law of Grace that supersedes the Laws of Karma. This demands conscious intent, however. Can we use this time to send out a different message to the Universe? Can we reach inside of ourselves and look at the denials and fears that keep us imprisoned in our lives? Can we encourage our communities, businesses and governments to do likewise? What if we look to this day, September 17, 2001, as a *Day of Truth*, to redirect our intentions toward the highest possibilities of our souls and for our beautiful planet?

"We can only go as high as we are willing to go deep, and it is often in the very depths that we find the greatest Light. This is where we find the power and the hope to sustain us, for it is only as we are willing to see and to embrace all of our deeply human fragmented realities that the Light of Grace can shine upon us.

"As we allow the Light of Grace to shine upon us, we open ourselves to a global spiritual initiation. We are seeing increasingly rapid expansions of consciousness on our planet. This emerging consciousness is 4th- and 5th-Dimensional in nature and can override the 3rd-Dimensional ecological realities on our planet. The nature of most spiritual initiations is the experience of a gradual ascent of consciousness followed by a quantum leap. When the time is right, this quantum leap could take place '*in the twinkling of an eye.*' We are collectively entering the birth canal of a New World. Will we birth ourselves into the Age of Light with grace and ease? Or will we continue on our collision course towards extinction?

"An astrological chart set up for Giza, Egypt, at 11:30 p.m., September 16, 2001, is very revealing. A perfect Star of David is formed. The descending triangle includes Saturn, Uranus and Mercury. Uranus and Mercury represent the energies of the Aquarian Age. Saturn joins them in a grand trine allowing these energies to be grounded into structure and form. Meanwhile, Venus, Chiron and the Midheaven come together in an ascending triangle. Joining together in another grand trine, these energies represent the ascent of the wounded feminine. The two triangles representing the descent of the Aquarian Age and the ascent of the feminine come together perfectly on this day, signifying possibilities for a great healing of our collective splits and shadows as we prepare for a planetary initiation. This Day of Truth recognizes that we are on the verge of a planetary spiritual awakening and is a call for deep self-examination. It is also a recognition that we are connected with a vast array of Beings who can assist us if we call for their assistance collectively.

"Although we cannot remain in denial about the ecological realities on our planet, the pathway to the Fifth World is in affirming the new realities among us. Somewhere between an ungrounded spiritual escapism based on denial and a narcissistic preoccupation with gloom and doom, we can choose to intentionally and purposefully envision a brave New World based on the deepest Truth of our Beings. In order to do this, we must consciously choose to face our own shadows, commit to rebirth and open to the Light of our guiding Truth.

"May this Day of Truth reflect the deepest Truth of our Beings. And may this be the message that we send out to the Universe as we prepare for the dawning Age of Light.

"May we walk in beauty."

[Author's note: The reason the 6000-year-old calendar encoded in the stone of the Great Pyramid of Giza ended on September 17, 2001, is because on that sacred and holy day, our Beloved Planet Earth was birthed into the initial impulses of her new reality as a 5th-Dimensional SUN. In that Cosmic Moment, her radiant Light expanded a thousandfold, and the Earth disappeared from the physical sight of the ancient seers.]

Buckminster Fuller said many insightful things in his lifetime. Two of his famous quotes are:

"The world will be saved by individuals of integrity freely joining together." and...
"In order to change something, we must not struggle to change the existing model. We must create a new model and make the old one obsolete."

People are waking up, and they are becoming more receptive to the Light of God. The Flame of Transfiguring Divine Love is finding a pathway into the deepest recesses of every heart. We are learning more profoundly than ever before that we are all in this together and that this is our moment of decision.

In order for all life on Earth to move forward with the rest of our Solar System, we must each make a choice. We can choose love, or we can choose hate. We can choose to Ascend into the Light, or we can choose to self-destruct. It is up to us.

Love and hate cannot exist in the same space. If we are expressing hate and judgment, there is no space for love and tolerance. It is just that simple. If we have not totally surrendered our hearts to Transfiguring Divine Love, our God Presences cannot integrate into our bodies, and we will not be the empowered Beings of Light we are capable of being.

When our hearts are centered in Transfiguring Divine Love, we clearly see and know that *we are all* Beloved Children of God doing the best we can do according to our wisdom and understanding. The Divine Intelligence within that Flame reveals that if we expand our own Light, we greatly expand the Light that is available to awaken our sisters and brothers who are still asleep.

The Lightworkers around the world have joined together in consciousness, and we are humbly and gratefully assisting in Humanity's awakening process. We are following the guidance of our God Selves and the Beings of Light in Realms of Illumined Truth. We are grasping every opportunity to expand the Light of God into Humanity's collective consciousness.

By invoking the Light, we are able to purify, transmute, consecrate and dedicate, *to the highest good* the energy released by people from every event on the planet that draws Humanity's focus of attention. We can use the collective energy from all of the celebrations associated with the world religions. We can also use the energy released by Humanity from every other holiday—whether it is spiritual, secular, political, national or global. We can use celestial events such as Equinoxes, Solstices, Full Moons, New Moons, Blue Moons, Solar and Lunar Eclipses, meteor showers, passing comets and the intensified Light from powerful Solar Flares. We can purify and raise up the energy from sporting events, musical events, movie, television and media events and every other opportunity that unifies the cup of Humanity's collective consciousness.

Simply by our conscious intention, we can join hearts and minds with the Lightworkers around the world who are networking and orchestrating global meditations and visualizations. These meditations create a vehicle through which the Sons and Daughters of God can join together to invoke the Light that will transform the maladies manifesting on Earth. Our opportunities are limitless. All we have to do is be willing to be the Open Door that no one can shut, then the Light of God will flow through us and continually bless all life.

Activating the Matrix and Archetypes for Divine Government

After the opening of the portal for the Causal Body of God in August 2000, the anchoring of the Flame of Transfiguring Divine Love in August 2001, and the opening of hearts that took place after the events of September 11, 2001, the vibratory rate on the planet had finally reached a frequency that would sustain the matrix and archetypes for *Divine Government*.

In order to grasp the significance of that, we must understand what Divine Government represents. First of all, Divine Government is *not* One World Government, a New World Order or any of the other concepts that have been used to describe the manipulative, controlling shadow governments ruled by the embodied forces of imbalance. Divine Government is the antithesis of that level of consciousness.

Divine Government reflects the Universal Law *"As above, so below."* It is a self-governing body guided and directed by the God Selves of all Humanity: a government *of* our God Selves, *by* our God Selves, *for* our God Selves. When we truly understand what that means, we will see the tremendous effect Divine Government will have on the world and all life.

Our God Selves are who we *really* are, and they transcend our fragmented, manipulative human egos. These aspects of our Divinity are multidimensional, and they are one with the Divine Heart and Mind of God. Our God Selves are our superconscious minds, and they understand the Divine Principles governing this Earth. They know the urgent need of the hour.

Our God Selves know that all life is interrelated and that if the family of Humanity is going to survive, we have to come together as one unified force of Divine Love, Harmony and Balance. Our God Selves also know that every evolving soul is going through a unique learning experience and that our various races, religions, creeds, beliefs, cultures, nationalities and lifestyles are part of that experience. Our egos are distorting much of what we are expressing through our diversities at this time, but when our God Selves are in charge, we will revel in the beauty and wonder of our differences.

When our God Selves are in control, we will understand that our diversities help us learn and grow. Then we will happily share our gifts, talents, wisdom, knowledge and abundance to enhance the lives of all people. We will know that we are cocreating this reality together and that God's Abundance and the God supply of all good things are limitless.

Once the matrix and archetypes for Divine Government are activated in the physical plane, the obsolete, fear-based cup of human consciousness will be shattered, and the patterns of perfection in the Causal Body of God that are associated with Divine Government will be available to flow into the hearts and minds of every Human Being.

That event will greatly expand the Divine Intelligence within the Flame of Transfiguring Divine Love in every Heart Flame. Then even the most resistant souls will awaken, and their God Selves will take command.

Eventually every country will be governed by the God Selves of the people abiding in that country. Since our God Selves know the full significance of the oneness of all life, they know that only by working toward the highest good of all concerned in every facet of life will we succeed in accomplishing the Divine Plan. Only by creating win-win situations in every governmental exchange, every human exchange and every exchange with the environment and the Nature Kingdom will there be Eternal Peace and Limitless Abundance on Earth.

When our God Selves are governing the planet, we will tap into the patterns of perfection in the Causal Body of God that govern the Universal Laws affecting energy, medicine, health, healing, the economy, food supply, shelter, technology, communication, travel, education, science, sacred geometry, music, art, movement, meditation, spiritual growth, enlightenment, peace and every other pattern of perfection.

Implementing the Divine Plan

We were guided by the Spiritual Hierarchy to arrange to have the Sixteenth Annual World Congress On Illumination in Washington, DC, in August 2002. Our guidance came two years before the event was to take place, so we did not understand the full magnitude at the time.

Every facet of the unfolding Divine Plan is contingent on how much is accomplished during the previous phase of the plan. Not even the Company of Heaven knows exactly how successful the Lightworkers will be with each activity of Light until it is completed. Only then is an evaluation made, and the next phase of the plan determined, according to the greatest need of the hour.

We were asked to organize the gathering in Washington, DC, because that location represents the *heart of government* for the most powerful country in the world. America represents the microcosm of the macrocosm for the planet. The original Divine Intent of this country was to model to the world how the family of Humanity could live together in harmony, prosperity, equality, happiness with liberty, freedom and justice for all—one unified nation under God. All of our sacred documents: the Declaration of Independence, the Constitution of the United States of America and the Bill of Rights proclaim that Divine Mission.

In spite of the terrible errors we have made as a country and the corruption that has been demonstrated in our government off and on since its inception, *the original Divine Intent for this nation has not changed!*

AMERICA is an anagram for the I AM RACE. The New World was to be a blueprint for Divine Government. The I Am Race was to be a race of God-Conscious souls comprised of every race, religion, culture, nationality, creed and lifestyle. Even though it seems like we have fallen far from the original plan, the blueprint for Divine Government is pulsating in the Spark of Divinity for this country, and it is now time for the matrix and archetypes for Divine Government to be activated.

Once the matrix and archetypes are activated for any creation, the unformed primal Light of the Universe is magnetized into them, and they become manifest form. That means that once the matrix and archetypes for Divine Government are activated, *nothing* can prevent Divine Government from eventually manifesting on Earth.

It was not a coincidence that the events of September 11, 2001, evoked unprecedented patriotism in the hearts of Americans. As people throughout the country rekindled the joy, pride and love in their hearts for this country, the Light of God flowed into Washington, DC, and created a powerful forcefield of unmanifest Divine Potential.

The Spiritual Hierarchy asked those of us at the New Age Study of Humanity's Purpose, Inc. to send forth a clarion call to inspire Lightworkers from all over the world to come to Washington, DC, to serve as instruments of God and surrogates on behalf of Humanity in the activation of the matrix and archetypes for Divine Government.

When we join together with other Lightworkers who have the

intention of fulfilling the Divine Plan and serving as instruments of God and surrogates on behalf of Humanity, our humble efforts are greatly empowered. Our God Selves take dominion of our Earthly vehicles, and full power of our multidimensional Divinity radiates through our Heart Flames. The intensity of that Light is unfathomable.

When all of the multidimensional facets of our God Selves blend with the God Selves of the other Lightworkers who are gathered with us, the Light expands exponentially. Through our unified Heart Flames, the Light of a *thousand* Suns is projected into the physical plane of Earth to accomplish that facet of the Divine Plan. The results are monumental! *Don't ever underestimate your ability to make a positive difference. You are a wondrous Child of God, and ALL that our Father-Mother God has is yours.*

In spite of all of the confusion and chaos happening in the world, there is convincing evidence that Humanity is awakening and that a profound shift of consciousness is taking place. All we have to do is observe what took place at the Winter Olympics in Salt Lake City, Utah, in February 2002, to confirm that Truth.

As I mentioned previously, the Olympic Games are the only events in the world that hold the attention of approximately four-billion people in a positive way for over two weeks. The collective cup of Humanity's focused attention during that time provides a tremendous portal through which Lightworkers can invoke the Light of God to assist with the unfolding Divine Plan.

During the 2002 Winter Olympics, the Divine Plan was to awaken the sleeping souls who were resisting moving forward in the Light and who had forgotten that they are Beloved Children of God. The goal was to help them through the storms of chaos and imbalance so they would trust enough to choose the Light. The Opening Ceremonies of the Olympic Games clearly demonstrated that facet of the plan.

The Opening Ceremonies were held on February 8, 2002, and the announcer began by stating that the theme of the Olympic Games was *Igniting the Fire Within*. After he made that announcement, a child skated into the arena carrying a lantern of Light. The announcer said the *Child of Light* was confronting storms as he searched for the Light within.

Next a skater dressed as a Flame entered the arena. The announcer said the Fire Within appears in order to show the Child of Light the way. Then, what seemed to be hundreds of children aged six to 12 skated into the arena carrying lanterns of Light.

Later five Native American tribes entered the arena in full native dress. They played their sacred instruments, and each tribe sounded a note with their flutes creating one harmonic chord. The audience all had flutes and joined in, creating a powerful Keynote for the Olympics' matrix.

After the matrix was formed, a representative from each tribe said a traditional prayer, asking the Great Spirit to bless the games. A Golden Eagle was released, and it encircled the stadium. Then 66 skaters dressed as Golden Eagles entered the arena with other skaters dressed as Flames.

Other statements the announcer used to describe the various aspects of the performance included:

"The coming of the Dawn."
"Recreating the Land of Enchantment."
"The Inner Light."
"The Fire that Lights your dreams."

At the conclusion of the Opening Ceremonies, the Olympic Torch was lit.

During the Olympic Flame's circuitous route to Salt Lake City, the torch was brought to Tucson, Arizona, for the very first time. When the torch passed through this portal of Light, the Flame of Transfiguring Divine Love was anchored within the Olympic Flame.

The moment the Olympic Torch was lit in Salt Lake City, the Flame of Transfiguring Divine Love expanded through the collective cup of Humanity's consciousness and intensified the Flame of Transfiguring Divine Love within the hearts of every man, woman and child.

That awesome activity of Light began the formation of a powerful, multidimensional *Bridge to Freedom* that expands the abyss from the densest frequencies of human pain and suffering into the 5th-Dimensional frequencies of Limitless Physical Perfection.

That Bridge to Freedom is building daily and hourly through the unified efforts of Lightworkers around the world. It is the bridge over which recalcitrant souls will be able to pass safely once they awaken and make the conscious choice to Ascend with the Earth. The Bridge of Transfiguring Divine Love is a gift of Divine Grace, Mercy and Compassion beyond our understanding.

The final piece of music played at the Opening Ceremonies

was Beethoven's *"Ode to Joy."* How perfect!

Interestingly, during the Olympic Games an American Bald Eagle was sighted in Tucson, and it remained for several days. That was indeed a very rare occurrence

The Canadian ice skaters who were involved in the controversy over the Gold Medal served an important part in the fulfillment of the Divine Plan. The Canadians were from Edmonton, an area not far from Mount Robson in Alberta, Canada. Pulsating above Mount Robson are the etheric Temples of the Elohim of the Third Solar Aspect of Deity, the Aspect of Divine Love. They are known as the Elohim Orion and Angelica. These mighty Builders of Form are the Silent Watchers of the Bridge of Transfiguring Divine Love.

As the world turned its attention to the Canadian ice skaters and heard their story over and over again, the Elohim Orion and Angelica were able to expand exponentially the Bridge to Freedom, moving this endeavor forward a quantum leap.

Another notable moment in the Olympic Games also involved ice skaters. During the ice dancing event, the couple from France put on a very poignant performance. The man was dressed in a costume that represented Humanity in bondage. The woman's costume represented fire, creation and freedom. Their music included the words from Martin Luther King's speech *"I Have A Dream."* The audience sat in reverent silence as the words *"Let Freedom Ring"* reverberated throughout the world. The French skaters won the Gold Medal. The Russian ice dancers won the Silver Medal as they danced to the music *"A Time For Peace."* The Italian ice dancers won the Bronze Medal as they danced to the song *"I Will Survive."*

The Olympic Games were God Victorious in every way, even in bringing to the attention of the world the flaws in the judging process and the need for new standards of integrity and honesty for the judges.

The Golden Christ Light Grid Activation

On April 13, 2002, at 3:00 p.m. Central Time, USA, Lightworkers all over the world joined together to anchor the Golden Christ Light Grid into the physical plane. That vitally important activation helped to accelerate Mother Earth's healing process and to increase her vibratory rate.

Lightworkers all over the world listened to their hearts and traveled to various areas to align along the Crystal Grid System. The physical Crystal Grid System of Earth is the same as the acupuncture meridians within our human bodies. Humanity's Solar Spines, with our Twelve Solar Chakras, serve as acupuncture needles. When we are physically aligned along a meridian or on an acupuncture point in the body of Mother Earth, we are capable of anchoring multidimensional frequencies of Light into the physical plane of Earth.

The Golden Christ Light Grid vibrates with the full spectrum of Christ Light which includes, among other things, Divine Consciousness, Eternal Peace and God's Limitless Abundance. The following vision of the Golden Christ Light Grid Activation was shared over the Internet in March 2002.

Turtle Woman's Vision
The Golden Christ Light Grid Activation
by Turtle Woman, Oma
(This was shared over the Internet)

"The Earth was far below in her entirety, a beautiful blue and white swirling marble in a sea of stars and space. Approaching the Earth, I noticed a grid overlaying the Mother, a five-pointed grid, one of mathematical pentagons, honeycombed, one next to another. There were lines that ran through each pentagon point, connecting to the center of each pentagon, creating a huge mesh which encompassed the Mother in her wholeness over land and sea.

"I knew the points of the pentagons and the intersecting lines in the center of each pentagon were the power points along the ley lines. I understood that each point was where a Lightworker needed to be to activate the Light Grid to bring full consciousness awakening to all on the planet. I was surprised to see and understand that, in reality, it would only take hundreds of Lightworkers worldwide instead of the thousands I had previously thought would be needed to activate the Light Grid. An understanding came over me that one Lightworker was needed to physically stand on each and every point on the grid. Once each Lightworker arrived at his or her assigned point, the Light activation would take place as each Lightworker implanted the Golden Light of Christ at exactly the same time, simultaneously, worldwide.

"Then I was shown that it would require several years for Lightworkers to disperse and move to the Light Grid activation points.

The breaking up of Spirit Groups would start to commence for this dispersion, but many would be reluctant to make these moves as many of the grid points would require people to leave the comfort of friends, family and spiritually supportive areas to move to rather undesirable locations, often areas of isolation in one manner or another with little surrounding spiritual support. Many Lightworkers would resist the promptings nudging them in this direction, and the longer the resistance, the more critical the timing would be in the long run, with the possibility of the grid not being activated with dire consequences for many souls.

"The vision transformed again, and I was unexpectedly shown a pleasant young Asian man standing in front of me vignetted. He was small in stature and frame, around five feet tall, somewhere in his late teens or early twenties and was walking across an open plain on a pleasant day in a short-sleeved, light or white knit shirt and khaki pants. He smiled at me, and I realized he could see me too. I understood that he was Chinese as he stepped to a certain point, stopped and smiled again. I instantly knew he was the last Lightworker to arrive in place on the Light Grid and that it was time to activate the grid. I knew he had made a great effort to get to his assigned point, that he had faced personal dangers to do so, and yet he treated it with ease, joy and knowingness. I knew that once he was in place that all that had to be done was for all Lightworkers to implant the Golden Christ Light at exactly the same moment, worldwide. I knew that it would take only hundreds, but all had to be in place, implanting the Golden Light of Christ at exactly the same moment. I wondered if all would follow the promptings they were being given and go to those many undesirable places they did not want to be.

"The vision suddenly shifted again, as if in answer to the question. I was standing in a front yard that I knew was 'mine,' but it was not where I was currently living. I had no idea where this yard, this place, was. It was a pleasant spring day in mid-afternoon. Somehow I knew it was 3:00 p.m. (Central Time - USA). I could see and feel a breeze and the Sun on my face, slightly to my right side. I was looking southeast down a street which 'T' intersected into the front of the house on the street on which I 'lived.' Southeast, the direction to simultaneously receive and manifest! (East, the direction of receiving and the Golden Light. South, the direction of manifestation and childlike innocence).

"I was standing in the front yard doing what I knew was my

daily exercise of implanting the Golden Light of Christ within myself, my relations, my property, my surrounding area, state, country, the entire Mother and radiating it out into all of Creation. I knew it was the day of the Light Activation, and I was starting to get concerned as a few minutes passed and nothing out of the ordinary happened. My heart began to sink as I thought the young Chinese man did not make it after all, that maybe he was asleep since it was night on his side of the world.

"As I stood facing the southeast verbalizing and visualizing the Golden Light of Christ, I realized people were walking their dogs, jogging, bicycling, and driving down the street with their windows open with their radios playing. I was not familiar with any of the music. I had never heard it before. People were starting to notice me as they went by, and I was a little embarrassed that I was being observed. I felt disappointed and sad as I continued invoking the Light while watching an alternative scenario start to play out of massive death and destruction in absence of the Lightworkers activation of the grid NOW!

"As the prayer went out, an enormous power surge shot into my body like a light switch flipped on in a dark room. I was instantly engulfed in a huge, visible pillar of Golden Light! It came from as far in the sky above as one could see, endlessly extending beyond sight. It surrounded my body several feet in diameter. It was a brilliant Golden radiance, surging with power and energy! I was instantly fully awake and felt like a cosmic spark plug connected directly to the Source. The joy, the knowing, the total awareness, the complete power of the Highest Good! I knew the young Asian man had just made the last connection in the grid. I could see him standing in the quiet hours of darkness with a sky filled with stars, his Golden Pillar standing out and illuminating all around him! An expression of bliss was on his face!

"My heart soared! I could also see all the others standing at their posts, every Lightworker on the grid engulfed in their individual Pillar of Golden Light! I could see all of our pillars extending out in all directions into space, shooting in all directions into ALL of Creation! My body was rigidly standing at attention, my arms down by my side, my eyes straight ahead, totally engulfed in holy Golden Light extending endlessly into the sky and beyond.

"I did not have to verbalize the Golden Light; I did not have to visualize the Golden Light; I *was* Golden Light in all its power and beauty! I was One and yet separate. I was in complete ecstasy, yet it was taking all my concentration to hold that Power of Light. I prayed silently to hold the Light, to not fail, to be worthy but, most importantly, physically able to withstand it!

"I prayed for help and strength. I became aware of people on the street stopping and staring, standing with their mouths open, some coming into the yard, amazed and shocked, wondering what was going on! How could this be? They were awed and yet somewhat fearful. I could hear their thoughts, 'What *is* this'?

"Someone I knew when I was young suddenly appeared in the yard in amazement, starting to comment on what was going on, but before she could finish what she was saying, she instantly awoke into full consciousness, overwhelmed and collapsing on the lawn in the power of her instant at Oneness. A chain reaction started to take place. As each person suddenly awoke, the people in the closest vicinity to them would suddenly wake up too in wonderment, amazement, shaking their heads and marveling at how they had been walking zombies all their lives, asleep until just seconds ago! I knew the miracle of total worldwide Enlightenment was unfolding!

"I could see that every Lightworker worldwide, thousands and thousands, were now standing in full Golden Pillars of Christ Light, at work, at home, at the grocery store, sitting in their cars on freeways. We were all connected as One to the Source, to our Selves and to each other. I could see the chain reaction expanding from each Lightworker to each and every Being worldwide as it spread truly at the speed of Light. I could hear the birds bursting out in song and see animals jumping around in pure glee as they witnessed and understood what was happening. I could hear the trees and all the plants giving praise to the Creator, the rocks and stones vibrating with awareness—everything connected at once in exuberance and song, singing with victory and praise and thanksgiving!

"Again the vision instantly shifted, and I was in space looking down upon the Earth Mother and was still within my Golden Pillar of Light, connected to myself on the Earth yet extending into eternity as the entire Mother radiated with the Golden glow, an immense halo of Golden Christ Light surrounding her way out beyond her atmosphere, the intensity of the Light magnifying exponentially as I watched.

"I saw thousands of ships surrounding the Mother and could see all the Beings from innumerable Galaxies, Universes, and Dimensions—literally all of Creation watching in stunned amazement as the Mother and all her children laughingly exploded with radiant

Golden Light shooting out through all of Creation like a supernova, transformed, transforming as it went.

"I could hear All of Creation exclaim in surprise, 'They have done it! They have shown us the way! We can all be this! Spirit and matter as One'!

"In this state of connection to Oneness, I knew the vision was to be released, that permission would be given when the time was right. The vision suddenly popped, and I was standing in the living room of my home of many years with tears streaming down my face. knowing both sides of the coin of whether or not the Light Grid is activated. The choice is ours, according to free will.

"The vision took place in 1991. I am now living in the place with the yard that was shown to me in that vision. Within the last few weeks (March 2002), I have finally been given permission to re-lease this vision. I have been shown that the reality of this vision requires every Lightworker who knows they are part of this Golden Christ Light Grid Activation to let themselves be guided right now to their activation point if they are not already there. It is imperative that this message reach as many Lightworkers as possible world-wide, as quickly as possible. As shown in the vision, the journey for some will be long and arduous. For the activation to take place, each Lightworker has to be on their point on the grid system, other-wise, the grid will not activate. The time is now. I thank you God NOW!

"Blessings to All! Stay in the Golden Light. All My Relations in Love and Light, Turtle Woman, Oma."

This activation was God-Victoriously accomplished on April 13, 2002. The vision reveals what took place in the multidimensional Realms of Cause. Now the Golden Christ Light is filtering into Humanity's consciousness, and a greatly accelerated awakening is taking place.

Cocreating a New Reality

Contrary to outer appearances, this is the dawn of unprecedented opportunities for our personal and planetary transformation. It has never been more vital for Lightworkers to recognize that we have the ability to cocreate a new reality. Our purpose and reason for being on this planet is to learn how to use our creative faculties of thought and feeling to cocreate Heaven on Earth. It is time for us to join together with our Father-Mother God and cocreate the beauty and wonder of the Heavenly Realms on Earth. As we accomplish this facet of the Divine Plan, we will fulfill the Divine Edict "*As above, so below.*"

Just for a moment, put aside your thoughts and fears of the chaos and confusion manifesting in the outer world, and go within to the deepest recesses of your heart. Ask your God Self to take full dominion, and ask that you be allowed to remember the vows you took in the Heart of God before this world was.

When you were first breathed forth from the Core of Creation as a Beloved Child of God, you were given two choices. One choice was for you to remain in the Heavenly Realms of Limitless Physical Perfection and bask in the radiance of God's Light for all Eternity. The other choice was for you to descend into the dense reality of the physical plane where you could learn to use your creative faculties to cocreate previously unknown expressions of Divinity. You realized that by choosing to become a cocreator with your God Parents, you would assist in expanding the Kingdom of Heaven throughout Infinity.

Obviously, you chose to become a cocreator or you would not be embodied on Earth at this time. Once you made that decision, you were given the gift of free will, and you were empowered with the knowledge and understanding "*All that my Father-Mother God has is mine.*"

Regardless of what direction your life has taken or what distorted human miscreations you are experiencing in your life at this moment, your original Divine Mission has not changed. Encoded in the Divine Blueprints of your RNA/DNA structures are the original patterns of your Divine Potential as a Child of God. You are an empowered cocreator. Everything you need to transform your life into the perfection of Heaven on Earth is already pulsating within your Divine Blueprints. All you have to do is remember that Truth, and start using your creative faculties as they were intended to be used.

Instead of using your thoughts and feelings to empower the pain and suffering caused by human miscreations, focus on your vision of Heaven on Earth. You now have the ability to reach up into the patterns of perfection blazing in the Causal Body of God. Through your meditations and prayers, invoke your God Self to reveal to you the viable solutions for the problems manifesting in your own life, and tap into the solutions for the various maladies existing on

Earth as well.

Don't ever underestimate your ability to change your reality. The Universal Law is "*Where your attention is, there YOU are. What you put your thoughts, words, actions and feelings into, you bring into form.*"

The clarion call has gone forth from the heart of our Father-Mother God. Humanity, individually and collectively, is being invoked to reclaim our Divine Birthright as Children of God. We are being asked to cocreate a new reality. Our Father-Mother God and the Company of Heaven are imploring us to fulfill the vows we took prior to this embodiment.

In order to be on Earth during the unique moment of her Ascension in the Light, the God Self of every embodied soul vowed to assist in some way to transform this sweet Earth and ALL her life into the perfection of Heaven on Earth. That statement is not just a lofty platitude. In spite of the negativity appearing on the screen of life and the horrendous things people are doing to each other, that statement is very real and a very possible achievement.

Each one of us holds a unique thread that must be woven into the tapestry of the unfolding Divine Plan in order for it to be brought to fruition God Victoriously. No two people have the exact same skills or will participate in exactly the same way. Only our God Selves can reveal what we must do in order to accomplish our part of the plan. We each need to listen to our inner guidance and respond according to our heart's call. The unfolding Divine Plan is incredibly complex. It is multifaceted and multidimensional. All facets of the plan are *equally* important and critical to the success of the whole.

Preparing for the Activation of Divine Government

Here is a brief description of some of the activities of Light that prepared us for the activation of the 5th-Dimensional matrix and archetypes of Divine Government. In 1987 during the first Harmonic Convergence, the Twelve Solar Aspects of Deity began pulsating through the Crystal Grid System. That influx of Solar Light began a 12-year process that activated Humanity's Twelve Solar Chakras and reconnected our Twelve Solar Strands of DNA. That cleared the way for the unique Ascension experiment that will take the Earth through the 4th- and 5th-Dimensional shifts in unprecedented time.

This Cosmic push is occurring so that the Earth will be ready for the Cosmic Inbreath that will be taken by the Cosmic I AM in the not-too-distant future. This Inbreath will raise ALL of Creation into higher frequencies of Light and will move our evolutionary process forward a quantum leap.

The Spiritual Hierarchy said that the experiment would take approximately 25 years—until the year 2012. They informed us that the first five years would be very tumultuous as the Twelve Solar Aspects of Deity expand through Humanity's newly-awakened Solar Chakras. Then there would be a shift, and for the next 20 years, the Light of God would increase on Earth causing the energy, vibration and consciousness of all life to accelerate at warp speed. During the 25-year period, anything conflicting with that Light would be pushed to the surface for purification.

In 1991, as we approached the fifth year after Harmonic Convergence, the Spiritual Hierarchy told us that it was time to implement the next critical phase of the Divine Plan. That phase of the plan was designed to create a momentous shift on the planet that would ensure the eventual manifestation of Divine Government.

The Legions of Light have always told us that Divine Government is an essential factor in manifesting God's Eternal Peace and Prosperity which are imperative elements in creating the perfection of Heaven on Earth. Divine Government is a government *of* the God Selves of Humanity, *by* the God Selves of Humanity, *for* the God Selves of Humanity. It embraces reverence for *ALL life* and works consistently to cocreate the highest good for all concerned.

The Spiritual Hierarchy said that in order for the quantum shift to be successfully accomplished, the *Immaculate Heart* for Divine Government needed to be activated. The Immaculate Heart contains the permanent seed atom which is imprinted with all of the unmanifest Divine Potential for that particular expression of Divinity. In order to activate the Immaculate Heart for Divine Government, the Spiritual Hierarchy set a plan into motion and invoked the assistance of the God Selves of all Humanity and dedicated Lightworkers in embodiment.

In May 1991, we were asked by the Company of Heaven to hold one of our seminars in Columbus, Ohio. The city of Columbus is named after Christopher Columbus, and in front of City Hall, there is a large statue of Columbus that was given to the city by his hometown of Genoa, Italy.

As many of you know, Christopher Columbus was one of the embodiments of St. Germain who is now an Ascended Master and an exponent of the Violet Flame of Liberty and Freedom. A powerful forcefield of Violet Flame blazes through the portal of Light in Columbus, Ohio. Columbus, Ohio, represents the *heart of America* and Washington, DC, represents the *heart of government* in America. St. Germain has been working diligently for centuries to assist Humanity in cocreating Divine Government and to bring the Divine Plan for the United States of America to fruition.

During our seminar, St. Germain informed us that it was time to activate the Immaculate Heart for Divine Government. He said the Light would first blaze through the portal of the heart of America in Columbus, Ohio, and then flow into the heart of government in Washington, DC.

The Lightworkers gathered at our seminar joined with the Company of Heaven and formed a Chalice of Light through which the Light of God poured to activate the Immaculate Heart for Divine Government. At the precise moment of the activation, President George Herbert Walker Bush, who was in Washington, DC, at the time, had a slight flutter in his heart, which was reported by the media to be a mild heart attack. News of the event spread like wildfire around the world. In an instant, the focused attention of the entire planet was turned to the *"heart of government in the United States of America."*

Nothing could have happened that would have more effectively, or instantaneously, focused the attention of the whole world on the *heart* and *Washington, DC.* Not surprisingly, it turned out that President Bush did not have a heart attack after all, but the mysterious flutter in his heart served its purpose perfectly. For several weeks, the Immaculate Heart for Divine Government was integrated and assimilated into the physical plane which cleared the way for the next phase of the plan.

From July 11, 1991, until January 11, 1992, we experienced what was known as *"Ascending through the Doorway of 11:11."* The events that took place during that six-month period created the quantum shift that the Spiritual Hierarchy told us would occur five years after the first Harmonic Convergence.

On July 11, 1991, we experienced a very powerful New Moon Solar Eclipse. The total Solar Eclipse lasted for a full seven minutes, which is very rare. During that time, fiery pillars of Divine Love and Power poured forth from the heart of our Father-Mother God. As these pillars of Light blended together in perfect balance, they formed an unprecedented frequency of the Violet Flame which flowed through the Twelve Solar Chakras aligned along the axis—the Solar Spine—of Mother Earth. That incredible gift of Light realigned the foundations of consciousness on Earth with Divinity and ensured the inclusion of the physical plane of Earth in a Solar Inbreath that involved our entire Solar System of Alpha and Omega.

A Solar Inbreath is a multidimensional activity of Light in which our Father-Mother God breathe all life closer to their own Divine Threefold Flame. This activity aligns the Threefold Flames pulsating in the hearts of all Humanity. The Threefold Flame in our heart is our focal point of unity with the whole of Creation. Even though Humanity is evolving in different directions with different goals and experiences, at certain points in each great Cosmic Cycle, all activity is suspended for a Cosmic Moment to reconfirm that all life is ONE and that this fundamental condition of the Universe remains primary and absolute.

The Spiritual Hierarchy revealed to us that when the Solar Inbreath was taken during the moments of the total Solar Eclipse, the Immaculate Heart for Divine Government was greatly expanded. That occurrence created the environment for the next phase of the Divine Plan which involved the activation of the 4th-Dimensional matrix and archetypes associated with Divine Government.

The Berlin Wall had been taken down on November 9, 1989, and Eastern Europe was experiencing the final throes of communism. Desert Storm was coming to an end, and the cold war was over. Everything was ready. The Spiritual Hierarchy set a plan into motion and requested our assistance.

The Beings of Light told us that prior to Earth's Ascension onto the Spiral of the 4th Dimension, the 4th-Dimensional patterns of Divine Government had to be in place.

In August 1991, the Spiritual Hierarchy asked us to hold the Fifth Annual World Congress On Illumination in Washington, DC, within the forcefield of the Immaculate Heart of Divine Government. Lightworkers from all over the world responded and came to Washington, DC, to serve with the Company of Heaven.

On August 18, 1991, after a wondrous week of preparation, the matrix and archetypes in all their glory were activated. Twelve hours after the activation, a coup in the Soviet Union was attempted against Mikhail Gorbachev. That attempted coup struck the final blow to communism in the Soviet Union and established a momentum of democracy and freedom that proved to be unstoppable.

The Light continued to build as we ventured through the six months leading up to our Ascension through the Doorway of 11:11. In September 1991, St. Germain and the Legions of Light associated with the Violet Flame joined with the God Selves of Humanity to open the Twelve Stargates of Aquarius.

Aquarius and the 7th Solar Aspect of Deity, which reverberates with the Violet Flame, will be the predominant influences during the 2,000-year cycle of this dawning New Age. The Violet Flame is a key ingredient in manifesting Divine Government and in our personal and planetary transformation.

On September 30, 1991, the Light of God poured through the Heart Flames of Lightworkers all over the planet. That influx of Light enveloped all life on Earth in an invincible forcefield of protection. Then, under the direction of St. Germain, mighty bolts of Violet Lightning were projected from the core of Creation through the Twelve Stargates of Aquarius and permanently opened those portals of the Violet Flame.

The Twelve Stargates of Aquarius are located in:

1. Giza, Egypt—The Lion's Gate
2. Thunder Bay, Canada
3. Southwestern United States of America
4. Cuba and the Caribbean Islands
5. Brazil
6. Sumatra—South Pacific
7. New Zealand
8. South Africa
9. Beijing, China
10. St. Petersburg, former Soviet Union
11. Arctic—North Pole
12. Antarctica—South Pole

Aeons ago when Humanity sank into the dense abyss of our own human miscreations, the Earth fell off of the Spiral of Evolution and was entrapped on the Wheel of Karma. With the incredible influx of the Violet Flame that occurred with the opening of the Stargates of Aquarius, a bridge was formed across the abyss from the Wheel of Karma to the Spiral of Evolution by the Mighty Elohim.

On October 4, 1991, through the dedicated efforts of awakened Lightworkers and the Company of Heaven, an unparalleled influx of the Ascension Flame poured through the Stargates of Aquarius and assisted the Earth to Ascend off the Wheel of Karma. On the wings of the Ascension Flame, the Earth Ascended over the Violet Flame Bridge and onto the Spiral of Evolution.

That incredible activity of Light allowed the Earth to reclaim her rightful position on the 3rd-Dimensional spiral which cleared the way for the final phase of preparation for Earth's Ascension through the Doorway of 11:11.

For three months, the new frequencies of the 3rd-Dimensional Spiral of Evolution were assimilated into every particle of life on Earth, and the Violet Flame transmuted the maximum amount of Humanity's negativity that Cosmic Law would allow. Then on January 11, 1992, the Earth Ascended through the multidimensional Doorway of 11:11 onto the first rung of the 4th-Dimensional Spiral of Evolution.

Eleven is the master number that reflects the transformation of the physical into the Divine, matter into Spirit. 11:11 is a code that our God Selves imprinted on our RNA/DNA structures aeons ago to signal the Cosmic Moment when the Earth would be given the opportunity to Ascend into the 4th- and 5th-Dimensional Realms of Limitless Physical Perfection.

Since our initial ascent onto the spiral of the 4th Dimension in 1992, myriad activities of Light have taken place through the selfless, individual and collective efforts of awakened Lightworkers all over the world. It is impossible to fathom how important our Lightwork has been in averting catastrophes and shifting the consciousness of the masses, but the Beings of Light in the Realms of Illumined Truth have said that we are succeeding beyond the greatest expectations of Heaven.

In January 2002, *eleven* years after the activation of the 4th-Dimensional matrix and archetypes for Divine Government, the Spiritual Hierarchy informed us that everything was in place for the activation of the 5th-Dimensional matrix and archetypes for Divine Government.

The Comet Ikeya-Zhang was detected on February 1, 2002, by two amateur astronomers in Japan and China. The comet passed closest to the Sun on March 18; then it began its journey across the skies over the northern hemisphere on its way back into deep space. The last time this ancient messenger was seen by observers on Earth was in 1661.

For several weeks, Comet Ikeya-Zhang shook the ethers and broke down the crystallized patterns and obsolete archetypes of Ages past. That Celestial Intervention assisted in creating a fluid field of unmanifest potential, which made it easier for Humanity to project visions of the New Heaven and the New Earth onto the atomic and subatomic particles of the physical plane.

During the last week of April and the first two weeks of May, a rare, planetary alignment allowed us to experience the radiance and power of Mercury, Venus, Mars, Saturn and Jupiter in the night sky all at the same time. A few hours later Uranus, Neptune and Pluto appeared. If we include the Earth, we were able to experience and absorb the Light and blessings of nine worlds in just one night. That was an event that few astronomers can say they have observed. It was a once-in-a-lifetime experience, and it won't occur again for 70 to 100 years.

On May 5, Venus, Saturn and Mars grouped together to form a perfect equilateral triangle in the western sky. That sacred symbol represents the love, wisdom and power of the Threefold Flame. The triangle was visible from just about everywhere, and it blessed all life with its luminous presence.

In the Middle East, the sacred triangle was directly above Bethlehem. It is interesting to note that during this momentous time, amid the war and turmoil in the Middle East, the ancient Roman Gods of Love/Venus, Wisdom/Saturn and Power/Mars gathered to project their Light into the holy land once again.

On May 10, Venus and Mars appeared to pass so close together that they seemed to become One. As the Roman God of Power and the Roman Goddess of Love united, they bathed the Earth with the Divine Balance of our Father-Mother God.

On May 26, 2002, we experienced a rare Saturn-Pluto alignment that occurred within just 12 hours of a Lunar Eclipse. Astrologers said that was more rare and more powerful than the Grand Fixed Cross that occurred on August 11, 1999, or the alignment of planets, the Grand Stellium in Taurus, that took place in early May 2000.

The energies of Pluto are deeply transformational and pierced through the rigid structures and crystallized blocks that were being brought to the surface by Saturn. Humanity was given an opportunity to resolve our inner conflicts so that we will individually, and collectively as a Human Race, merge with our God Selves and create a lasting inner peace.

On June 10, 2002, we experienced a very powerful Solar Eclipse. That eclipse enhanced the affects of the activities taking place through the alignment of Pluto and Saturn and accelerated the transformation of the frequencies of chaos and discord. Those events helped paved the way for the activation of the matrix and archetypes of the 5th-Dimensional frequencies of Divine Government.

The Beings of Light told us that in order for the Earth to Ascend into the 5th-Dimensional frequencies of Limitless Physical Perfection, the patterns for government must be compatible with the 5th Dimension. They said that once the 5th-Dimensional matrix and archetypes for Divine Government are activated , the obsolete, fear-based patterns of human miscreation will be shattered. Then the patterns of perfection from the Causal Body of God that are associated with the governments of the world will begin to flow into the hearts and minds of every Human Being. When that occurs, even the most resistant souls will awaken, their God Selves will take command, and they will begin fulfilling their Divine Potential as Beloved Sons and Daughters of God. When our God Selves are governing the planet, they will easily reach into the Realms of Illumined Truth and tap into the viable solutions for every problem manifesting on Earth.

Victory is Ours!

The collective body of Lightworkers on the planet has proven once again that the Light of God is ALWAYS Victorious and that WE are that Light. The following miraculous events took place during the 16th Annual World Congress On Illumination in Washington, DC, August 17-22, 2002. These activities of Light were accomplished through the unified efforts of not only the Lightworkers gathered in Washington, DC, but the God Selves of all Humanity and the entire Company of Heaven.

Prior to the World Congress On Illumination, the House of Representatives and the Congress went into recess, and all of the politicians left Washington, DC. That created a clear space for a powerful cleansing and healing to occur throughout the entire area.

In early August, the Perceid Meteor Shower swept through the atmosphere of Earth and as it did, the obsolete matrixes and archetypes of corruption in world governments and political and military depravity were shattered. This allowed the Mighty Elohim to create a fluid field of unmanifest Divine Potential in Washington,

DC, in preparation for the activation of the 5th-Dimensional matrix and archetypes for Divine Government.

During the Opening Ceremonies of Light on August 17, 2002, the various aspects of Deity throughout the Universe projected their luminous Presence into the atmosphere of Earth. First came the resplendent Solar Logos, the masculine and feminine aspects of our Father-Mother God from Suns beyond Suns:

> *The White Fire Being of Helios and Vesta,*
> *the representatives of our Father-Mother God*
> *from our physical Sun;*
> *The White Fire Being of Alpha and Omega,*
> *the representatives of our Father-Mother God*
> *from our Central Sun;*
> *The White Fire Being of Elohae and Eloha,*
> *the representatives of our Father-Mother God*
> *from our Great, Central Sun;*
> *The White Fire Being of El and Ela,*
> *the representatives of our Father-Mother God*
> *from our Great, Great Central Sun;*
> *And the White Fire Being of the*
> *omniscient, omnipresent, omnipotent*
> *Cosmic I AM—All That Is.*

Then, in a magnificent procession of Light, the entire Company of Heaven came forth from the Great Silence to join the Solar Logos:

> *Crowns, Thrones, Principalities, Galactic Beings, Archangels,*
> *Seraphim, Angels, Cherubim, Ascended Masters,*
> *the Mighty I Am Presences and the Solar Christ Presences of*
> *ALL Humanity, the Directors of the Elements and the Devas*
> *and the Devas Rajas serving the Earth.*

With one voice, this august body of Divinity spoke to the Light-workers gathered in Washington, DC:

"Beloved Sons and Daughters of the most high, living God, this is an event of Cosmic significance. We in Heaven's Realms have been in the Great Silence preparing for this illustrious gathering. We have come into the atmosphere of Earth to join you this sacred and holy night, and we will remain with you

until the victorious activation of the 5th-Dimensional matrix and archetypes for Divine Government which will take place at the conclusion of this sacred conclave.

"It is vital that you comprehend the magnitude of this moment for it is heralding an awakening and a shift of consciousness that is taking place at an atomic, cellular level for every soul evolving on Earth. You have responded to your heart's call, and you have selflessly volunteered to come and serve as surrogates on behalf of all Humanity. For that, precious Ones, your names are being written in the Golden Book of Life for all Eternity.

"For the past year, the Flame of Transfiguring Divine Love has been blazing through every Heart Flame. The Divine Intelligence within this sacred Flame is exposing, through the Light of Divine Clarity, the illusions of the human ego that are perpetuating the distorted beliefs that are being used to justify Humanity's inhumane behavior toward one another. As a result of this activity of Light, the Earth and Humanity are, at long last, vibrating at a frequency of vibration that will sustain and maintain the 5th-Dimensional matrix and archetypes of Divine Government.

"The patterns of perfection from the Causal Body of God that are encoded in this matrix and these archetypes will result in a government OF the God Selves of Humanity, BY the God Selves of Humanity, FOR the God Selves of Humanity.

"Ages ago the clarion call for assistance rang forth from the Heart of Beloved Mother Earth. You, Blessed Ones, with mercy and compassion, responded to her heartfelt plea. You have come from Galaxies beyond Galaxies and Suns beyond Suns to serve Humanity and to save the Earth.

"Time and again you volunteered to embody on Earth, immersing yourself in the humanly-created sea of negativity that was smothering this planet. Time and again through lives of toil and pain, you struggled to create a pinpoint of Light through the psychic-astral plane. In the midst of the most heart-wrenching adversity, you held aloft the Cup of your consciousness creating an open portal through which the Light of God could flow to reach the withering souls of Humanity.

"For thousands of years, your success was limited, and your progress was ever so slow. But you continued undaunted by the discouraging appearances of the outer world, clinging

tenaciously to the Immaculate Concept of the Divine Plan for Planet Earth, which was revealed to you by your Father-Mother God and encoded in the cellular memory of every fiber of your Being.

"Now it is time for you to reap the fruits of your labor. Your selfless efforts in unison with the selfless efforts of myriad Lightworkers around the world have at last succeeded to the point that will allow the patterns of perfection for Divine Government to be securely established and encoded through all levels of consciousness on Earth. The fluid field of unmanifest Divine Potential has been prepared in Washington, DC, and throughout this week, We, in Heaven's Realms, will join with you and guide you through the final steps of preparation for the activation of the 5th-Dimensional matrix and archetypes for Divine Government.

"Listen to your Inner Guidance. You have been preparing for aeons of time to fulfill your facet of this glorious Divine Plan. Know that everything you need is already within you. All you have to do is be the loving, peace-commanding Presence you are destined to BE.

> *"The Divinity within our hearts salutes, with honor and reverence, the Divinity within your hearts.*
> *I Am that I Am."*

The complexity and the synchronicity of the Divine Plan is awesome to behold. During the week of the World Congress On Illumination, there were several specific, astrological alignments and events including the *second* Full Moon in Aquarius (the Blue Moon on August 22) that gave maximum support to the unfolding activities of Light. There were also many global meditations for personal and planetary transformation as well as scheduled global prayers for Peace. In addition to all of the above, there was another amazing event in Washington, DC, involving St. Germain and the Freemasons that assisted immensely in fulfilling the Immaculate Concept of the Divine Plan.

St. Germain is known as the Son of Freedom. He is an Ascended Master and an exponent of the Seventh Solar Aspect of Deity, the Violet Flame, which will be the predominant influence on Earth during the Age of Aquarius. His Divine Complement is Ascended Master Lady Portia who is also aligned with the Violet Flame.

She is an exponent of Divine Justice, Opportunity, Victory, Liberty and Freedom.

For literally centuries, St. Germain has embodied to initiate various facets of the Divine Plan that would pave the way for the establishment of Divine Government on Earth.

St. Germain was Merlin, the mystical tutor and mentor of King Arthur during the late-5th and early-6th centuries. In that embodiment, he taught Arthur the spiritual Truths that allowed him to become king. Merlin worked with King Arthur to form the Knights of the Round Table, a group of dedicated men who established a model of Divine Government that moved the people into a new state of civility.

It is said that King Arthur and the Knights of the Round Table held back heathen barbarians, and with might and wisdom preserved their country. They created and maintained an orderly and decent system of government that preserved the city, rescued the beleaguered and brought peace to the land. King Arthur is now known as the Ascended Master El Morya, and his beloved Guinevere and Divine Complement is Ascended Master Lady Miriam.

El Morya and Lady Miriam are exponents of the First Solar Aspect of Deity, which pulsates with the full momentum of God's First Cause of Perfection, Divine Will, Illumined Faith, Power, Authority and Protection.

St. Germain, Lady Portia, El Morya and Lady Miriam have been working together, both in and out of embodiment, for millennia. They have all been instrumental in bringing this Cosmic Moment to fruition.

In the 1300s, St. Germain embodied as Christian Rosenkreuz and founded the Mystery School known as the Rosicrucians or The Order of the Rosy Cross. The Rosicrucian teachings incorporated the teachings of the Essenes and other sacred knowledge.

In the 1400s, St. Germain embodied as Christopher Columbus. In that embodiment, he was given the Divine Mission of finding the land that would be the location where souls would come from all over the planet to, one day, model a New World. It was destined to be a land in which the family of Humanity would demonstrate to the rest of the world how to live together as one unified nation under God in harmony, liberty, justice and freedom, expressing equality and prosperity for all. Even though we have fallen far from the original vision, that Divine Potential still pulsates in the permanent seed atom in the heart of this sacred land and is awaiting its moment of manifestation.

In the 1600s, St. Germain embodied in Europe as Count St. Germain. During that embodiment, he initiated the structuring of the Freemasons and formed a secret, mystical society. Many of the ideas and rituals of Masonry originated in the period of cathedral building from the 900s to the 1600s. At that time, stonemasons formed associations called guilds in various European cities and towns. With the decline of cathedral building in the 1600s, St. Germain inspired the Masons became a secret, spiritual fraternal organization.

Masonry, also called Freemasonry, is one of the oldest and largest fraternal organizations in the world. The organization's official name is Free and Accepted Masons. Masonry is dedicated to the ideals of charity, equality, morality and service to God. Masons donate millions of dollars each year to charitable projects, including hospitals, homes for widows, orphans and the aged, relief for people in distress and scholarships.

Masons promote morality in which all men agree to be good men and true. Throughout its history, Masonry has sought to bring together men of different religious beliefs and political opinions. Men of any religion who profess belief in one God may join.

The original Divine Intent of the secret ceremonies and mystical philosophy of the Masons was to build a New World. Masons call God the "*Great Architect of the Universe.*" Their teachings reflect many of the teachings of the Essenes and the Rosicrucians.

Most of the Founding Fathers of the United States of America were Freemasons. Many of the symbols in the Great Seal of the United States and on our dollar bill are sacred symbols of the Freemasons.

Their beliefs and concepts are woven into the principles that this nation was founded on, and the Declaration of Independence, the Constitution of the United States and the Bill of Rights all reflect the philosophy of the Freemasons.

On occasion, as has happened in all of the world religions and even the original plan for this country, the Divine Intent of the Freemasons has been overlooked, and power has sometimes been abused, but the Immaculate Concept of the original Divine Purpose of this organization is still intact.

Amazingly, during the World Congress On Illumination, the Masons were holding their 109th Imperial Session in Washington, DC. There were 50,000 33-degree Masons from every state in the nation in attendance. Throughout the week of the World Congress, 50,000 Free Masons met daily and conducted their sacred ceremonies and meetings.

In 1931, through Guy Ballard and the Mystery School known as the "I AM Activity," St. Germain said:

"One by one, great awakened souls are coming forth who will become clearly conscious of their own mighty, inherent God-Power, and such as these will be placed in all official positions of the government. They will be more interested in the welfare of America than in their own personal ambitions and private fortunes. Thus will another Golden Age reign upon Earth and be maintained for aeons."

In 1952, St. Germain and El Morya decreed that it was time for the teachings of the Ascended Masters to be brought out of the Mystery Schools and for those teachings to be made available to every soul who has *eyes to see and ears to hear*. Since that time, the Ascended Masters' teachings and the Realms of Illumined Truth have been openly available to every evolving soul. All ESOTERIC teachings are now EXOTERIC.

For *fifty years,* St. Germain, Lady Portia, El Morya and Lady Miriam have served with the rest of the Spiritual Hierarchy to prepare Humanity to be the Open Doors through which Divine Government will manifest on Earth.

On August 18, 2002, Archangel Michael directed the great Lords of Power and Protection who serve in his Regal Court to descend into Washington, DC, and to traverse the city north, south, east and west. His Legions entered all of the embassies, chanceries, consulates and all offices of the international representatives. They entered the Capitol Building, the Congressional Office Buildings and the Senate Office Buildings. They entered the State Department, the White House, the Executive Office Building, the Pentagon, all military bases and every office and business concerned with government and military affairs in any way.

Archangel Michael then directed additional Lords of Power and Protection to traverse the Earth and to enter *every* government and military building and facility in the world. As a final step of preparation, he stationed an Angel of Power and Protection in the auras of every man, woman and child on Earth.

When all of his Legions were in their strategic positions, Archangel Michael sounded his Cosmic Tone. Then he directed his Legions to use their Swords of Blue Flame to cut free every line of force that was not of the Light. The Angels swept through the buildings and the energy fields of every soul, cutting the negativity free from all time frames and dimensions. When that activity of purification was complete, Archangel Michael blazed the purifying Flame of God's Will into every facet of life.

In overwhelming gratitude, Beloved Mother Earth then released waves of Divine Love to envelop the Elemental Beings who had selflessly sustained her Crystal Grid System in the face of horrendous adversity. She held every Elemental in the embrace of her Heart Flame and reinforced the crystals to withstand more Light.

When that activity was complete, the Solar Elohim came to the fore. Through the Twelvefold Solar Spines of the Lightworkers gathered in Washington, DC, the Elohim infused the crystals in the Grid System with the highest 5th-Dimensional frequencies of the Twelve Solar Aspects of Deity they were able to endure.

On August 19, 2002, Orion and Angelica, the Elohim of the Third Solar Aspect of Deity, and the Silent Watchers of the Bridge of Transfiguring Divine Love, came forth to guide us through the next phase of the Divine Plan. These exponents of Divine Love and Adoration invoked the Solar Christ Presence of every soul evolving on Earth into the Temples of Light above Washington, DC.

As the Solar Christ Presence of all Humanity entered the loving embrace of Orion and Angelica, we merged into one luminous Being of Light. We then breathed in the breath of the Holy Spirit, and our unified Light Body expanded to engulf the entire Planet Earth. The planet was cradled in our Heart Flames, and the full radiance of our collective Solar Christ Presence bathed every particle of life with Divine Love.

Elohim Orion and Angelica then invoked the Solar Logos from the Suns in our Universe to escort our collective Solar Christ Presence into the heart of the Cosmic I AM—All That Is—for a Cosmic Initiation. In an instant, we Ascended through myriad Dimensions of Light into the heart of our omniscient, omnipresent, omnipotent Father-Mother God.

Within this forcefield of unfathomable Divine Love, the luminous Presence of St. Germain, Lady Portia, El Morya and Lady Miriam appeared before us. They revealed that every soul responsible for establishing Divine Government on Planet Earth is already in embodiment. Some have reached their maturity and some are still infants, but all are prepared and ready to fulfill their unique facet of the Divine Plan.

As the Initiation began, St. Germain and Lady Portia breathed the patterns for Divine Government into their Heart Flames. Then, the Cosmic I AM sounded a Keynote, and the souls who are destined to establish Divine Government on Earth stepped forth from Humanity's collective Solar Christ Presence. They stood before St Germain and Lady Portia, and in deep reverence and knowing, they acknowledged the moment at hand.

On the Holy Breath, St. Germain and Lady Portia breathed the Violet Flame containing the patterns of Divine Government into the Heart Flames of the souls standing before them. As the Violet Flame merged with the Divinity in each soul's heart, a magnificent Violet Maltese Cross was formed. The souls breathed in the Violet Flame and, as they did, the Maltese Cross expanded to envelop their physical, etheric, mental and emotional bodies.

St. Germain and Lady Portia then invoked the Goddess of Liberty, the Goddess of Justice, the Goddess of Freedom and the Goddess of Victory to come to the fore to assist these souls in their Earthly sojourn.

The Goddess of Liberty stationed an Angel of Liberty above every soul to blaze the Flame of Liberty through the upper arm of the Maltese Cross.

The Goddess of Justice stationed an Angel of Justice to the left of every soul to blaze the Flame of Justice through the left arm of the Maltese Cross.

The Goddess of Freedom stationed an Angel of Freedom below every soul to blaze the Flame of Freedom through the lower arm of the Maltese Cross.

The Goddess of Victory stationed an Angel of Victory to the right of every soul to blaze the Flame of Victory through the right arm of the Maltese Cross.

These selfless Angels volunteered to remain within the auras of these souls until their missions are accomplished and Divine Government is a manifest reality on Earth.

The Violet Maltese Crosses in the energy fields of the souls who are responsible for establishing Divine Government will now serve to identify them to Humanity at a heart level. When these souls run for elected office or accept governmental positions, we will recognize them intuitively. We will be inspired to support them in their efforts to establish Divine Government, and we will assist them in bringing forth and implementing the viable solutions that will heal the maladies of the world.

Once that initiation was complete, the souls again entered the collective Solar Christ Presence of Humanity and became one with that Body of Light.

Next Alpha and Omega came to the fore. They were joined by Helios and Vesta and Elohim Orion and Angelica. After a moment of pure silence, the Cosmic I AM sounded a resounding Tone that reverberated to the core of Humanity's Solar Christ Presence. As the Tone held our focused attention, Alpha and Omega sent forth a clarion call and invoked every soul on Earth who was refusing to move forward into the 5th Dimension to come forward.

Amazingly, every recalcitrant soul came forward. Some responded in spite of their ego's defiance; some came out of curiosity; some responded out of confusion; some out of fear and some out of inner knowing, but they ALL came and stood before Alpha and Omega.

When the very last laggard soul came forward, Alpha and Omega directed Elohim Orion and Angelica to expand the Flame of Transfiguring Divine Love in each soul's heart. As the Divine Intelligence within the Flame was intensified, the Truth of each soul's Divinity was revealed. With a new level of clarity unprecedented since their fall aeons ago, each laggard soul was shown the Truth of their Divine Heritage as Beloved Sons and Daughters of God and the pathway they would need to take in order to return Home.

Then Alpha and Omega gave each laggard soul *one last chance* to choose to Ascend into the 5th Dimension with the rest of the Solar System. To the amazement and elation of the Solar Christ Presence of Humanity who were witnessing this Divine Initiation, *every single laggard soul took vows before Alpha and Omega to do what is necessary to Ascend into the 5th Dimension.* In that instant, their agreements and their vows were recorded in their Heart Flames and their etheric bodies. These commitments will now filter into their conscious minds day by day until they are fulfilled.

Once that Divine Initiation was complete, the Solar Logos escorted Humanity's collective Solar Christ Presence back to our rightful position in the System of Alpha and Omega. As we passed through the various dimensions, we heard the Cosmos rejoicing, and the Angels were singing.

That afternoon the Lightworkers at the World Congress On Illumination walked around the city of Washington, DC, and infused the fluid field of Unmanifest Divine Potential with the 5th-Dimensional frequencies of Divine Love and Victory.

On August 20, 2002, there were several activities of Light to allow the laggard souls to integrate their experience from the day before. Throughout the day, their Solar Christ Presence gently prepared them for the changes they will have to make in order to be ready for their shift into the 5th Dimension. The Lightworkers gathered in Washington, DC, held the space for every awakening soul to quickly integrate this new awareness. We also worked with the Legions of Illumined Truth to assist all souls to accept their vows on a conscious level, as they hear and respond to the still, small voice within.

On August 21, 2002, a God-Victorious event occurred that was beyond even the expectations of Heaven. For over 50 years, we had been told by the Spiritual Hierarchy that even though many souls on Earth were awakening enough to warrant the salvation of the Earth, there were still millions of souls who would probably not be ready to make the shift into the 5th Dimension. The Spiritual Hierarchy said that when it was time for the shift to take place, the souls who were not able to withstand the frequencies of the 5th Dimension would be transferred to another planet to continue their slow, painful progress in a 3rd-Dimensional reality.

When the first Harmonic Convergence took place in August 1987, the Elohim were given permission by our Father-Mother God to create a *second* Earth. This New Earth interpenetrated the existing Earth, but it pulsated with more rarefied 4th-Dimensional frequencies of Light. The Divine Plan was for souls who were awakening and lifting up in energy, vibration and consciousness to be integrated into the New Earth in preparation for their Ascension into the 5th Dimension. The souls who were refusing to move into the Light, however, would remain in the 3rd-Dimensional frequencies of the old Earth in preparation for their transfer to another 3rd-Dimensional reality.

Since 1987, Lightworkers all over the world have known and talked about the fact that there are actually two Earths and that we are all being given a chance to choose which Earth we want to exist on.

In 1998, the Spiritual Hierarchy said that the unprecedented awakening that had taken place within Humanity since the first Harmonic Convergence had created enough Light on the planet to awaken the laggard souls *if they choose to awaken*. Unfortunately, many of those souls did not understand that they were being given an opportunity to move into the Light, and they were afraid that if Earth Ascends into the 5th Dimension, they will perish. Consequently, they have been fighting tooth and nail to prevent the Earth and the rest of Humanity from moving forward in the Light.

In 2001, Alpha and Omega decided to try one last experiment to see if the recalcitrant souls would awaken and choose to move into the Light. That experiment was the gift of the Flame of Transfiguring Divine Love. To the elation of all involved, the experiment worked and, as I have just shared with you, as of August 19, 2002, every laggard soul has now vowed to do what is necessary for them to Ascend into the 5th Dimension with the rest of Humanity.

That glorious accomplishment meant that there was no longer a need for two Earths. So, during an incredible activity of Light on August 21, 2002, which involved the Mighty Elohim, the Directors of the Elements, the Elemental Kingdoms, the Solar Christ Presences of all Humanity and the Spiritual Hierarchy, the 3rd-Dimensional Earth Ascended over the *Bridge of Transfiguring Divine Love—the Bridge to Freedom*—into the initial frequencies of the 4th and 5th Dimensions. During that Cosmic Moment, the old Earth merged and became ONE with the New Earth.

Once the merging of the two Earths was complete, the Directors of the Elements released the 3rd-Dimensional Elementals who had volunteered to remain on the old Earth when the rest of the 3rd-Dimensional Elementals were released in May 2001. These precious Sylphs of the air, Undines of the water, Salamanders of the fire and Gnomes and Nature Spirits of the Earth joyously Ascended into the Heart of Alpha and Omega. Then, new 5th-Dimensional Elemental Beings descended in a glorious procession to take their place.

There is now ONLY ONE EARTH, and through the amazing Grace of God, every soul evolving on Earth is going to make their Ascension into the 5th Dimension.

A Special Gift

With the cooperation of the Elohim and the new 5th-Dimensional Undines, a forcefield of protection has been placed around the dolphins and the whales. This is a powerful circle of white lightning called the *Ring-Pass-Not of God's First Cause of Perfection*. This forcefield will be sustained and energized through the invocations and prayers of Lightworkers everywhere. It is specifically designed to deflect the harmful ELF sonar rays that the Navy is using so that they will not harm the dolphins and the whales just in case the Lightworkers are not able to convince the Navy to stop this horrific activity.

On August 22, 2002, all was in readiness for the activation of the 5th-Dimensional matrix and archetypes for Divine Government. As the activity of Light began, members of the Spiritual Hierarchy who have been teaching Humanity the principles of Divine Government in the Inner Schools of Learning descended into Washington, DC.

They were followed by a procession of the Founding Fathers of the United States of America. George Washington, Thomas Jefferson and Abraham Lincoln led this august procession and took their positions above the monuments dedicated to them. As they did, a 5th-Dimensional portal of Light opened above each of the three monuments.

The rest of the Founding Fathers, joined by the Solar Christ Presences of the 50,000 Freemasons gathered in Washington, DC, stood shoulder to shoulder and formed an invincible forcefield of protection around the city. Together they created an Circle of Divine Love and Divine Will around the Heart of Divine Government for Planet Earth.

Next, the Goddess of Liberty took her position at the cardinal point to the north of Washington, DC. The Goddess of Justice stood to the east. The Goddess of Freedom stood to the south, and the Goddess of Victory stood to the west.

St. Germain, Lady Portia, El Morya and Lady Miriam then descended into the evolving forcefield of Light bringing with them the full-gathered momentum of Divine Government for the dawning Permanent Golden Age of Spiritual Freedom, Eternal Peace and Limitless abundance.

The Beings of Light then invoked the Solar Christ Presence of the embodied souls who will be the instruments for Divine Government on Earth. The souls came from the far corners of the Earth and reverently entered the Circle of Divine Love and Divine Will. These souls were joined by the loving, supportive Solar Christ Presenc of all Humanity.

Then, as one unified consciousness of Infinite Divine Love and Divine Will, that body of souls created a forcefield of Light that will permanently maintain and sustain the 5th-Dimensional matrix and archetypes for Divine Government.

When all was in readiness, the masculine aspects of our Father God sounded a Cosmic Keynote and projected the 5th-Dimensional matrix for Divine Government into Washington, DC, the Heart of Government for the United States of America.

Once the matrix for Divine Government was in place, the feminine aspects of our Mother God projected forth a blazing Sun of Divine Love and permanently secured the archetypes for Divine Government in the heart of the matrix.

Now it is our responsibility as Lightworkers to bring these patterns of perfection into physical manifestation. This will be accomplished through our thoughts, words, actions and feelings, as we deliberately energize and empower *only* those things that support the creation of Heaven on Earth.

Self-Government

We must remember that Divine Government involves not only the governments of the world, it involves *self-government,* which consists of each of us being governed by our *God Selves*. It is time to love our lower human egos into the Light and time to give our God Selves full dominion in our lives.

Self-government determines what we choose to empower with our thoughts, words, feelings and actions. It determines how we use our lifeforce and what we allow ourselves to cocreate.

During this incredible moment of planetary Ascension, it is very important for each of us to evaluate whether or not we are allowing our dysfunctional, fragmented human egos or our God Selves to govern our lives. Fortunately, that is not a difficult assessment to make. All we need to do is simply pay attention throughout our day and monitor what we are thinking and feeling.

Are our thoughts and feelings based in fear, anxiety, chaos, disappointment, frustration, anger, hatred, failure, exhaustion, boredom or other expressions of negativity? Are we allowing ourselves to be manipulated by the media and the appearances of the outer world? Are we buying into the gloom and doom reports flooding the Internet? Or are we focusing the power of our attention on creating what we want to manifest in our lives instead of those distorted human miscreations?

Are we empowering and holding the vision of Heaven on Earth in spite of the adversity appearing on the screen of life? Are we energizing through our thoughts, words, feelings and actions *only* the things that will enhance the quality of life for ourselves and our loved ones? Are we expecting miracles and truly understanding that the Light of God is *always* victorious and that *we* are that Light?

Very simply, if we are empowering negativity, then our egos are governing our lives. If we are holding the vision of Heaven on Earth and empowering what we want to create in our lives, then your God Selves are governing our lives.

I know it takes a lot of work to monitor every thought, word, feeling and action, it seems much easier to just mindlessly muddle through our daily experiences. The problem is that everything is being greatly accelerated. It used to take a long time for our negative thoughts and feelings to catch up with us. Now, things are manifesting almost instantaneously.

If we don't give full dominion of our lives over to our God Selves NOW, we are in for a very tumultuous and painful road ahead. If we do allow our God Selves to govern our lives, we can truly create Heaven on Earth right here and right now. The choice is up to us.

We have everything to gain and nothing to lose by accepting this Truth as a possibility. Let's make a commitment to ourselves to allow our thoughts, words, feelings and actions to express *only* the positive things we want to empower and create in our lives. For the next six months, let's not allow ourselves to worry, talk about or empower the negative things we hear through the media or elsewhere.

Instead, every day let's focus our attention on the most positive visions we can create for ourselves and the Earth. Let's see the family of Humanity living in peace, abundance, health, harmony and joy as we envision the maladies of the world being healed and reverence for all life becoming the order of the day. Let's envision our lives filled with loving relationships, rewarding jobs, abundance, health, enlightenment, joy, happiness and spiritual fulfillment.

I promise you that if we allow our God Selves to govern our lives *faithfully* for six months, we will see miraculous changes, and then we will be motivated to continue giving dominion of our lives to our God Selves forever

Everything is in place, as never before, to empower us to accomplish this mighty feat. All we have to do is consciously act and live out of that knowing and that Divine Truth. If we are willing to put forth the effort, our victory is assured!

The Heart of America

The Heart of Divine Government is Washington, DC, and the Heart of America is Ohio. Interestingly, just before the matrix and archetypes for Divine Government were activated in the physical plane, two of the politicians in Ohio modeled to the world the old and new archetypes for government. Congressman James Traficant SYMBOLICALLY represented the old archetypes being removed from government. He was indicted for fraud and corruption, removed from office and sent to prison for eight years. At the same time, Congressman Dennis Kucinich, also from Ohio, SYMBOLICALLY represented the new archetypes being established in government when he gave a speech that perfectly expresses the consciousness for Divine Government. This is his speech.

Spirit and Stardust
by U.S. Representative Dennis Kucinich

This message was given by Rep. Kucinich at the Praxis Peace Institute Conference in Dubrovnik, Croatia, on June 9, 2002.

"As one studies the images of the Eagle Nebula, brought back by the Hubble Telescope from that place in deep space where stars are born, one can imagine the interplay of Cosmic forces across space and time, of matter and Spirit dancing to the music of the spheres atop an infinite sea of numbers.

"Spirit merges with matter to sanctify the Universe. Matter transcends to return to Spirit. The interchangeability of matter and Spirit means the starlit magic of the outermost life of our Universe becomes the soul-light magic of the innermost life of our self. The energy of the stars becomes us. We become the energy of the stars. Stardust and Spirit unite, and we begin: one with the Universe— whole and holy from one source, endless creative energy bursting forth, kinetic, elemental—we, the earth, air, water and fire, source of nearly fifteen billion years of Cosmic spiraling.

"We begin as a perfect union of matter and Spirit. We receive the blessings of the Eternal from sky and Earth. In our outstretched hands, we can feel the energy of the Universe. We receive the blessings of the Eternal from water, which nourishes and sanctifies life. We receive the blessings of the Eternal from the primal fire, the pulsating heart of Creation. We experience the wonder of life, multidimensional and transcendent. We extend our hands upwards, and we are showered with abundance. We ask and we receive. A Universe of plenty flows to us, through us. It is in us. We become filled with endless possibilities.

"We need to remember where we came from—to know that we are One, to understand that we are of an undivided whole: race, color, nationality, creed, gender are beams of Light refracted through one great prism. We begin as perfect and journey through life to become more perfect in the singularity of 'I' and in the multiplicity of 'we,' a more perfect union of matter and Spirit. This is human striving. This is where, in Shelley's words, '. . . hope creates from its own wreck the thing it contemplates.' This is what Browning spoke of, our 'reach exceeding [our] grasp.' This is a search for Heaven within, a quest for our eternal Home.

"In our souls' Magnificent, we become conscious of the Cosmos within us. We hear the music of peace; we hear the music of cooperation; we hear music of love. We hear harmony, a celestial symphony in our souls' forgetting; we become unconscious of our Cosmic birthright, plighted with disharmony, disunity, torn asunder from the stars in a disaster welldescribed by Matthew Arnold in Dover Beach: '. . . the world, which seems to lie before us like a land of dreams, so various, so beautiful, so new, hath really neither joy, nor love, nor Light, nor certitude, nor peace, nor help for pain. And we are here, as on a darkling plane, swept with confused alarms of struggle and flight where ignorant armies clash by night.'

"Today Dover Beach is upon the shores of the Potomac River in Washington, D.C. Our leaders think the unthinkable and speak of the unspeakable inevitability of nuclear war, of a nuclear attack on New York City, of terrorist attacks throughout our nation, of war against Iraq using nuclear weapons, of biological and chemical weapon attacks on civilian populations, of catastrophic global climate change, of war in outer space.

"When death (not life) becomes inevitable, we are presented with an opportunity for great clarity, for a great awakening, to rescue the human spirit from the arms of Morpheus through love, through compassion and through integrating spiritual vision and active citizenship to restore peace to our world. The moment that one world is about to end, a New World is about to begin. We need to remember where we came from because the path HOME is also the way to the future.

"In the city I represent in the United States Congress, there is a memorial to Peace, named by its sculptor, Marshall A. Fredericks, the 'Fountain of Eternal Life.' A figure rises from the flames, his gaze fixed to the stars, his hands positioned sextant-like as if measuring the distance. Though flames of war from the millions of hearts and the dozens of places wherein it rages may lick at our consciousness, our gaze must be fixed upward to invoke universal principles of unity, of cooperation, of compassion, to infuse our world with peace, to ask for the active presence of peace, to expand our capacity to receive it and to express it in our everyday life. We must do this fearlessly and courageously and not breathe in the poison gas of terror. As we receive, so shall we give.

"As citizen-diplomats of the world, we send Peace as conscious expression wherever, whenever and to whomever it is needed: to the Middle East, to the Israelis and the Palestinians, to the Pakistanis and the Indians, to Americans and to al-Qaida and to the people of Iraq and to all those locked in deadly combat. And we fly to be with the bereft, with those on the brink, to listen compassionately, setting aside judgment and malice to become peacemakers, to intervene, to mediate, to bring ourselves back from the abyss, to bind up the world's wounds.

"As we aspire to universal brotherhood and sisterhood, we harken to the cry from the heart of the world and respond affirmatively to address through thought, word and deed conditions which give rise to conflict: economic exploitation, empire building, political oppression, religious intolerance, poverty, disease, famine, homelessness, struggles over control of water, land, minerals and oil.

"We realize that what affects anyone anywhere affects everyone everywhere.

"As we help others to heal, we heal ourselves. Our vision of interconnectedness resonates with new networks of world citizens in non-governmental organizations linking from numberless centers of energy, expressing the emergence of a new organic whole, seeking unity within and across national lines. New transnational, web-based e-mail and telecommunications systems transcend governments and carry within them the power of qualitative transformation of social and political structures and a new sense of creative intelligence. If governments and their leaders, bound by hierarchy and patriarchy, wedded to military might for legitimacy, fail to grasp the implications of an emerging world consciousness for cooperation, for peace and for sustainability, they may become irrelevant.

"As citizen-activists merge the world over, they can become an irresistible force to create Peace and protect the planet. From here will come a new movement to abolish nuclear weapons and all weapons of mass destruction. From here will come the demand for sustainable communities, for new systems of energy, transportation and commerce. From here comes the future rushing in on us.

"How does one acquire the capacity for active citizenship? The opportunities exist everyday. In Cleveland, citizens have developed the ability to intercede when schools are scheduled to be closed and have kept the schools open. Citizens can rally to keep hospitals open; to save industries which provide jobs; to protect neighborhood libraries from curtailment of service; to improve community policing; to meet racial, ethnic and religious intolerance openly and directly.

"Active citizenship begins with an envisioning of the desired outcome and a conscious application of spiritual principles. I know. I have worked with the people in my own community. I have seen the dynamic of faith in self, faith in one's ability to change things, faith in one's ability to prevail against the odds through an appeal to the spirit of the world for help, through an appeal to the spirit of community for participation, through an appeal to the spirit of cooperation, which multiplies energy. I have seen citizens challenge conditions without condemning anyone while invoking principles of non-opposition and inclusion of those who disagree.

"I have seen groups of people overcome incredible odds as they become aware they are participating in a cause beyond self and sense the movement of the inexorable, which comes from unity. When you feel this principle at work, when you see spiritual principles form the basis of active citizenship, you are reminded once again of the merging of stardust and Spirit. There is creativity. There is magic. There is alchemy.

"Citizens across the United States are now uniting in a great cause to establish a Department of Peace, seeking nothing less than the transformation of our society, to make nonviolence an organizing principle, to make war archaic through creating a paradigm shift in our culture for human development, for economic and political justice and for violence control. Its work in violence control will be to support disarmament treaties, peaceful coexistence and peaceful consensus building. Its focus on economic and political justice will examine and enhance resource distribution, human and economic rights and strengthen democratic values.

"Domestically, the Department of Peace would address violence in the home, spousal abuse, child abuse, gangs, police/community relations conflicts and work with individuals and groups to achieve changes in attitudes that examine the mythologies of cherished world views such as 'violence is inevitable' or 'war is inevitable.' Thus it will help with the discovery of new selves and new paths toward peaceful consensus.

"The Department of Peace will also address human development and the unique concerns of women and children. It will envision and seek to implement plans for Peace education, not simply as a course of study but as a template for all pursuits of knowledge within formal educational settings.

"Violence is not inevitable. War is not inevitable. Nonviolence and peace are inevitable. We can make of this world a gift of Peace, which will confirm the presence of universal Spirit in our lives. We can send into the future the gift which will protect our children from fear, from harm, from destruction.

"Carved inside the pediment which sits atop the marble columns is a sentinel at the entrance to the United States House of Representatives. Standing resolutely inside this 'Apotheosis of Democracy' is a woman, a shield by her left side, with her outstretched right arm protecting a child happily sitting at her feet. This child holds the lamp of knowledge under the protection of this patroness.

"This wondrous sculpture by Paul Wayland Bartlett is titled 'Peace Protecting Genius.' Not with nuclear arms, but with a loving maternal arm is the knowing child genius shielded from harm. This is the promise of hope over fear. This is the promise of love, which overcomes all. This is the promise of faith, which overcomes doubt. This is the promise of Light, which overcomes darkness. This is the promise of Peace, which overcomes war."

For more information on how you can participate in the Department of Peace you may E-mail Representative Kucinich at: Dkucinich@aol.com *or* info@thespiritoffreedom.com.

We were asked by the Spiritual Hierarchy to hold one of our Free Seminars in Columbus, Ohio, on September 8, 2002, which is the day celebrated as Mother Mary's birthday. During that seminar, we fulfilled the Divine Plan of anchoring into the permanent seed atom of the Heart of America the newly activated 5th-Dimensional matrix and archetypes for Divine Government. Amazingly, when we walked into the hotel lobby where the seminar was to be held, we encountered several Free Masons and their wives all dressed in formal wear. They were having their annual ball at the hotel. I have been participating in seminars and conferences for 30 years, and I have only seen Free Masons at the two events involving the establishment of 5th-Dimensional Divine Government. Isn't the synchronicity of the unfolding Divine Plan incredible?

I would like to reiterate that from every conceivable Light Source, we are being encouraged, prompted, implored and guided to focus the power of our attention on the vision of the New Earth in all her resplendent glory. In spite of all of the saber rattling and war drums we are being bombarded with by the media, every credible Lightworker is gently turning his or her attention back to the reality of cocreating Heaven On Mother Earth—HOME. This is our purpose and reason for being, and it is why we volunteered to be on Earth during this Cosmic Moment.

We have each been preparing for aeons of time to develop the strength, skill, courage, wisdom and trust to hold true to our mission during these challenging times. Our training was successful, and we already have everything within our hearts that we need to succeed God Victoriously. Our responsibility now is to monitor our thoughts, words, feelings and actions daily and hourly to be sure we are empowering *only* the perfection patterns of Heaven on Earth from the Causal Body of God instead of the horrors of our fragmented, fear-based human egos.

Every world religion has taught us, in one way or another, that we are responsible for the circumstances occurring in our lives. What we send out returns to us. This is true whether we are sending out love or hate.

There is a grassroots awakening taking place, and literally millions of people all over the world are genuinely striving to create lives of joy, peace, abundance, health and comfort for themselves and their loved ones. The majority of people everywhere want the same thing. They want to know that their families are safe and that they can provide food, shelter, security, health care, education and comfort for their loved ones.

The majority of people sincerely care about other people and want the best for Humanity and all life evolving on Earth. Most people truly desire to create a lifestyle that not only supports their basic needs, but honors the Earth as well. The people who are willing to deprive others of their livelihood, comfort, security, prosperity and safety for their own greed are a small minority. Those who are willing to kill people and destroy the Earth for the sake of power and money are a mere fraction of Humanity as well.

It will help immensely if we all invoke the Flame of Transfiguring Divine Love pulsating in every person's heart, and ask the Divine Intelligence within that Sacred Flame to reveal the distortion and corruption in their thinking process that allows them to justify harming another part of life for their own selfish gains.

If, moment to moment, we focus the power of our attention on the New Earth and all that means to us in the way of love, peace, harmony, joy, happiness, abundance, health, beauty, limitless physical perfection, fulfillment, spiritual growth, enlightenment, wonder and awe, we will victoriously cocreate...

Heaven On Mother Earth—HOME.

ADDITIONAL OPPORTUNITIES
for
New Age Study of Humanity's Purpose
cofounded by
Patricia Diane Cota-Robles
and
Kay Eileen Meyer

❐ I would like to be on the *E-mail* mailing list.

❐ I would like to be on the *postal* mailing list.

❐ I would like a *brochure* of your books and tapes.

❐ I would like a sample of your postal newsletter
Take Charge of Your Life.

❐ I would like to receive information on the next
World Congress On Illumination.

❐ I would like information on your upcoming
FREE Seminars.

❐ I would like *ALL of the above.*

Please print:

NAME_____

ADDRESS_____

CITY_____

STATE_____ZIP_____PHONE_____

COUNTRY_____POSTAL CODE_____

E-MAIL_____

Please mail to:
The New Age Study of Humanity's Purpose
PO Box 41883, Tucson AZ 85717
FAX: 520-749-6643 or Phone: 520-885-7909
E-mail: eraofpeace@aol.com
Website: www.1spirit.com/eraofpeace

IT IS TIME FOR *YOU* TO BE FINANCIALLY FREE

by
Patricia Diane Cota-Robles

Our lack and financial limitation is based in *poverty consciousness*. In order for us to be poor, we must first accept poverty as our reality.

This incredible book clearly describes how we can change our attitudes and beliefs about money and naturally open up to the FLOW OF GOD'S LIMITLESS ABUNDANCE through prosperity consciousness.

This timely book also reveals a *Sacred Gift* given to Humanity by the Company of Heaven. This gift will reverse the plague of poverty on Earth and open the door to our financial freedom.

— —

I would like to order_____copy(ies) of the book
IT IS TIME FOR **YOU** TO BE FINANCIALLY FREE
for $7.00 each plus postage and handling.

NAME_____

ADDRESS_____

CITY_____STATE_____ZIP_____

COUNTRY_____POSTAL CODE_____

TELEPHONE_____E-MAIL_____

Name on Card_____ Amt_____
Card #_____ Exp_____
Visa ____ MasterCard ____ Discover____ Am Express ____

POSTAGE AND HANDLING

Up to $20.00.............$5.00 $20.01-$36.00.............$6.00 $36.01-$50.00.............$7.00 $50.01-$75.00.............$9.00 $75.01-$90.00...........$10.00 $90.01 and over.........$11.00	For all Canada & Mexico orders, please add an **additional 6% of the *subtotal*.** For all other foreign countries, please add an **additional 8% of the *subtotal*.** Please do not send personal checks. Send International Postal Money Orders. Thank you.

If paying by check or money order, please make payable to
New Age Study of Humanity's Purpose (or NASHP)
PO Box 41883, Tucson AZ 85717
You may also order via:
www.1spirit.com/eraofpeace
Fax: 520-749-6643
Telephone: 520-885-7909
E-mail: eraofpeace@aol.com

THE GIFT TO RECLAIM YOUR PROSPERITY
by Patricia Diane Cota-Robles

The greatest need of the hour is for awakening Light-workers to attain our financial freedom so that we can be FREE to fulfill our individual Divine Plans and quickly implement the viable solutions for the world's problems that are flowing into our conscious minds from the Causal Body of God.

This tape contains incredible information that has been given to Humanity by the Beings of Light in the Realms of Illumined Truth to help us open up to the limitless abundance of God, so that we will quickly attain our financial freedom.

I would like to order ____copy(ies) of the tape **THE GIFT TO RECLAIM YOUR PROSPERITY** for $9.00 each plus postage and handling.

NAME_____

ADDRESS_____

CITY_____STATE_____ZIP_____

COUNTRY_____POSTAL CODE_____

TELEPHONE_____E-MAIL_____

Name on Card_____ Amt_____

Card #_____ Exp_____

Visa ____ MasterCard ____ Discover ____ Am Express _____

POSTAGE AND HANDLING

Up to $20.00..............$5.00	For all Canada & Mexico orders, please add an
$20.01-$36.00..............$6.00	**additional 6% of the *subtotal*.** For all other
$36.01-$50.00..............$7.00	foreign countries, please add an **additional 8%**
$50.01-$75.00..............$9.00	**of the *subtotal*.** Please do not send personal
$75.01-$90.00............$10.00	checks. Send International Postal Money Orders.
$90.01 and over..........$11.00	Thank you.

If paying by check or money order, please make payable to
New Age Study of Humanity's Purpose (or NASHP)
PO Box 41883, Tucson AZ 85717
You may also order via:
www.1spirit.com/eraofpeace
Fax: 520-749-6643
Telephone: 520-885-7909
E-mail: eraofpeace@aol.com

BECOMING AN INSTRUMENT OF GOD
by Patricia Diane Cota-Robles

There has never been a moment in time when it was more imperative for us to fulfill our highest potential as Lightworkers. This is the moment we have been preparing for, and we have everything we need within us to be powerful Instruments of God.

The information on this tape is a gift from the Beings of Light in the Realms of Truth to help us remember who we are and why we are here. It will inspire us to join hearts with Lightworkers all over the world who are also remembering that they are powerful Instruments of God. Together we will enhance our lives and transform the world..

— —

I would like to order ____copy(ies) of the tape **BECOMING AN INSTRUMENT OF GOD** for $9.00 each plus postage and handling.

NAME_____

ADDRESS_____

CITY_____STATE_____ZIP_____

COUNTRY_____POSTAL CODE_____

TELEPHONE_____E-MAIL_____

Name on Card_____ Amt_____

Card #_____ Exp_____

Visa ____ MasterCard _____ Discover _____ Am Express_____

POSTAGE AND HANDLING

Up to $20.00..............$5.00	For all Canada & Mexico orders, please add an **additional 6% of the *subtotal*.** For all other foreign countries, please add an **additional 8% of the *subtotal*.** Please do not send personal checks. Send International Postal Money Orders. Thank you.
$20.01-$36.00..............$6.00	
$36.01-$50.00..............$7.00	
$50.01-$75.00..............$9.00	
$75.01-$90.00............$10.00	
$90.01 and over..........$11.00	

If paying by check or money order, please make payable to
New Age Study of Humanity's Purpose (or NASHP)
PO Box 41883, Tucson AZ 85717
You may also order via:
www.1spirit.com/eraofpeace
Fax: 520-749-6643
Telephone: 520-885-7909
E-mail: eraofpeace@aol.com

NEW TECHNOLOGY OF THE VIOLET FLAME
by Patricia Diane Cota-Robles

We are now capable of receiving previously unknown frequencies of the Violet Flame, which contain a *NEW TECHNOLOGY* that will greatly assist in transforming our Earthly bodies and our Earthly experiences into the perfection of Heaven on Earth.

This tape contains specific guidelines and instructions from the Company of Heaven that will enable us to utilize the powerful New Technology of the Violet Flame effectively and easily.

— —

I would like to order____copy(ies) of the tape
NEW TECHNOLOGY OF THE VIOLET FLAME
for $9.00 each plus postage and handling.

NAME_____

ADDRESS_____

CITY_____STATE_____ZIP_____

COUNTRY_____POSTAL CODE_____

TELEPHONE_____E-MAIL_____

Name on Card_____ Amt_____

Card #_____ Exp_____

Visa _____ MasterCard _____ Discover_____ Am Express_____

POSTAGE AND HANDLING

Up to $20.00.............$5.00	For all Canada & Mexico orders, please add an **additional 6% of the *subtotal*.** For all other foreign countries, please add an **additional 8% of the *subtotal*.** Please do not send personal checks. Send International Postal Money Orders. Thank you.
$20.01-$36.00.............$6.00	
$36.01-$50.00.............$7.00	
$50.01-$75.00.............$9.00	
$75.01-$90.00............$10.00	
$90.01 and over..........$11.00	

If paying by check or money order, please make payable to
New Age Study of Humanity's Purpose (or NASHP)
PO Box 41883, Tucson AZ 85717
You may also order via:
www.1spirit.com/eraofpeace
Fax: 520-749-6643
Telephone: 520-885-7909
E-mail: eraofpeace@aol.com